VENUS AND FURS
The Cultural Politics of Fur

Julia V. Emberley

I.B. Tauris
London

Published in the UK in 1998 by

I.B. Tauris & Co Ltd

Victoria House

Bloomsbury Square

London WC1B 4DZ

Copyright © 1997 by Cornell University

A full CIP record for this book is available from the British Library

ISBN 1 86064 230 6 hardback

ISBN 1 86064 227 6 paperback

Manufactured in the United States of America

FOR ELIE KORKMAZ

Contents

Figures

Preface

During the 1980s the fur-trapping and fashion industries came under increasing criticism from animal rights activists and animal welfare organizations for the cruel procedures used to obtain furs. Profit margins in the fur industry plummeted. Fashion designers and advertisers created new ways of disguising furs, confounding the boundary between real and fake. While environmentalists cast "fur" as the lead character in an ecological tragedy, the fashion apparatus reacted with all its powers of artifice to resituate fur as a figure of dissimulation, as far removed from "nature" as any commodity could be. Moral agendas and processes of commodification seemed directly at odds with each other, the one substantiating the need to protect animals, the other ruthlessly exploiting their exchange value.

The relationship between the environmental struggle and the fur fashion industry is not, however, as oppositional as it appears. Anyone interested in the environment, for example, must be concerned with what constitutes "nature" or the "natural," in other words, what social, political, discursive, and economic forces construct "nature" in general and fur specifically as a proper object around which to mount a political pro-ecology campaign. Producing nature is not an inexpensive enterprise. The "green" marketplace can be as demanding as any other commodity system of exchange. High investments in media and advertising, along with the production of ecologically correct consumables, have contributed to an aesthetization of this expression of political justice. Concurrently, fur fashion ideologues have as much at stake in the values and meanings ascribed to fur, for an ideology of artifice needs an already known discourse of nature from which to dissociate itself. The attack on fur brought substance, content, and social significance to fur fashions. They were no longer mere symbols of wealth, decadence, and prestige. Fur and fake-fur industries embraced the social discourse on nature precisely in order to have it subvert its own culture.

While a battle between commodities and dominant ideologies of nature and artifice occupied the media-infused public and political spheres during the anti-fur season of the 1980s, this symptom of social unrest took on a different significance for aboriginal trappers, Inuit fur fashion designers, and fur factory workers in the so-called Third World. Even bourgeois women felt the loss of whatever symbolic agency they had accrued as consumers of fur's symbolic power. A heterogeneous opening of antagonisms invaded the ideological field: middle-class anti-fur activists accosted middle-class and bourgeois fur-clad women with spray paint in metropolitan centers such as London, New York, and Toronto; British feminist graffiti artists protested the misogynist images of women in the anti-fur media campaign of Lynx; aboriginal constituencies in northern Canada, Alaska, and Greenland formed Indigenous Survival International to protest the misinformation disseminated by animal rights organizations such as Lynx as well as to support fur's symbolic value and the economic basis of fur trapping for northern indigenous communities. During the 1980s fur seemed entirely necessary to bring closure to a troubled post–World War II liberal political consciousness that had lost its political and economic ground to the right-wing governments of Thatcher and Reagan and yet had difficulty adjusting to the new complexities and contradictions of the political field, otherwise known as the new social movements. Fur was to be a postliberal comfort zone, in part in resistance to a historically transformed society.

The anti-fur challenge made use of media and other information technologies, calling for the demystification of fashion ideologies of luxury, status, and other spectacles of commodity wealth and symbolic power. But demystifying the masses only produced new mechanisms of mystification. A complex tapestry of political articulations and contradictory tensions emerged, and this book is about pulling at the strands that make up this rich text of social and material contestation, both historically and transculturally.

The contradictions that shape the current battle over fur's significance are historically overdetermined. Legislative acts in medieval Britain sought to regulate the wearing of fur as a symbol of landowning wealth and class privilege. They also sought to regulate material consumption in general by introducing a moral discourse on the detrimental effects of material excess. This discourse became increasingly linked, through the sixteenth and seventeenth centuries, with controlling women's sexuality and the outward signs of gender and adornment. Not only was fur a significant commodity fetish during the rise of the fur trade between Britain and the New World in the seventeenth century; the link between sexual and material excess contributed to fur's signification as a sexual fetish. The symbolic and material fetishisms ascribed to fur and especially the fur-clad upper-class white European woman, were further supported by an aesthetics of adornment, fashion, and style. Documentary and fine visual arts, fashion history books, and literary texts, including such notable works as Leopold von Sacher-Masoch's late nineteenth-century novel *Venus in Furs*, contributed to the libidinal investments in fur — as an object of desire, as a central figure in the ideology of female artifice.

The introduction of new technologies of representation — film and photography — in the late nineteenth century produced new ways of representing the symbolic agency of the fur-clad woman and the symbolic power invested in fur fashions. In G. W. Pabst's film *The Joyless Street*, made in Germany in 1925, a fur coat functions as a soft currency of libidinal exchange, there to mediate a moral and economic crisis in the post–World War I Weimar Republic. In the late twentieth century, fur fashions in North America became objects of parody, signs of sexual transgression, and codes of gender and race deregulation in *Unzipped* (1995) and *Paris Is Burning* (1991). Fur, the primary industry of fur trapping, and fur fashions also emerged as important codes in Inuit and Dene discourses of decolonization, especially those produced by cultural workers, including northern fur fashion designers, storytellers of the Sahtú-Dene such as George Blondin, and the photographer of contemporary Dene life Dorothy Chocolate.

This book traces the discursive and nondiscursive practices that institutionalize, subvert, and transgress the meanings of fur — as article of trade, sexual fetish, commodity, sign of wealth, protective clothing — in order to understand the contest over the meanings and values of fur as a struggle between people: between, for example, consumers and producers of fur. The antagonism that surrounds fur in the late twentieth century provides an opportunity to trace the cultural materialisms that shape the social practices and activities of various libidinal, symbolic, historical, cultural, and material agents: white bourgeois and aristocratic women of fashion, aboriginal fur fashion designers, models, photographers, and storytellers, fur femme "realness" queens, South Korean fur factory workers, white and black Venuses in fur, and the many other faces of the fur-clad subject. By rediscovering the complex relations between and among words, things, and people, we may begin to see the validity of arguing for a much-needed ecological movement that, in its search for ways to use and sustain the earth's natural resources, can no longer afford to overlook both the history of the construction of sexual difference and the history of imperialism (especially its relationship to the global trade in goods and natural resources). Perhaps, then, this movement, poised at a unique place in our contemporary world, can take up the challenge to re-present, radically and democratically, politically and symbolically, the voices of many "natures," human and animal, animate and inanimate, real and imagined.

This project was made possible by the help of many individuals and institutions. I gratefully acknowledge the generosity of the Society of the

Humanities, Cornell University, for a postdoctoral fellowship during the academic year 1992–1993 which made it possible to devote invaluable time to the early stages of its conception and writing. Many thanks to Jonathan Culler, then the Director of the Society of the Humanities, and Dominick LaCapra, the current Director, the administrative staff at the A. D. White House, and the Fellows during the 1992–1993 academic year, especially Emily Apter, Meaghan Morris, Jay Tribby, Jane Schneider, and Peter Schneider, for a rewarding and memorable time. I am also grateful for a research grant from the Social Sciences and Humanities Council of Canada as well as exploratory funding from the University of Northern British Columbia and Trent University, which made possible important research at archives.

Many thanks to Russell McDougall for inviting me to take up a Canadian Studies Fellowship at the University of New England in Armidale, Australia, in August 1996, where I had the opportunity to present my work, and to Jane O'Sullivan and Don Beer for their stimulating conversation, hospitality and kindness.

I am grateful to friends, family, and colleagues for suggestions of material to include as well as for support; thanks to Adrian Emberley, Alex Emberley, Marcelle Gareau, Lynette Hunter, Mary Ellen Kelm, Peter Kulchyski, Donna Landry, Antonia Lant, Ross Leckie, Peter Lichtenfels, Gerald MacLean, Pamela McCallum, Tilottama Rajan, Debbie Simmons, and Kathryn Taglia. I gratefully acknowledge my research assistants Johanna Ens and Adeja Chrisara for their hard work in tracking down sources and coping with the organization of the illustrations. To Alison Shonkwiler at Cornell University Press, for her expert editorial guidance and support throughout the entire process, my sincere gratitude. I would also like to extend my thanks to other members of the editorial staff at the Press, especially Terry McKiernan and Kay Scheuer, for their scrupulous care in the final stages of preparation for this book.

I benefited a great deal from the input of two anonymous readers for the Press whose wonderful suggestions and recommendations came at a critical time in the writing process. Thank you to these thoughtful scholars. I have tried my best to respond to their concerns.

The following previously published articles were revised for this book: "The Libidinal Politics of Fur," *University of Toronto Quarterly* 65 : 2 (1996): 437–43; "Fantasies of Contact in a Transnational Frame: A Transactional Reading," *Tessera* 17 (1994): 52–74; and "Simulated Politics: Animal Bodies, Fur-Bearing Women, Indigenous Survival," *New Formations* 24 (1994): 66–91. I am grateful to these journals for permission to reprint.

On a personal note, I thank my mother and father, Jean and Sidney Emberley, without whom I would never have written this book, intertwined as it is in obscure and indirect ways with their wonderfully varied and positively profound influence on my life. I credit Jean with teaching me what possibilities lay at the back of the wardrobe — including her very own (pre–environmentally enlightened) silver fox stole — for coming to terms with the sensuous uncertainty of critical thought.

This book is dedicated to Elie Korkmaz, for his love, his friendship, our lively conversations, and his wonderful family in Lebanon — Fadwa, Jean, Yolla, Michel, Dolly, Aida, Gabi, Andrée, Aline, and Eliane—who provided an extraordinarily loving and warm environment that sustained me during summers of writing. Love and thanks to you all.

JULIA EMBERLEY

Prince George, British Columbia

VENUS AND FURS

Introduction
An Obscure Object of Desire

FUR: *Sign of Wealth*

Gustave Flaubert, *Dictionary of Received Ideas*

*In an aversion to animals the predominant feeling is fear of being
recognized by them through contact. The horror that stirs deep
in man is an obscure awareness that in him something lives so akin
to the animal that it might be recognized. All disgust is originally
disgust at touching. Even when the feeling is mastered, it is only by
a drastic gesture that overleaps its mark: the nauseous is violently
engulfed, eaten, while the zone of finest epidermal contact remains
taboo. Only in this way is the paradox of the moral demand to be
met, exacting simultaneously the overcoming and the subtlest
elaboration of man's sense of disgust. He may not deny his bestial
relationship with animals, the invocation of which revolts him: he
must make himself its master.*

Walter Benjamin, *One-Way Street*

The cultural politics of fur has achieved a significant place in our contemporary world. Consider a newspaper article from a 1992 British Sunday paper, the *Observer*, which ran with the following headline: "If Sarajevo had fur, there would be an international campaign to save it." [1] This headline plus the title of the article that follows by Colin Smith, "A City Slowly Bludgeoned to Death," recall the media buzz surrounding the anti-sealing campaign of the 1970s, which depicted sentimental images of cuddly seals nestled under Brigitte Bardot's chin, juxtaposed with other images of baby seals bludgeoned to death and scattered over the ice floes off the coast of

Labrador in Canada. The anti-sealing campaign spread during the 1980s in Britain into a strong and effective general campaign against furs and trapping. The reference in the *Observer* headline to the anti-fur lobby prompts at least two possible readings. On the one hand, I read the headline with a somewhat cynical eye as if it were demanding an answer to the question: How is it possible that the anti-fur political lobby can so capture the urban imagination that it takes precedence over the genocide in Sarajevo? In other words, the environmental struggle is minor by comparison, and the significance attributed to the anti-fur lobby — a single aspect of an ecological movement that has come to stand for the whole — detracts from the urgency of political struggles elsewhere. On the other hand, I read the headline in the context of the success of the anti-fur movement in mobilizing public opinion against fur. Pressures from animal liberation and welfare activists during the 1980s effectively challenged the fur industry and its profit margins.[2] Fur sales in Britain reportedly fell 75 percent between 1985 and 1990.[3] The headline capitalizes on this success, suggesting by way of guilt politics that similar energies might be directed elsewhere, into struggles to defeat global political and economic forces that severely threaten and damage the lives of other people, especially those very far removed from the privileges of postindustrial metropolitan centers. The internationally minded reader may put another spin on this headline, substituting "oil" for "fur," thereby recalling the importance of natural resources to United States intervention in the Gulf War the previous year.

The multiple interpretations surrounding the headline indicate just how symptomatic "fur" became in Britain as a metonymic sign for the environmentalist movement and its hegemony in the domain of political struggle. There are, however, other social and historical realities displaced by Britain's symbolic investment in fur during the 1980s. As successful as the anti-fur lobby was in changing consumer habits in a world of "real material limits," to quote Raymond Williams, it was equally successful in distracting attention from the history of the British fur trade and its effects on aboriginal history and culture in Canada.[4] The earlier Greenpeace anti-sealing campaign was to have devastating effects on Inuit, Dene, and other First Nations communities that relied on seal harvesting to supplement their cash flow. Hugh Brody observed: "Sealskin prices tumbled and the International Whaling Commission was pressured to effect an international ban on all hunting of whale and dolphin species — though some special consideration was given to aboriginal subsistence hunters. Ringed sealskin prices fell from approximately $30 to as little as $2 or $3 each. The economic basis of hunting families and, in the eastern Arctic, whole communities collapsed."[5] Organizations such as Indigenous Survival International, composed of indigenous people from Alaska, Greenland, and Canada, formed in the mid-eighties in protest of the misinformation disseminated by anti-fur organizations about the gathering and hunting peoples of the far north. For northern indigenous peoples, fur trapping represents one means of material support, as well as a symbolic tie to traditional ways of life, in an otherwise poverty-inducing economic system. Seen in this light, anti-fur organizations constitute, as Hugh Brody remarks, a "new example of southern, imperialist intrusion" that has done harm to indigenous peoples in Canada, rather than furthered the cause of sustainable communities and economies.[6]

Nowhere has the conflict over the significance attributed to fur become more apparent than in the debate between animal liberationists, such as the British animal rights organization Lynx, and Inuit and Dene claims for self-determination, which include collective rights to live off the land, to hunt animals, and to engage in various cultural and economic activities involving the selling, processing, and use of animal fur. Out of this global tension spirals a productivity of imaginary spaces, textual and visual, from which to begin to tell a story of fur.[7]

Historically, the significance of fur has largely been viewed in the context of the fur trade and its political and economic interests. The fur trade in North America during the early modern period provided a source of mercantile wealth to Western Europe. For the indigenous peoples of North America, the political economy of this trade brought new forms of exchange value which eventually came to dominate indigenous modes of gatherer-hunter production. Fur was the principal object of exchange for guns, kettles, other tools, food staples, and luxury goods. The abundant scholarship on the fur trade has tended to focus on this aspect of the material production of fur. Harold A. Innis, in his seminal account *The Fur Trade in Canada: An Introduction to Canadian Economic History* (1930), argues that Canada came into existence as a country not in spite of its geography, as has often been suggested, but because of it, a geography centered on the waterways and trade routes created by the economic exigencies of the fur trade. Innis begins his introduction by observing that the "beaver (*Castor canadenis* Kuhl) was of dominant importance in the beginnings of the Canadian fur trade. It is impossible to understand the characteristic developments of the trade or of Canadian history without some knowledge of its life and habits."[8] Innis concentrates on the beaver because its fur was the primary economic unit from the mid-sixteenth century to the 1870s in the fur trade. Indeed, it came to occupy a privileged position as a monetary equivalent in the design of the "Made-beaver," a prime-quality beaver skin used to represent a standard of currency for a century and a half.

The work of Innis and other economic historians and anthropologists on the fur trade and the commodity status of fur as a luxury good or article of trade clearly demonstrates the significance of this object of material culture to colonial relations among Britain, France, and North America. The contemporary scene of fur's contested *symbolic value* suggests, however, that fur is a more complex sign of political, poetic, and I would suggest, erotic power than Innis and subsequent scholars have understood it to be. In this book, then, I do not offer an alternative narrative to traditional economic histories. I leave aside many questions, for example, about the relationship between the economic history of the fur trade and the demands of the fur fashion industry.[9] Rather, this book traces the material and symbolic modes of differentiation in the cultural history of fur.

To address the complex scene of fur's current configurations, the cultural study of fur must take as its subject not only the material production of fur (the fashion industry, fur trapping, fur farming, and the fur trade, historically and presently) but also the symbolic production of fur, the production of its material values and social significance in a variety of signifying practices including literary works; visual materials such as fine art, etchings, and photography; and other symbolic venues such as film and museums, as well as the figuration of fur in historical, juridical, and fashion discourses.[10] I contend that the current configuration of the cultural politics of fur can best be understood by analyzing how fur acquires its value not only as a commodity, a luxury good, an article of trade, but also as an object invested with libidinal desires. In the European or North American context, fur, in its various symbolic and material forms, circulates within libidinal as well as political economies. In other words, the symbolic production of fur cannot be separated from questions of desire such as the libidinal codification attributed to fur as a sexual fetish or the rise of the fur coat in the twentieth century as essentially a feminine fashion commodity. Fur would appear to be a multilayered object, sought after for both its desirability and its profitability. As commodity fetish, it appears to fulfill the needs of a "modernizing" capitalist and patriarchal society. As a libidinal fetish, however, it becomes the object which creates those needs.

More than an object of material culture, a commodity, fashion garment, animal skin, or sexual fetish, fur circulates as a *material signifier* in the transnational discourses of political and libidinal exchange. In *The German Ideology* Marx and Engels write: "The cherry-tree, like almost all fruit-trees, was, as is well known, only a few centuries ago transplanted by *commerce* into our zone, and therefore only *by* this action of a definite society in a definite age it has become 'sensuous certainty' for Feuerbach."[11] Feuerbach's notion of sensuous certainty, Marx and Engels insist, cannot be abstracted from the realm of deterministic limits, a definitiveness of time and place produced by the exchange of wealth and objects. To suggest otherwise is to posit a fetishistic ideal in which a thing exists simply as a thing, endowed with meanings and values that are intrinsic, mythical, and immutable. In the passage I have quoted, a demystification of the fetishism of sensuous certainty takes place and the cherry tree is placed in a field of trans-*actions*. For Marx, those transactions are largely of a commercial sort, where an exchange of economic interests determines the facticity of the cherry tree's existence in Europe. What we perceive to be nature, and therefore natural, Marx and Engels would have us understand as a product of highly mobile circulations and transactive exchanges. Those exchanges may be determined primarily by economic exigencies, but I am just as convinced that the values and meanings attributed to objects are produced in libidinal, ecological, or discursive modes of exchange. It is in these possible discursive and nondiscursive sites of transaction that fur, as much as the cherry tree, constitutes itself as a *material signifier*. Meanings are attributed to it, such as that of "natural object" or "sexual fetish," and material and social values accrue.

The process of exchange must already involve the identification of codes of exchange value. In the social production of values for fur, textual, ecological, libidinal, and economic transactions both necessitate recognizable codes of exchange and put those codes of exchange value into circulation in order to produce effects of identification. The exchange value of fur exists in our ability to recognize or misrecognize its figuration as commodity, currency, sexual fetish, luxury good, article of clothing, animal hide, natural product. At a more general level of transaction, codes of exchange would include the larger categories of money, women, and natural resources. These categories, both the specific and the general, figure in material and discursive economies as the effects of exchange and the values necessary to effect exchange. I propose a transactional reading that traces the representation of exchange value in various symbolic forms such as language, film, media, literature, as well as in the marketplace.

Gayatri Chakravorty Spivak explains that "the definition of Value in Marx establishes itself not only as a representation but also [as] a differential. What is represented or represents itself in the commodity-differential is Value."[12] Sexual difference is a good example of a code that produces "woman" as an identifiable object of exchange, sometimes explicitly, other times as a hidden mediation who is nevertheless central to a link between two men.[13] It is possible to read the cultural inscription of sexuality as a mode of differentiation upon which a negotiation of value is set in motion. A transactional reading, then, is also committed to citing at any particular historical or cultural conjunction what "social production of a differential" (to borrow Spivak's phrase) is at work.[14] Why is the social production of differentials important to the codes of exchange ascribed to cultural artifacts such as fur? It is important because social differences encode the value of fur for the consumer, the reader, or the spectator. It is the social transaction of fur as a material object as well as the values and meanings ascribed to it that constitutes subjective relations of exchange — economic or discursive — between or among consumers, readers, and spectators. Cultural artifacts such as fur, which have a long history of trade between and within domestic and foreign entities, mediate social as well as economic relations of reciprocity or contestation.

A transactional reading not only maps the commerce of textual exchange; it also participates in the negotiations and has the potential to mobilize antagonistic oppositions such as woman/man and human/animal out of their fetishistic regimes of truth. Sexual or anthropocentric differences that give relative value to these dualities can then be subject to a disassemblage whereby the imperial violence (specific to the history of the traffic in furs) that constructs *fine distinctions* is displaced and the fluidity and permeability of borders set in motion.

The differential play of oppositions, such as human/animal, animate/inanimate, feminine/masculine, words/things, partially determines the boundaries of this field of inquiry. The effects of these oppositions are most poignantly registered on the configuration of subjects, defined in relation to one another: men and women, among women of different social and economic classes, and between American, French, or British and Canadian imperial and indigenous subjects. The circulation of fur in the symbolic economies of desire and power further suggests a mode of symbolic agency in which subjects actively and strategically negotiate, acknowledge, and transform their appropriation of fur's value, individually or collectively.

Libidinal Economies of Fur

Chapter 1, "Simulated Politics," analyzes the fur debate that took place in England during the 1980s. In particular, I focus on the dominance of mass media as a vehicle for altering public opinion about the purchase and wearing of fur. The use of various kinds of mass media by the animal rights organization Lynx, including cinema commercials, billboard signs, and made-for-in-home-viewing videos, places Lynx's strategy within a particularly prevalent mode of aestheticized politics in the late twentieth century. Access to dominant ideological apparatuses of representation, such as the media or, even more pressing today, the Internet, creates conditions under which it is possible to aestheticize political interests, to produce, in other words, a simulated or virtual politics. My interest here is to politicize the aestheticization of these interests, to highlight the significance of gender and culture differences to this practice, and thereby to disclose the tension between political and aesthetic modes of representation as well as to dramatize those tensions between political and symbolic powers and agents in the fur debate.

The Lynx media campaign of the mid-1980s set out to implicate in cruelty to animals not only the fur fashion industry but, by virtue of her complicity in wearing the fur coat, the female bourgeois consumer. Demonized images of fur-clad women dominated the media landscape of the metropolis of London during the mid-eighties. Hanif Kureishi incorporated the anti-fur attack on women into his screenplay for Stephen Frears's film *Sammy and Rosie Get Laid* (1987). Near the conclusion of the film, when caravans are forced to leave the waste ground because of property development, the property developer's wife stands on the periphery observing the scene in her long sable coat. The feminist, anti-imperialist, lesbian activist in the film, Rani, crosses behind her and spray-paints an "X" on the back of the coat. Kureishi records in his published *Diary* that he got the idea for the scene when he went to "the opera . . . with a vegetarian friend. A woman in a long sable coat sits next to us. My friend says: I wish I carried a can of spray paint in my bag and could shoot it over her coat. Thought it might be an idea to stick in the film. But where?" [15] Even if this "progressive" act of protest originates in the pores of its contradictory class affiliations "at the opera," Kureishi, nevertheless finds an appropriate place for this image in the film, using it to represent a burgeoning developer's paradise under Thatcher relentlessly dispossessing the urban poor.

I read Kureishi's figure of the white, heterosexual, fur-clad bourgeois woman, the enemy of the urban dispossessed, as a feminist allegory on the limits of gender in representing the economic violence of capital-intensive property development. On a more mundane level, however, the bourgeois woman, because of her heterosexual-class affiliation, figures as an accessory to the crime of exploitation and oppression. The figure of the fur-clad bourgeois woman holds a remarkable degree of symbolic power. For Audre Lorde that power not only circumscribes the intolerable hierarchies of class difference but also enters into the dynamics of racial superiority. Lorde writes about an encounter, as a child, on the AA subway train to Harlem:

I clutch my mother's sleeve, her arms full of shopping bags, christmas-heavy. The wet smell of winter clothes, the train's lurching. My mother spots an almost seat, pushes my little snowsuited body down. On one side of me a man reading a paper. On the other, a woman in a fur hat staring at me. Her mouth twitches as she stares and then her gaze drops down, pulling mine with it. Her leather-gloved hand plucks at the line where my new blue snowpants and her sleek fur coat meet. She jerks her coat closer to her. I look. I do not see whatever terrible thing she is seeing on the seat between us — probably a roach. But she has communicated her horror to me. It must be something very bad from the way she's looking, so I pull my snowsuit closer to me away from it, too. When I look up the woman is still staring at me, her nose holes and eyes huge. And suddenly I realize there is nothing crawling up the seat between us; it is me she doesn't want her coat to touch. The fur brushes past my face as she stands with a shudder and holds on to a strap in the speeding train. Born and bred a New York City child, I quickly slide over to make room for my mother to sit down. No word has been spoken. I'm afraid to say anything to my mother because I don't know what I've done. I look at the sides of my snowpants, secretly. Is there something on them? Something's going on here I do not understand, but I will never forget it. Her eyes. The flared nostrils. The hate.[16]

Lorde's passage brings to light a gendered depiction of racial superiority and class elitism. In the Lynx campaign, however, the contradictions of class, race, gender, sexuality, and World (First, Third, New, Old) differences are ideologically resolved through the media depiction of brutality to animals. Class hierarchies, racism, ethnocentrism, and heterosexism still remain alive and well in their images and pamphlet literature. A seemingly politically progressive act of moral justice toward animals takes on new meanings: environmental imperialism, environmental sexism, environmental racism?

The image of the fur-clad bourgeois woman in the Lynx campaign is full of contradictions. It depicts bourgeois, and middle-class, female consumers as morally responsible for the exploitation and oppression of other humans and animals, even if, politically and economically, they are largely denied access to such realms of power. And yet this figure also serves to deny such women power where they do exercise it — as symbolic agents who through the visual display of their bodies must manipulate the field of symbolic power to gain, however tenuously, class affiliation and commodity-based material wealth. It was, perhaps, this contradictory reproduction of visual violence toward female bourgeois and middle-class consumers in conjunction with the sanctioned ignorance on the part of Lynx and other animal liberationist and welfare organizations in Britain, the United States, and Canada, displayed toward aboriginal cultural and economic disempowerment, that prompted me to inquire into a gender history of sexual difference and ideologies of cultural difference.[17]

Symbolic Historiographies of Fur

The libidinal investments in the symbolic production of fur can be traced to the sumptuary laws of England from the fourteenth to the early seventeenth century. Chapter 2, "The Sumptuous Details of History," examines the legislation against extravagant living which restricted food consumption and the quality of cloth and apparel worn by nobility, clergy, and peasantry, as well as fur apparel. Although there is little evidence that this legislation was or could be strictly enforced, it did serve to regulate class and gender distinctions socially by establishing fur-clothing styles as ideological codes of economic status and wealth. The effects of this codification have been long lasting. Flaubert's definition of fur — "Sign of Wealth" — is perhaps the most succinct expression of the signifying force sumptuary laws were to exercise over time.[18] Signs of the monarchial privileges accorded fur survive in a contemporary advertisement for Swedish Crown Mink (see Figure 1). The advertisement plays on royalty's privileged access to certain furs as a metaphor for the quality of the fur and the aesthetic taste of the consumer; it also plays on the idea that sumptuary laws were designed, in part, to prohibit the middle classes from acquiring the visual signs of monarchial privilege and therefore challenges the monarchial monopoly over the codes of symbolic power.

The hierarchy of furs and social positions created by these regulatory acts also influenced notions of sexual propriety among different classes of women and contributed to the construction of feminine and masculine genders and sexual differences between men and women. For example, prostitutes were forbidden to wear fur in order to differentiate them from "respectable women." The regulation of sumptuousness in relation to sexual and economic propriety took an interesting twist in the contemporary moment when Richard Nixon in his now-infamous "Checkers speech" used the metaphor of sartorial display with respect to his wife, to distinguish an honorable from a dishonorable use of political funds: "I should say this, that Pat doesn't have a mink coat. But she does have a respectable Republican cloth coat, and I always tell her that she would look good in anything."[19] Nixon's use of the mink coat (countered by the domestic animal, the family pet named Checkers) as a sign of unacceptable material extravagance carries connotations of sexual excess into the sphere of economic (im)propriety and the misuse of public monies. That Mrs. Nixon's sexual propriety can stand as a metaphor for Nixon's politicoeconomic propriety turns on the historical constructions of the libidinal and political investments conjoined in the oppositional figure of the prostitute/ respectable woman in fur.

What appears to be a relatively minor aspect of sumptuary legislation in medieval Britain gained increasing importance through the sixteenth and seventeenth centuries — that is, the link between material excess, female sexuality, and women's attire. The ideology of artifice that emerges in Puritan discourse was designed to attack female dissimulation and masquerade. This chapter also examines these attacks on artifice and women.

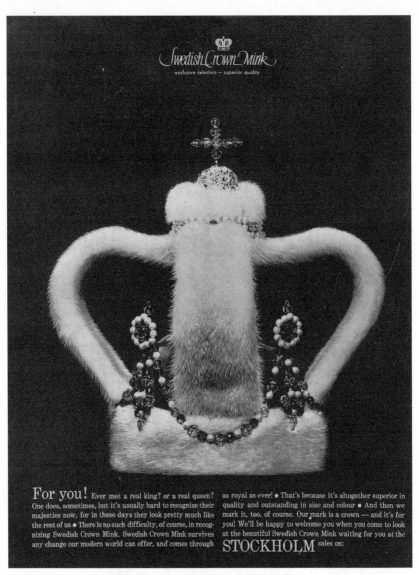

For you! Ever met a real king? or a real queen? One does, sometimes, but it's usually hard to recognize their majesties now, for in these days they look pretty much like the rest of us ● There is no such difficulty, of course, in recognizing Swedish Crown Mink. Swedish Crown Mink survives any change our modern world can offer, and comes through as royal as ever! ● That's because it's altogether superior in quality and outstanding in size and colour ● And then we mark it, too, of course. Our mark is a crown — and it's for you! We'll be happy to welcome you when you come to look at the beautiful Swedish Crown Mink waiting for you at the STOCKHOLM sales on:

FIGURE 1. Swedish Crown Mink advertisement (1965).
Reproduced by permission of Sveriges Pälsdjursuppfödares Riksförbund (Swedish Fur Breeders Association) and the British Library (P 445/1).

Clearly, an ideology of artifice serves to support contempt for women who figure as spectacles of symbolic power. But such "material girls" also use modes of symbolic agency to resist figuration as the passive embodiment of male desire or economic dependency. Madonna flings her white fur stole over her shoulder in her music video "Material Girl" in defiance of female economic dependency, transforming Marilyn Monroe's theme song "Diamonds Are a Girl's Best Friend" into a radical pro-sex anthem that could easily be paraphrased as "Sexual Commodification Is a Girl's Best Friend."[20] Madonna transforms her value as a sexual commodity into something far more desirable than mere diamonds. In Madonna's video, it is men who desire her, not she who desires diamonds. Compare Madonna, with her defiant commodification of sexual independence, to the woman who is accosted on the street for wearing fur, the current popular icon of an invidious spectacle of symbolic power.

Chapter 3, "The Masochist's Gift," explores the invention of the fur-clad feminine despot in the theoretical context of psychoanalytical constructions of sexual fetishism, masochism, and sadism and Leopold von Sacher-Masoch's late-nineteenth-century novel *Venus in Furs*. Along with the psychoanalytical discourses of the late nineteenth century, Masoch's sexualized version of the master/slave dialectic provides interesting and complex representations of relations of power and femininity, sexual and commodity fetishisms, and sexual and political violence. The figure of the fur-clad woman in Masoch's novel suggests that by the nineteenth century fur had become invested with a surplus of sociosymbolic meanings; indeed, it had become a representative figure of the vicissitudes of a European cultural inscription of violent excess, both sexual and material, par excellence. Constitutive of this cultural inscription of excess and violence is the concurrent European expansion. In order to understand how the figure of the fur-clad feminine despot emerged as a bearer of an imperialist sexualized violence, we need to take Edward Said's suggestion that while it is difficult "to show the involvements of culture with expanding empires, to make observations about art that preserve its unique endowments and at the same time map its affiliations . . . we must attempt this, and set the art in the global, earthly context."[21] I, therefore, read the figure of Wanda in *Venus in Furs* as a charged characterization of a European fantasy of Oriental despotism. Masoch's use of European orientalism in circumscribing the meaning of feminine despotism is especially important inasmuch as it brings into view constellations of power and desire which cut across several maps of imperial and sexual conquest.

In *Venus in Furs* Leopold von Sacher-Masoch exploits Titian's representation of the fur-clad women as an exemplary moment in the visual history of fur's sexual fetishism. The sexual fetishism attributed to the fur-clad woman can be traced to the extraordinary mid-seventeenth-century etchings of Wenceslaus Hollar. In his collection titled *The Four Seasons*, of which Hollar produced four versions, the plates for *Winter* stand out for their depiction of an allegorical figure of woman in fur. These images along with Hollar's etchings of women's fashion accessories, including fur muffs, deserve notice as an earlier atypical and anticipatory contribution to the libidinal investment in fur and its importance to the invention of the fur-clad feminine despot. A study in the kinds of images reproduced over time which constitute the visual lexicon of fur fashions provides an opportunity to elaborate on Walter Benjamin's important essay "The Work of Art in the Age of Mechanical Reproduction." For my purposes Benjamin's essay foregrounds the iteration, functionalism, and image/text relationship of etchings, engravings, and fine art images, especially as they are used for pictorial evidence in twentieth-century fashion historiography. My intention here is to illustrate that the iteration of such images overdetermines the social and political, as well as economic, values that we attribute to fur in our present moment. Although Benjamin's essay focuses on a mode of ideology critique based in class relations, other modes of social differentiation, such as gender, sexuality, and race, support the visual overdetermination at work in the aestheticization of political power which Benjamin himself is particularly concerned to critique. The kind of aestheticization of politics I observe in the Lynx campaign, for example, is entirely indebted to a history of pictorial reproduction which inscribes, especially through the use of "works of art," an aesthetic value for fur overdetermined by the artistic representation of white, upper-class or aristocratic female bodies.[22] Chapter 4, "The Fecundity of Fur," examines the pictorial history of fur. The history of the visual representation of fur and women indicates what images have over time come to stand as authoritative signs from which to "read" fashions of the day. It is particularly notable that after the seventeenth century, portrait paintings by Rembrandt, Holbein, Titian, and Rubens became authoritative visual reproductions in fur fashion discourse. Fur fashion has always been viewed as an elite commodity, signifying an exclusivity and aesthetic value similar to the very art in which it was — and still is — depicted.

The Cultural Politics of Fur

People for the Ethical Treatment of Animals (PETA), the largest national animal-rights organization in the United States launched a "Naked" campaign in the early 1990s which enlisted celebrities and fashion models to make the anti-fur position as "fashionable" as the season's clothing trends. Using some aspects of the fashion industry to critique others certainly conforms to a kind of fragmented, postmodern selective consciousness by which we rely on advertising companies to inform the general public about what's in and what's out, defining who can be discriminated against and who cannot. This irony has not been lost on fashion industry ideologues themselves.

FIGURE 2. "How to Control Wild Animals" (1992).
Reproduced by permission of Diesel USA.

The problem with the kind of simple moralities favored by Lynx and PETA is not so much their simplicity as the ease with which they can be appropriated for the rather sophisticated purposes of ideological recontainment by the fashion industry itself. Diesel Jeans advertisements parody the self-righteous tone of much of the Lynx and PETA promotional literature, appealing to a consumer perceived as too sophisticated to be taken in by the naive strategies of an increasingly socially conscious "green" marketplace. You needn't buy fur coats, but you can still spend a small fortune on designer jeans. Fashionable activism demands fashionable "active wear."

One advertisement shows "how to control wild animals" (see Figure 2). Domestication is the answer, a neolithic resolution to the problem of waste: "wasting space, wasting time, using the planet as a toilet!" The schizo-rhetoric of the advertisement flows from a suggestive association of the black woman/wild animal with all the baggage this eye-catching racist inscription of the untamed, uncivilized black woman carries, to an ironic displacement in the call to build zoos and metal cages for the production of a not "natural" beauty — all too reminiscent of caged animals in fur factories and the other Diesel Jeans advertisement, titled "Pet Shop" (see Figure 3). The woman on the zebra skins is both the sacrificial black sheep and the redemptive figure of irony, signaled no less by the cross hanging around her neck. The engineers of this image signal their position — in what is

FIGURE 3. "Pet Shop" (1994). Reproduced by permission of Diesel USA.

quickly becoming a popular quest for political simulation — in a further appropriation of another redemptive figure: the Indian. The signature of the Mohawk brave is stamped above another logographeme: "Number 7, in a series of Diesel 'How To . . .' Guides to SUCCESSFUL LIVING for PEOPLE interested in general HEALTH and mental POWER." The multiplicity of logos suggests a desire to cover all bases, to enter the fashion code into a polyvocal political discourse, because it is only in the realm of ideological codes that our liberty of choice lies. Nothing about this advertisement tells us, the spectators, about the exploitative conditions under which women labor in the textile industries of the Philippines, Mexico, and South Korea, even if we are talking about "workwear."[23] In fact, one could almost be convinced by the rhetoric of political simulation that the domain of exploited labor has disappeared from the face of the earth and we are left with only an ideological mode of resistance illustrated in the advertisement by its call to "general HEALTH and mental POWER." At least this advertisement is clear about one thing: the inscription of racism, together with an ironic disclaimer, tell us that complicity is afoot, and its location is elsewhere: "Shopping malls, mega parking-lots, golf courses." Isn't that what First Nations' lands are for? Isn't that what the Third World is for? Isn't that what the "wilderness" is for?

Commodities, notes Marx, are very strange things. They appear to be

animate, alive, "abounding in metaphysical subtleties and theological nice-
ties."[24] They speak to each other as if they constituted a collectivity. The
fur coat in the Lynx campaign signifies a complex discourse on the ethics
of consumer decision making. In an increasingly "green" marketplace, ethical concerns rest with ecologically correct consumables. Fur coats speak to
us of unethical consumer habits. On the other hand, Lynx T-shirts and
billboard signs speak to us, quite literally with slogans and captions, of
a new order of proper consumption. In dialogue with each other they
compete for our attention. Shopkeepers swing with the current sea change,
turning the color of U.S. money, the color of envy, into the color of ecology:
don't be surprised if you feel a little nauseated by this daunting wave of
green capital that is threatening to crush us between Scylla and Charybdis.
And as if to give the fur coat a measure of human authenticity, a representation of an identifiable living creature stands in to support it, to give the
illusion that its voice derives from nature. She is called "Woman." By and
large she is mute, dumb; at best she mimics the voice of reason. If she did
otherwise, she would tempt us into wasteful expenditure, hedonistic excess,
and other perversions of desire, enchantment, and fantasy. Once you get
past the fur coats at the end of a stuffy wardrobe and enter the chilly climate
of virtual politics where fur coats speak louder than women, you feel as if
the world has turned inside-out. How is it that women came to figure as
derisive spectacles of such demonlike consumerism? How is it that Lynx
cannot let go of the enormous symbolic capital invested in this figure of
the fur-clad bourgeois woman? She is, to be sure, rather captivating, mysterious and enigmatic.

A study of the gender significance attributed to fur fashions reveals that
what is "new" (as only commoditization itself depends upon the reinscrip-
tion of the "new") to this century's configuration of fur's symbolic value
is the explicitly feminine connotation given to wealth and prestige. The
practice of putting the meanings and values ascribed to fur into motion in
the symbolic world of the metropolis rests with the female spectacle. As
consumers, as spectacles of luxury, class privilege, and racial superiority,
European bourgeois women actively participate in achieving their status
through the accumulation of the symbolic capital invested in "femininity."
The spectacle of the fur-clad woman, who invests "femininity" with cultural capital, achieves symbolic value, then, by way of a gendered mode of
social differentiation. The accumulation of cultural capital is entirely necessary for bourgeois women in order to invert their disproportionate lack
of control over access to economic capital due to their material dependency
on bourgeois men. While she acts as an agent of display and thereby accrues social prestige through the very activity of luxury-commodity exchange, she also increases her subjective value as "Woman" and enters into

circulation as an object of exchange among the wealthy class. Her practices of consumption participate in the making of the bourgeois woman; as a bourgeois female consumer she reproduces the social and symbolic values of her gendered class position in the purchase and display of a fur coat.

Chapter 5, "How to Misread Fashion," examines how the fur coat circulates in the twentieth century primarily as a feminine fashion commodity worn by women to display the twin signs of wealth and social prestige. The female bourgeois consumer of fur fashion is an entity constructed by a set of coordinated components, including, among others, the fashion magazine, fashion writers, critics, photographers, the trade journals of the fur industry, media and other signifying practices such as film, not to mention the intellectual production of fashion criticism and theory in the academy, which delineates the legitimacy of fashion as an aesthetic or pre-aesthetic object of analysis. The combined efforts of all these signifying practices produce consumers capable of "misreading" their material and symbolic interests and thereby able to participate as *symbolic agents* in the arena of fur fashion display and consumption. In this chapter I discuss an earlier twentieth-century film by G. W. Pabst, *The Joyless Street* (*Die freudlose Gasse*, 1925). In this film a fur coat occupies a significant place as a sign of female sexuality and its libidinal profits of exchange. Jennie Livingston's documentary on the gay balls in Harlem, *Paris Is Burning* (1991), and *Unzipped* (1995), which documents the creation of a fashion show by the American designer Isaac Mizrahi, are two late-twentieth-century films that overturn, through parody, the conventional association of fur and female erotic power. In all three films, however, the fur coat exists as a symbolic object of wealth and prestige conjoined with an ideology of female sexual power because it is known and recognized as such; that is, it is socially instituted and received by spectators and consumers who have acquired the cultural capital necessary to decipher the codes that make the fur coat a desirable object for aspiring middle-class women as well as bourgeois women. These films not only help to create that very cultural capital; they also open up the possibility for a critical account of how such "capital" circulates both economically and libidinally.

This book is necessarily selective and partial, concentrating on those inscriptional spaces in which fur takes on remarkable, exemplary, or in some cases, atypical degrees of valuation. I do not aim to provide a chronological narrative of a continuous transformation of fur from one signifying category to another, nor do I want to reduce the symbolic status of fur's history to an atemporal flow of random or aleatory events. As Walter Benjamin writes, history is "the subject of a structure whose site is not homogeneous, empty time, but time filled by the presence of the now [*Jetztzeit*]." Benjamin continues: "Thus, to Robespierre ancient Rome was a past charged with the time of the now which he blasted out of the continuum of history. The French Revolution viewed itself as Rome reincarnate. It evoked ancient Rome the way fashion evokes costumes of the past. Fashion has a flair for the topical, no matter where it stirs in the thickets of long ago; it is a tiger's leap into the past. This jump, however, takes place in an arena where the ruling class gives the commands. The same leap in the open air of history is the dialectical one, which is how Marx understood the revolution."[25] Like the history of the luxury status of fur and access to it by the ruling classes, a study of the history of fur, and perhaps especially fur fashion, is its own special "tiger's leap" into the past.

I read the current contest over fur, fur-bearing animals, and fur fashion as evoking, right down to its soft and sensuous fibers, the history of class exploitation, imperialism, and the oppression of women. Fur fashions not only evoke "costumes of the past"; they conjure up a history that is often too preoccupied with its own glory to bear the nakedness of its devastating effects on North America's indigenous peoples. The material and symbolic history of fur and fur fashions has had an enormous impact on the lives of European, aboriginal, and immigrant women from all classes — laboring, aristocratic, and bourgeois — most notably in the dominant construction of female subjectivity as a sexual sociosymbolic prop for the edifice of imperial trade and colonization in the "New World." This is not to say that women are collectively victimized or exploited to the same degree, or that women use similar strategies or tactics to resist oppressive circumstances. What women do do collectively, regardless of the class, race, and colonial specificities of their situation, is act as agents in the world, reproducing, transforming, or in some way negotiating their social relations and material existence. To that extent, we're all "material girls." But how Inuit and Dene women negotiate their interests as producers of fur hides for the fur fashion or tourist markets in the late twentieth century and how European aristocratic women in the early modern period deploy symbolic agency in their display of fur fashions constitute significant differences, primarily in their access to economic capital.

The political and libidinal economies of fur have come together in startling ways in the contemporary moment. Part of the agenda of the animal rights' movement is resistance to fulfilling the fetishistic desires of a ruling social and economic class whose pleasure derives from the slaughter of animals. Implicitly, the human/animal opposition, which structures both criticism of and support for animal rights activism, contributes to a new kind of fetishism, the spectacle fetishism of mass media and their images of sadistic violence and cruelty to animals. From status symbol to sadist symbol, "Fur: Sign of Wealth" conjoins with "Fur: Sign of Animal-Victim."

The reproduction of imperialist practices on the part of the ecological movement, which, in Britain at least, chose to ignore the effects of its anti-fur campaign on the economic and political self-determinacy of northern indigenous peoples in Alaska, Canada, and Greenland, has produced several strategic responses among aboriginal fashion designers and storytellers. Chapter 6, "Furs in Disguise," discusses these strategic responses in light of the politics and ideologies of cultural difference that pervade not only the work of mainstream fashion designers such as Issac Mizrahi and Jean Paul Gaultier but also the Inuit fashion shows held at the Museum of Civilization in Ottawa in 1995 and 1996. Storytellers such as George Blondin in *When the World Was New: Stories of the Sahtú Dene* and Julie Cruikshank's ethnographic approach to the stories of Angela Sidney, Kitty Smith, and Annie Ned in *Life Lived like a Story: Life Stories of Three Yukon Native Elders* offer new insights into animal-human and human-land relations that support the value of fur in indigenous struggles for cultural and political self-determination.[26] These texts not only challenge the idea that the fur trade is a historical component of indigenous peoples' lives but also question whether the trade, in its present reality, would be necessary if Dene and Inuit women and men had access to organized labor.

"Furs in Disguise" can be read as an allegory of the simulated economic and libidinal investments in fur in our postmodern times. It dramatizes the ideological operation of *misrecognition* essential to the commodity, ethnographic, and sexual fetishisms of an object such as fur. Misrecognition informs a disinterested stance, a neo-Kantian perception of the autonomous aesthetic object, which not only brackets off material existence but preserves the objective mechanisms of exchange.[27] In the figure of the fur-clad female spectacle, it is women's bodies that mediate these objective mechanisms of exchange. In the ideologies of cultural difference which permeate the political and symbolic appropriations of aboriginal labor practices on the land, an ethnographic fetishism mediates the legitimacy of mainstream fashion production of fur clothing and images. The erotic and exotic commodity fetishisms attributed to the economic and libidinal investments in fur, while seemingly working to circumscribe the meaning and value of fur, effectively inscribe the figure of the white bourgeois woman and aboriginal gatherers and hunters as spectacles of political, poetic, and symbolic exchange.

This book analyzes the contemporary meanings of fur in light of the various historical contexts and political and libidinal economies in which it has circulated. The current structure of meanings can be seen as a palimpsest of the past values and new concerns that overdetermine the use of the fur concept. In the early twentieth century the fur trade declined drastically, and fur became, in the Western economic context, a marginal commodity, its marginality serving to redouble its inaccessibility as a luxury commodity: as certain fur-bearing animals became rare and extinct, so too the fur coat itself was to become a rare and reified commodity, while retaining its trace as sexual fetish.[28] Meanwhile, in other worlds, fur retained its economic value as staple for aboriginal people, and its symbolic value increased as it became a vital support for modern aboriginal cultures. A newspaper headline for an article on the cosmetics industry in Canada's national newspaper, the *Globe and Mail*, "For Today's Fashions, We'd Rather Dance with Wolves Than Skin Them," recalls a residue of colonial relations layered by current ecological correctness and the spectacle fetishism of cruelty to animals.[29] I believe that we can read in this excess of significations a postcolonial allegory of the history of imperialism and, further, that the history of fur in its various value-laden contexts constitutes a treasure-house of signs from which to trace the gender and colonial character of early European expansion and its continuing effects in the late twentieth century.

Simulated Politics

Millions of animals are trapped each year in steel-jawed traps, then cruelly killed, like this North American coyote dying slowly beneath the boots of a hunter. And millions more are incarcerated for brief lives in tiny, squalid cages on fur farms, before being gassed, electrocuted or lethally injected and stripped of their pelts. All this waste and misery to serve the whims of the fashion trade. It's a cruel, despicable business. Because no-one needs a fur coat. They are simply status symbols — luxury garments bought at a heavy price in animal pain and suffering.

No civilised country should tolerate the cruelties of the fur trade. And people who wear fur coats should be shamed out of the belief that fur is glamorous. Furs are beautiful — but only on their rightful owners, the fur-bearing animals.

Join the moral majority. Oppose the fur trade.

Leaflet produced by Lynx

One of the most important moments in the film is when Rafi and Rosie are having their row in the restaurant. Rafi's line is that she doesn't know what it is like in decolonized countries and she's giving the line about there being no excuses for torture. They're screaming at each other and everybody in the restaurant forms a sort of audience so that it becomes a public performance. At a certain moment the camera holds on a close-up of Rosie so that it almost looks like a still. Rosie has very sharp weapon-like earrings, and the profile is frozen in such a way that it looks as though a caged beast has been cornered: the beleaguered position of the civilized conscience for whom torture is bad under any circumstances.

Gayatri Chakravorty Spivak, *"Sammy and Rosie Get Laid"*

Blasphemy protects one from the moral majority within, while still insisting on the need for community.

Donna Haraway, "A Cyborg Manifesto"

The conflict over fur, international in its scope and effects, is the most recent and perhaps the most politically charged context in which fur emerges as a complex sign of cultural, political, and social conflict. The anti-fur/pro-fur polarization is like a metaphysical binary opposition and as such can be subject to a deconstructive turn that would disclose not only the subordination of the pro-fur side articulated by First Nations to the anti-fur side of the duality but also their relative complicity in each other's disparate political agendas. On the anti-fur side, an ecological puritanism demands the strict regulation and control of animal conservation, preservation, and economic utility. From the pro-fur side such desire to regulate and control the use of animals and trapping practices conforms to a much longer history of British imperialist strategies to eradicate indigenous economic, political, and social practices, not least through a Christian missionizing zeal all too present in the "crusade for animal rights."[1] Yet, while anti-fur moralists attempt to reconceptualize the dominant anthropocentric metaphysics that have shaped a hierarchical relation between human and animal and pro-fur supporters stress the importance of disparities between human consumers and producers of animal products, both share a common interest in competing for the meanings and values ascribed to fur, fur-bearing animals, and purchasers of fur products.[2]

The contradictory interests in the contemporary arena of cultural politics with respect to fur trapping signal a certain tension in both textual and visual fields of political and aesthetic modes of representation. This tension is clearly marked by a struggle among different political, economic, and cultural values — for aboriginal hunters, on the one hand, and animal welfare or rights organizations such as Lynx, on the other hand. What is less obvious is the degree to which the values and meanings ascribed to the fur object in particular and the fur trade in general are inflected by libidinal investments. In these various discursive fields fur as an object is constituted by divergent and at times competing meanings and values. The stories this written object relates are by no means unique to the paleonomic narratives of European expansion into North America, the effects of the early fur trade between England and France and North America, and the globalization of the fur industry in the twentieth century.[3] Fur also circulates within a libidinal economy. When fur is constructed as a desirable object, sustaining or rejecting that desirability can only be accomplished for capitalist patriarchy through the mediation of sexual, ethnographic, and commodity fetishisms.

In Lynx's use of mass media to disseminate politically charged messages, fashion photographic images of a psychic fantasy of woman were recoded through a provocative and disturbing set of depictions in which the un-evenly gendered and racially oriented relations among woman, animals, in-digenous hunters, and Third World fur-factory workers are recontained and reproduced in all their sumptuous and fetishistic appeal. This chapter addresses the images and texts of the Lynx media campaign. It also explores the other side of the environmental debate, the discourse on northern hunters such as that of Hugh Brody and the formation of Indigenous Sur-vival International (ISI). In order to counter the effects of the Lynx public media campaign, Brody, in consultation with ISI, organized the exhibition *Living Arctic* at the British Museum. The problem with the discourse on northern hunters and indigenous cultures is that it excludes the specificity of aboriginal and Inuit women as gatherers and their work in the treatment and selling of furs. Although I am critical of both sides of the debate, this feminist intervention concentrates primarily on Lynx while taking the dis-course on northern hunters as an occasion to address an important debate within feminist theory on the epistemological characterization of egali-tarian gendered relations in modern gatherer-hunter cultures.

Selling Politics to the Masses

In September 1984 Greenpeace International announced in England that it would launch a campaign against the fur trade with the intention of "sham[ing] the wearers of fur coats off the streets."[4] With the aid of the bad boy of 1960s fashion photography, David Bailey, and a "celebrities charter" of forty signatories supporting the campaign, Greenpeace geared up for a massive media assault on the cruel sensibilities of the rich and glamorous. When Greenpeace withdrew its support over a controversy in-volving the potential effects of this campaign on the already tenuous eco-nomic stability of indigenous trappers in northern Canada, the media-based animal rights organization Lynx consolidated its existence.[5]

The Lynx campaigners outlined their media strategy in their promo-tional literature:

> Our aim is to create a new climate of opinion which ensures that wearing fur garments is no longer acceptable. In this way we will strike at the heart of the fur industry depriving it of customers for fur products and so dramatically reducing the number of animals killed for their fur. This is being achieved by a spectacular and innovative advertising campaign using billboard and bus shelter posters and cinema commercials, which show the unpleasant reality behind the glamorous image portrayed by the fur industry.

Lynx also announced a commitment to parliamentary reform. Its resolutions, however, which include lobbying the government to legislate against fur factory farms in England and the European Union and prohibiting fur imports from countries that still use steel-jawed leg-hold traps (although they were banned in the United Kingdom over thirty years ago), were far less prominent during the mid-1980s than the media campaign, into which Lynx poured its energy and its money. Later, the success of the campaign contributed to the European Union's introducing a ban on the import of wild fur from countries using the leg-hold trap, which was to go into effect in January 1996. The ban was temporarily postponed until January 1997 and was delayed again pending an international agreement on humane trap standards among Canada, the United States, Russia and the European Union. According to Richard Maracle, a member of the Mohawk Nation and principal adviser to ISI (Canada), the ban would affect "over 73,000 Aboriginal adults and their families."[6]

The advertising medium is one ideological apparatus of representation capable of disseminating political as well as commercial interests. As the Benetton fashion advertising campaign of the fall and winter of 1992–1993 demonstrated, with its use of documentary photographs of "real-life" events previously published in news magazines and dealing with themes of "immigration, AIDS, terrorism, violence, and the plight of political refugees," the aestheticization of political events is a highly profitable enterprise, capitalizing as it does on the twin currencies of provocation and mystification.[7] In the case of Lynx the distinction between the political and commercial seemingly all but disappears as the high production values of its protofashion images provide a protective gloss for the simulation of its political agenda.

Like astute semioticians of the political economy of the sign, the Lynx advertising campaigners used the seductive power of the image, especially high-production-value fashion images of sumptuously clad fur-bearing fashion models, though turning these images to other purposes. Lynx purported to engage in a form of image critique when it announced its intention to "show the unpleasant reality behind the glamorous image portrayed by the fur industry." In several of their glossy posters, fashion photographs of women in fur remind the spectator of these already symbolically invested signs of social distinction. Contrary to what one might expect, however, the symbolic recoding of the fur fashion images by the Lynx campaigners does little to challenge the ideological effects of such images in interpellating the female or feminine consumer; rather, the fashion photo is reproduced precisely for the fetishistic voyeurism that dominates its spectral reception. In the poster captioned "Fur coat with matching accessories" a model in a fur coat and hat wears an expensive-looking silver earring made

The leg-hold trap.
For animals that
don't get strangled,
beaten, gassed or
electrocuted.

ur coat with
matching
accessories.

LYNX

Fighting the fur trade.

P.O. Box 509, Dunmow, Essex CM6 1UH.

FIGURE 4. Lynx anti-fur poster (1984). Reproduced by permission of
Respect for Animals, P.O. Box 500, Nottingham, NG1 3AS, U.K.

from the foot of an animal and dripping with blood (see Figure 4). A thick
silver chain with a small leg-hold trap, also stained with drops of blood,
hangs around her neck as though the chain were just another fine accessory,
and the image just another fashion photograph. In this "anti-fashion" statement, the written image is articulated through the primary text: "Fur coat
with matching accessories."[8] A supplementary text in smaller print at the
bottom lefthand side of the image alters the significance of this fashion
photograph for its anti-fur spectators: "The leg-hold trap. For animals that
don't get strangled, beaten, gassed or electrocuted." In this tainted fashion
image the so-called referent — the real woman who wears the fur coat —
is brought into the realm of individual accountability, where she looks more
like a social scapegoat than a model for ethicopolitical behavior. The fur-
bearing woman, as a class unto herself, collectively comes to figure as a cold
and cruel monstrosity, an accessory to the crime, who would wear her capacity for terror and violence on her sleeve.

Raymond Williams maintains that to change the deepest habits and assumptions of a consumer society is a sound ecological approach to the
problem of diminishing resources.[9] Lynx predicates its "radicality" on this
argument that consumer habits must change in a world where resources,
that is, wild animals, are limited. One way to effect such a change, for Lynx,
has been to offer alternative consumer markets, a kind of "green" radical
chic. Underlying Lynx's use of various media and ideological apparatuses
to change public opinion has been an extensive commercial enterprise. And
Lynx, until its dissolution in early 1993, was very much in the business of
fighting the fur trade through a competitive commercial strategy, which

ranged from selling T-shirts, coffee mugs, and glossy posters to distributing a mail order catalog that sells these and other commodities representing commercially invested signs of cultural rebellion such as Doc Martens boots and shoes, made with "the finest non-leather material available." Lynx's mass media advertising campaign not only sold an anti-fur morality; it also sold commodities. Indeed, all these libidinally and ideologically invested images are deployed to develop, as ironic as it seems, a commercially viable political constituency: or is it a politically viable commercial constituency? In either case, the aestheticization of commodities, "as a dimension of the semiotic, celebrates the transformation of the material by the abstract," as Susan Stewart notes. "The capacity of all play and fictions to reframe context is a transformation performed by means of signifying practices, the transformation of use value into exchange value by means of signification. It is not surprising that the age of late capitalism is marked by the aestheticization of commodities and the commercial exploitation of sexuality." [10]

Although Williams may have anticipated, however much he may have deplored, the opening of new consumer markets as one strategy to affect consumer habits, I doubt he could have foreseen the ideological twists and turns that would be manufactured to bring about such shifts. In blaming a social referent for the continuation of the fur trade in the late twentieth century by casting as enemies those women who wear fur coats, Lynx abstracted consumption from the real processes of the world's economy in trade. This scapegoating mechanism represents one important means by which the radicality of Lynx was ideologically engineered to make it a leading voice within the politicized field of ecological struggles.

Some of the questions we might ask include: What kind of "aestheticized politics" are publicized by this animal liberation agenda? What kinds of gendered and racially oriented myths are subjected to aestheticization to convey Lynx's political message? And what interests does Lynx's commercial enterprise hold for advertising a politics of cruelty to animals? The peculiar combination of media advertising, fragmentary focus on a single aspect of ecological struggle, and commercial investment gives way to what I call simulated politics. In one sense I use the term to draw attention to the technological media of photography, film, and video, used by Lynx to simulate a relatively closed world in which a tragic drama is enacted between animal victims and glamorous women whose complicity as consumers of fur coats is taken as lending support to the perpetuation of this cruel and barbarous enterprise. I also use the term to describe a political agenda that pretends to be a popular political struggle even though no political constituencies are being represented, supported, or advocated. On the contrary, the moralistic and aggressively self-righteous political voice of Lynx was designed, like its American moral-majority counterpart, the pro-life campaign, to represent those who cannot represent themselves and, therefore, must be represented: animals and fetuses. Is it accidental that Lynx and other self-righteously moralistic organizations developed in the 1980s as new social movements asserted the right of politicized constituencies to speak for themselves? The simulated politics of Lynx tends to silence the voices of these new social movements. Moreover, this postmodern aestheticization of political representation points to a problem of political agency for those liberal-minded individuals who participated in and supported the Lynx enterprise; the need to represent an especially problematic animal constituency that cannot represent itself signals an attempt on Lynx's part to reinstate hegemonic equilibrium for its supporters where the established voices of a post–World War II regime of power were being openly challenged.[11]

Whereas Lynx's simulated politics did not represent a social group and its agenda did not consider the social relations between human and animal or the human/animal organism and technology, the campaign had very real material and ideological effects on such social groups as European bourgeois women, fur factory workers in South Korea, and Inuit and Dene hunters, trappers, and treaters of fur. The following three sections explore the simulated politics of Lynx through some examples of the images used.

Natural Automata and Fur-Bearing Women

The notion of the "dumb animal," devoid of both speech and reason, not to mention a soul, is at the basis of an anthropocentric modern philosophical tradition in the West, which uses the animal/human opposition to produce a hierarchical equation between the inferior faculties of the animal and the superior ones of the human (that is, "Man"). Descartes, for example, reasons in his *Discourse on Method* that animals differ from humans. In a somewhat ironic anticipation of the cybernetic realities of postmodern life, Descartes employs a cyborg figure to dramatize the human/animal distinction, comparing the machine animal or natural automaton to the human:

> This will not seem at all strange to those who know how many different automatons, or moving machines, the skill of man can construct with the use of very few parts, in comparison with the great multitude of bones, muscles, nerves, arteries, veins and all the other parts that are in the body of any animal. For they will regard this body as a machine which, having been made by the hands of God, is incomparably better ordered than any machine that can be devised by man, and contains in itself movements more wonderful than those in any such machine.

I made special efforts to show that if any such machines had the organs and outward shape of a monkey or of some other animal that lacks reason, we should have no means of knowing that they did not possess entirely the same nature as these animals; whereas if any such machines bore a resemblance to our bodies and imitated our actions as closely as possible for all practical purposes, we should still have two very certain means of recognizing that they were not real men.[12]

Animals differ from humans, first, because "they could never use words, or put together other signs, as we do in order to declare our thoughts to others" and, second, because "even though such machines might do some things as well as we do them, or perhaps even better, they would inevitably fail in others, which would reveal that they were acting not from understanding but only from the disposition of their organs."[13] Note that it is not simply the ability to use words or to speak which is in question but the ability to assemble signs in a particular syntax or grammar, in other words, in a rational manner that can be communicated or recorded, that is written (videotaped? photographed?) for the benefit of others and hence constitutive of the production of a cultural text.[14]

From Descartes we learn that animals are truly dumb: they do not speak, nor do they reason with the capability of a rational soul. The dumb animal, then, serves as the anthropocentric other to the rational and belief-bound human, who is also always already "Man."

The implications of this Cartesian logic are strikingly apparent in a Lynx advertising poster that presents an image of a woman shown from the waist down in a short black skirt and stiletto heels dragging a fur coat that leaves a trail of blood behind her (see Figure 5). In representing the rights of fur-bearing animals that "lack speech," the image of the woman, cut off at the waist, is also rendered speechless. But the attribution of dumbness to women evokes yet another, perhaps more spurious, meaning: women are also, it would appear, stupid. But how are they stupid and what form of stupidity is being called to the spectators' attention? Clearly a fur coat is not in and of itself a stupid thing to desire. The lack of intelligence on the part of women would seem to lie elsewhere.

Part of what constitutes the making of a female consumer is an individual-subject interpellated as passive when confronted by advertiser's persuasive marketing tactics. For Cathy Griggers, in American consumer discourse the female consumer has become "as splintered as the markets which women comprise." In other words, women are susceptible within the social discourse of consumption to competing changes in the meanings and values ascribed to commodities. In keeping with this feminized logic of consumption, women "represented a major market to be divided and redi-

It takes up to 40 dumb animals to make a fur coat.

But only one to wear it.

LYNX

Fighting the fur trade

If you don't want animals gassed, electrocuted, trapped or strangled, don't buy a fur coat. P O Box 509 Dunmow, Essex Tel: 0371 872011

FIGURE 5. Lynx anti-fur poster (1984). Reproduced by permission of Respect for Animals, P.O. Box 500, Nottingham, N G I 3A S, U.K.

vided, and the dark continent of their desire meant new terrain, unmapped territories of objects for satisfaction as they entered consumer markets either newly opened to them or newly created in the name of their desire." [15] If we were to apply Griggers's critique of the imperial logic of passive commodity acquisition to the Lynx mandate, we would conclude that the fur coat, which once represented an object to be consumed by white bourgeois women or aspiring middle-class women in order to exhibit their materially superior social status, now represents an object to be rejected in order to exhibit a morally superior social status. Lynx, then, represents the primary consumer for the fur market in the figure of the white bourgeois woman whose purchasing power is deemed unstable and subject to relatively easy manipulation. I want to pause here for a moment and reflect on the use of advertising by Lynx and note the contradictory assumptions contained by its psychic fantasy of woman as the female consumer-cum-politicized subject.

The ostensible stupidity of the female consumer manifests itself in her susceptibility to a value system that privileges the fur coat as a mark of social distinction. She has been duped by the fashion advertising system, which is held responsible for producing the desires needed to maintain the values of a hierarchical class society. And yet, despite the implicit critique of the fashion advertisements for promoting fur coats, Lynx uses the advertisement format to promote an anti-fur morality. In theory, then, the logic of female passivity which pervades the advertising genre will condition women's consumer habits whether the fashion advertisers promote furs or Lynx's advertisers promote anti-fur morality. In either case, the construction of women as dumb — silent and stupid — is essential to the success of Lynx's media campaign.

But while for Lynx it could be said that every advertising viewer is equally dumb, it could also be said that Lynx interpellates the viewer as intelligent whereas other advertisements do not. The implication of intelligence is essential to Lynx's mandate to provoke the necessary critical response that would shift consumer registers from wanting desirable commodities to amassing intelligent ideas.[16] Their cinema commercial, "Scavengers," is a representative attempt to interpellate an intelligent female spectator, although a particularly circumscribed one. The commercial depicts a rather conventional bourgeois fabula in which Sugar Daddy purchases a fur coat for Mistress Woman. The commercial is shot using avant-garde filmic techniques of distortion and fragmentation to create an effect of moral degeneracy. At the conclusion the woman pulls away the front of a fur coat hanging on what appears to be a seamstress's dress form (otherwise known as a "dummy"), only to find rotting flesh teeming with maggots and flies. This scene is followed by a black background on which appear the words: "When animals are killed for fur, two kinds of scavengers move in. The difference is the flies don't know any better." Whereas in the "dumb animal" poster women are passively positioned as lacking the capacity to reason or voice intelligent choices, in the cinema commercial women are positioned paternalistically as intelligent enough to know better, or at least more intelligent than the flies. The problem with the intelligent woman, however, is that she would compromise herself by trafficking both her intelligence and her sexuality merely for the sake of possessing a fur coat. Not surprisingly, Lynx provoked a kind of critical response it had not hoped for. Feminist graffiti artists voiced their own particular brand of criticism on one billboard (see Figure 6).[17] Contrast this graffiti commentary with the spray-painted back of a luxurious fur coat in Stephen Frears's *Sammy and Rosie Get Laid*. Women who wear fur coats have reacted, according to one major fashion magazine, by "refusing to be intimidated" and insisting on their right to wear their precious and expensive possessions.[18]

If women are intelligent enough to know better than to wear a fur coat, then for the woman who does wear fur, the implication is that she must be a cruel sort of person. In a poster designed by Linda McCartney, who, along with her famous husband Paul McCartney, supported the Lynx campaign, the sadomasochistic motif of the cold and cruel woman justifies Lynx's use of the derogatory and demeaning curse, Bitch! (see Figure 7). The contradictory dichotomies that make up the psychic fantasy of woman — the classic opposition being the virgin/whore — also operate in this poster to divide the good female consumer — the good bitch who would disown her class-based gender privilege — from the bad female consumer

FIGURE 6. Feminist graffiti on Lynx anti-fur poster, London (1985).
Reproduced by permission of the photographer, Jill Posener.

— the rich bitch who would flaunt her class privilege at the expense of exploiting animals (but not workers, of course). The discontinuous relationship between real women who wear furs and the fashion images that promote the wearing of fur constitutes the "specular logic" of Lynx's anti-fur-trapping media campaign. This collapsing of the imaginary into the real is, in large part, what gives Lynx's images their rhetorical force.[19]

Lynx's dramatization of moral justice in the form of a spectacular media campaign substitutes for the voices of political constituencies of disenfranchised groups, such as women. Lynx's aestheticized politics simulates political struggle, the struggle of writhing animals trapped in the video advertising images of their campaign, while other political struggles and politicized constituencies are agitating elsewhere. Through its presence on the media landscape in the urban environment Lynx's simulated politics could be said to silence the voices of those new social movements that represent a complexity of articulations among the categories and political realities incorporating gender, race, class, sexuality, and decolonialization, including the women's movement, anti-racist and anti-imperialist struggles, new forms of socialism, gay and lesbian liberation movements, and the ecological movement or, as it has also come to be known, the "green" revolution.[20]

Bailey's and McCartney's use of the stereotype of the dumb blond woman should alert us to the powerlessness of bourgeois women within their own relatively privileged class and imperial positions, for in this

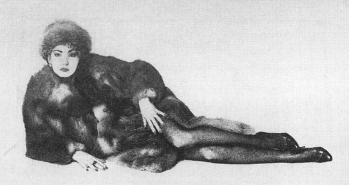

Rich bitch.

Poor bitch.

If you don't want millions of animals tortured and killed in leg-hold traps don't buy a fur coat.

Visit the Lynx Shop at 79 Long Acre, London WC2.
Or write to: PO Box 509, Dunmow, Essex.

FIGURE 7. Lynx anti-fur poster (1984). Reproduced by permission of Respect for Animals, P.O. Box 500, Nottingham, NG1 3AS, U.K.

media campaign such women are quite obviously "fair game."[21] The racial privileging of the wealthy white women in this campaign, however — both as targets, those who are being "shamed into not wearing fur coats," and as advocates, those who are its greatest supporters, such as Linda McCartney — signals that another, more insidious politicoeconomic border is being sharply policed by the ideological effects of the Lynx campaign. All non-European peoples are rendered invisible and nonexistent in the media campaign, only to surface in the educational videos as part of Lynx's condemnation of fur farms, termed fur factories, in so-called newly industrializing countries such as South Korea.

Of Wild Dogs and Domesticated Spectacles

The first Lynx video, *The Roar of Disapproval* (1989), sets out to "show the fur trade as it really is."[22] The "truth" about fur trading and trapping can be summed up with the descriptive terms, barbarous and cruel, usually applied to the use of steel-jawed leg-hold traps that are designed to trap an animal without killing it immediately. Bullets rank as an unacceptable method for obtaining fur pelts because they damage the fur. The video begins with several distressing shots of fur-bearing animals struggling to free themselves from traps. The narrative voice-over informs the viewer that animals often mutilate themselves by chewing off the caught limb in order to escape. The images of these trapped animals effectively portray their powerlessness and their status as victim. As much to heighten the emotional response of the viewer as to underscore the pain these animals suffer, the video also represents images of domestic animals, such as pet dogs, who have lost limbs in accidental encounters with leg-hold traps. Trapping is indiscriminate, the viewer is told, victimizing both wild and domestic animals. The difference between the wild and domesticated trapped animal is determined by the value of their skins; wild animals constitute a treasure, whereas domesticated pets or other undesirable animals constitute "trash," and are so labeled.

The borderline between wild and domestic animal is further breached in the discussion of fur factory practices. Fur farms began in the United States and then moved to the USSR and Scandinavia before they emerged in Korea. During one particular segment, also reproduced in another Lynx video called *Fur Factories*, images of mink and foxes confined in small cages are accompanied by the authoritative commentary of a zoologist and sociobiologist, Desmond Morris, who explains that the erratic behavior of the animals in the cages is a symptom of psychosocial distress caused by the animal's inability to exercise its naturally wild instincts. Morris's commentary is compelling precisely because of the anthropocentric mimesis of human suffering which is projected onto the caged animals. The methods of "execution" range from neck breaking through lethal injection, gassing, and electrocution. The viewer is shown images of all methods of killing, including a longer segment on electrocution in which the viewer witnesses the insertion of a prod into the anus of an animal. When the electric current is administered for a few seconds the body of the animal stiffens and it dies immediately. The Korean fur factory, which produces pelts for the Jindo fur coat manufacturing corporation, uses somewhat more "primitive" and less efficient means. For example, a Korean man demonstrates a method — no animal is actually shown in this presentation — which uses two long planks of wood between which the neck of the animal is presumably squeezed until it dies. This specific discussion of the Korean factory in *The Roar of Disapproval* is supplemented with another seemingly related representation of cruelty. The viewer is shown a large dog being strung up by a noose and left to hang, writhing and struggling. In the following set of frames, presumably the same dog, now dead, is having its outer body hair burned off with a blow torch. These images have very little to do with fur factories and it is interesting to note that in a second video, *Fur Factories*, they do not appear although the rest of the footage on fur factories is reproduced in its entirety. The images of the dog's death and the removal of its fur reproduce an ethnocentric contempt for the treatment of an animal the West holds sacred as a symbol of successful animal domestication. That Korean culture should treat a domesticated pet of the First World as merely another animal without sentimental or emotional status — just another piece of trash — identifies the men depicted in these images as essentially barbarous, not only capable of torturing wild animals in the fur factories but, more important, unable to understand a foundational neolithic distinction between the wild and the domesticated.[23]

In the Lynx mandate, it is a categorical imperative that "no *civilized* country should tolerate the cruelties of the fur trade" (Lynx leaflet, emphasis added), and another that "people who wear fur coats should be shamed out of the belief that fur is glamorous." The suggestion is unmistakable that the demon of barbarity in the figure of the white wealthy British female citizen — the Rich Bitch — can be exorcised through its projection onto Korean factory workers and their culturally specific (represented as uncivilized) use of dogs — the Poor Bitch — for food rather than companionship. What the video sublimates for the First World viewer is a vision of these men as wild, out of control, and equally in need of domestication. The subject of this domestication, however, is the First World viewer's gaze, domesticated into an unquestioning acceptance of these images as a comfortable and comforting affirmation of already ingrained anthropocentric and ethnocentric imperial assumptions. Yes indeed, fur sells politics and the "politics" it sells are culturally imperialist.

Lynx's images are at times all too reminiscent of those that recall twentieth-century human atrocities. Heaps of pink mink carcasses resemble the piles of bodies associated with genocide. These images evoke a structure of experience for the generation of individuals who have constructed this media campaign and whose memory encompasses the rise of German nationalism and the Holocaust.[24] The significant changes in the political field since World War II, the rise of new social and political movements, have left this predominantly white, liberal-minded constituency confused about the exercise of the democratic participation that had hitherto given them their "voices," but at the cost in some cases of the global exploitation of non-European peoples. It is worth noting, I think, that the Falklands War (1982) and the new political movements in Britain in the early 1980s represent instances of how the dominant British classes have been determined, as John Solomos and his colleagues put it, "by the historical development of colonial societies which was central to the reproduction of British imperialism."[25]

Korean factory workers and bourgeois European women emerge as the primary scapegoat figures in the Lynx media campaign and educational videos.[26] Further reproducing British cultural and economic imperialism is Lynx's equally problematic characterization of the extent to which northern indigenous hunters are involved in the contemporary fur trade.

The Discourse of Indigenous Survival

The Lynx media campaign belongs to what Donna Haraway calls the "informatics of domination," a rearrangement of global relations through science and technology. According to Haraway, "We are living through a movement from an organic, industrial society to a polymorphous, information system." Produced within the context of this worldwide shift, Lynx represents a contradictory formation, a commercial enterprise masked as a political movement, a simulation of a political movement through microelectronically produced images that rely on old-fashioned modernist tropes of "depth," "integrity," "organic sex role specialization," and nature/culture hierarchies of difference to construct their message.[27] How surprising, then, that this simulated progressive movement is structured around the social residues of sexism and ethnocentrism. Its position on fur trapping and trading by aboriginal people in North America is even more alarming.

Lynx was part of a general shift in the 1970s and 1980s toward a broadly based international approach to animal liberation. A very successful lobby to prohibit the harvesting of harp seals off the Labrador peninsula in the early 1970s soon spread, as Hugh Brody notes, "into a general campaign against sealing and trapping." Indigenous communities such as the Inuit, which relied on seal harvesting to supplement their cash flow, were devastated. Brody concludes: "In the grip of moral righteousness, animal rights activists have been slow to recognize that their campaign had become a new example of southern, imperialist intrusion."[28]

When Greenpeace withdrew its support from Lynx over the issue of aboriginal economic security, Lynx minimized the importance of aboriginal peoples in fur trading and shifted the attention of its political spectatorship toward the "enemy within," the largely white middle- to upper-class women who wear fur coats. In response to Greenpeace and anyone who was concerned about the effects of its campaign on indigenous cultures, Lynx assured them in a "fact sheet" that the part played by aboriginal people in international fur markets was negligible, insufficient to warrant any major concern for their economic well-being:

> Most trapping by truly native people [as opposed to non-native people who trap and hunt "like" the native] is carried out in the Yukon and North West Territories (N.W.T.) in Canada. During the 1982–83 trapping season, 200,000 animals were taken (by all categories of trapper) in these two provinces compared with the 4 million trapped in all Canada and 25 million in N. America as a whole. That is less than 1% of North American trapped animals originate from native peoples. In other words, native people are responsible for around a quarter of 1% of furs produced worldwide. In the N.W.T. trapping AND fishing represents 1% of the Territorial Gross Domestic Product as well as 1% of the labour force.
>
> In the N.W.T. the cost of trapping with even a minimum amount of equipment exceeds the average fur income and only 5% of trappers claim that trapping is their occupation. The vast majority are part-time trappers.
>
> In a discussion document entitled "Defence of the fur trade" (1985) the Canadian Department of External Affairs stated that, "Defence of aboriginal cultures could be a good counterbalance to anti-fur or anti-trapping campaign."

What does this information connote? There are at least three points I wish to raise. First, the well-educated and liberal-minded reader will pick up on the closing paragraph as a sign of how the Canadian state, because of its own vested interests, will readily exploit its indigenous population to ensure that the benefits it derives from the fur-trading market will be maintained. In other words, if it speaks to us, it says "Don't you, the educated liberal reader, fall into the same trap of defending aboriginal fur trappers. You will only be supporting the Canadian state's economic interests." And of course, it is true that the Canadian state has actively qualified its continuing economic interest in the fur trade by enlisting the symbolic powers signified by aboriginal people. An article published in the *Times* reports that the House of Commons Committee on Aboriginal Affairs and Northern Development "produced a report which describes the [animal rights] activists as 'a wealthy growth industry.' It said the fur industry and the livelihood of about 100,000 trappers, the majority of them Eskimos and Indians, were in danger of destruction." In defense of its "$Can 600 million in direct earnings" and about "$Can 200 million a year for allied industries, such as transport," the Canadian government maintains that "trapping 'has always been and should remain' an essential part of Canada's cultural and economic mosaic." [29]

A second issue raised by the Lynx fact sheet concerns the definition of fur trapping as an occupation, which can be quantified as full or part-time work; this characterization misrepresents what has largely been an unquantifiable activity. [30] The Inuit in northern Canada hunt and trap to acquire sufficient cash to live their gathering-hunting way of life. By "way of life" I mean specifically that gatherers-hunters constitute a competing mode of production apart from the multinational capitalism that dominates the globe. The way in which postmodern gatherers-hunters acquire and use cash does not conform to the neat capitalist model Lynx imposes on what could more accurately be described as a kind of "mixed economy" that permits, as Brody points out, hunting peoples, such as the Inuit, to incorporate wage employment opportunities and the sale of products into a gatherer-hunter system. According to Brody, periodic wage labor, such as trapping, carving walrus ivory for the art market, and making moccasins, jackets, and beadwork, "reinforces hunters' flexibility: if periodic wage labour can ensure that they, or some other member of their household, can hunt and trap with maximum effectiveness, then a wage labour job is part of what is wanted and needed." [31]

And this brings me to the third and final point I want to make about the so-called facts in Lynx's information pamphlet. When Lynx writes that "1% of North American trapped animals originate from native peoples" and, further, that "native people are responsible for around a quarter of 1% of furs produced worldwide," what this foray into statistical authority does not tell us is that the minimal amount of cash that gathering-hunting peoples earn as trappers, until the recent plunge in fur prices caused by the anti-fur-trapping lobby, represented a primary source of cash income. In other words, that 1 percent contribution to the global economy of fur trading translates into approximately 100 percent of the total cash resources of a Dene or Inuit trapper.

Brody's *Living Arctic: Hunters of the Canadian North*, which emerged as a prominent counterdiscourse to the earlier animal rights' opposition to seal harvesting in the 1970s and to the anti-fur campaign of Lynx, was commissioned as the official publication of a British Museum exhibition held during 1987 and 1988.[32] The exhibition and Brody's text were produced in collaboration with ISI to help their readers and museum spectators to unlearn stereotypes about the hunting peoples of the far north, their cultural practices and strategies for economic and political survival. In the face of these educational efforts to influence animal welfare/rights organizations, Lynx remained willfully ignorant, maintaining a singularly misinformed representation of northern indigenous hunters. The mass media campaign launched by Lynx in conjunction with the publication of Brody's book for the British Museum and the formation of ISI indicates that the discourse on fur trapping both inside and outside Britain was fractured along different lines of counterhegemonic struggle. It would appear that what conditions the popularity of the struggle depends on access to the ideological apparatuses of technological reproduction, in particular, mass media.

Cyborg Politics

The question of technology is an important aspect of the debates in green cultural politics. In the arena of cultural production, the technological mediations of television and the satellite have come to play a significant role in the lives of Inuit people.[33] In her groundbreaking essay "A Cyborg Manifesto," Donna Haraway ironically reconfigures the "cyborg," half human/animal organism and half machine, as a postmodern exemplar of detotalization capable of projecting an ecologically blasphemous, and far from correct, fantasy for social transformation. Among the multiple articulations that can be made in the current political field of new social movements, Haraway is particularly interested in hinging together feminist, marxist, and environmentalist struggles. In keeping with the cyborg's irreverent disposition toward the idea of a coherent and unified human subject, Haraway's own political assemblage resists the conventional unifying origin myth at the heart of ecofeminist utopias, which would have us return to an innocent, natural, organic past in the name of protecting mother earth. Cyborgs represent a critical opposition, a more flexible mediation capable of incorporating rather than repudiating science and its strong arm, technology. Thus, the cyborg is designed to incorporate the contradictory relationship technologies occupy in the nature-transforming societies of industrial and postindustrial modes of production.[34] In a controversial move, Haraway situates her cyborg figure against the competing ecofeminist representative of political change, the reinvented mother goddess that has become so fundamental to ecofeminism's self-representation.[35] Given a choice between the comforts of divine resolution and the contradictions of everyday material life, Haraway writes, "I would rather be a cyborg than a goddess." It must be said, however, that the main trouble with cyborgs, as Haraway points out, "is that they are the illegitimate offspring of militarism and patriarchal capitalism."[36] As both symptom and critique of the expansion of the "military industrial complex," cyborg politics are, then, tricky business.

Haraway's argument is relevant to an examination of the redemptive place gatherer-hunter peoples have come to occupy in the discourses of deep ecology, there to cure the ills of the West's deep-seated nature-destroying and pollution-causing pathologies. As an imaginary resolution of the contradictory place of an ecopolitics of conservation in late-capitalist social life, gatherer-hunters represent a stable emblem of a "traditional" and therefore more truly "conservative" way of life. What presupposes this utopian investment in gatherer-hunter peoples is a fetishistic containment of them as stable, fixed, and traditional, belonging to an (ab)original past from which European and Euro-American civilizations can trace their origins, development, and progress. Gatherer-hunter peoples still exist, venturing into various kinds of technological applications in order to survive as well as derive profit and pleasure in the postmodern world. The postindustrial aspects of Inuit paleolithic existence include, among other things, the use of snowmobiles and rifles, an economic and somatic dependency on southern commodities and foodstuffs, and an active trade in craft goods and artifacts. The presence of industrial and postindustrial economic, military, and political forces in the Canadian north, especially in the period from the 1930s to 1950s, radically transformed Inuit cultural practices. Nevertheless, Inuit cultures, in the face of a southern Canadian government's wish to vanish and vanquish them and multinational desire for control of oil and gas resources, continue to fight back the frontiers of development and have engaged in a politics of survival I would call after Donna Haraway a "cyborg politics."

In "The Postmodern and the Paleolithic," Peter Kulchyski argues for a doubly inflected hypothesis about the relationship between technologies and social change: "The first thesis is that technology alone is not a sufficient agent of change that leads to the destruction of gatherer-hunter societies. . . . The second thesis is that advanced technology itself contains an emancipatory possibility and lends itself to emancipatory social projects, such as that of the Inuit." The example Kulchyski uses to test his hypotheses is the Inuit Broadcasting Corporation, established in the early seventies in response to Inuit demand for television shows and documentaries broadcast in the Inuktitut language and containing issues and themes related to Inuit experience, as well as programing produced by Inuit themselves. IBC began by simply sending out video cameras to small communities. As Kulchyski observes, "with a minimum of training support, the visual results often showed no predispositions as to what television 'should' look like." Kulchyski describes a video program made by Sac Kunnuk of Igloolik, *Hunting a Seal*. Unlike our usual experience of television programing, which consists of names and faces employed by multinational broadcasting corporations with little or no personal relationship to the larger spectatorship (in fact, one could define stardom as the reification of nonpersonal relations par excellence), "in the paleolithic-postmodern . . . the community speaks its own language and sees itself on television."[37]

To the degree that Inuit culture is a product of such industrial technologies as the snowmobile and the rifle and such postindustrial technologies as the satellite, Lynx is also a product of such postindustrial technologies as microelectronics and a range of media outposts, from made-for-home-viewing video to cinema advertisements. Their respective methods for incorporating technologies into the political sphere would suggest, however, that what for the Inuit and Dene constitute the tools for political survival in the postmodern world are for Lynx the means by which to maintain hegemony over the political field by simulating a radical political movement that in effect attempts to silence European women, and indigenous and non-European women and men.

This chapter has situated the British animal welfare organization Lynx within a frame of multiple competing political narratives. The geopolitical space in which these narratives emerge spans the historical distance between the British–New World colonial trade routes of the sixteenth and seventeenth centuries and their re-presentation through a sea change into the global communication networks of the late twentieth century. The use and exchange values inscribed on commodities, such as fur pelts, that once traveled on the surface of the ocean in human- and cargo-bearing vessels now travel, semiotically, through a vast network of microelectronic transmissions and satellite technology. The contradictions and clashes to emerge from the contemporary simulcast of competing discourses help to constitute the vicissitudes of cyborg politics, not least because of the communications technologies and ideological apparatuses used to deploy and create Lynx's anti-fur "green" political constituency, Brody's anti-imperialist constituency, and ISI's decolonial constituency.

In conclusion, I want to consider one more mode of cultural contestation, specifically Brody's attention to Inuit women as gatherers. This final intervention in another geopolitical scene of representation is predicated on an important debate within feminist theory between minoritized and universalized conceptions of women's oppression. Perhaps the most significant challenge to the thesis of women's universal oppression stems from Eleanor Leacock's research into the sexual division of labor among the Naskapi and Montagnais peoples of the eastern Labrador coast. Leacock's reading of the gender relations of precapitalist social formations challenges the conventional idea that a sexual division of labor is symmetrical to gendered divisions in the distribution of power. Leacock, along with Mona Etienne, explains that the division of labor in gatherer-hunter societies

> is by sex only, and relations between the sexes are based on the reciprocal exchange of goods and services. . . . in egalitarian society [i.e., that of the gatherer-hunter] a "private," familial female domain is not defined and made secondary to a public, political male domain. Instead, authority is dispersed and decisions are by and large made by those who will be carrying them out. All manner of social arts are used by both women and men to influence people, resolve problems, and hold groups together.[38]

Brody adopts the egalitarian gender thesis put forth by Leacock and Etienne to support the kinds of rhetorical gestures of equivalency he evokes throughout *Living Arctic* in his repetitive usage of the phrase "men and women." Nevertheless, his consistent assumption that hunting is an exclusively masculine activity points to an inequality elsewhere: Inuit and Dene women's work and experience are rarely specified beyond either the inclusive rhetorical gesture of equivalency or the exclusive presuppositions of Brody's privileging of hunting over other activities such as gathering and the treating of fur and hides.

Man-the-Hunter occupies a significant place in Western ideologies of human-nature interaction. In her essay "Teddy Bear Patriarchy," Donna Haraway tells a series of stories about the early twentieth-century hunter, taxidermist, inventor of cameras, and photographer Carl Akeley, and the visual, specular, and sculptural productions of his life which inform the discourse of natural history at the beginning of this century. In her reflections on the construction of nature by Akeley in his stuffed-animal dioramas, Haraway writes that "Akeley sees himself as an advocate for 'nature' in which 'man' is the enemy, the intruder, the dealer of death. His own exploits in the hunt stand in ironic juxtaposition only if the reader evades their true meaning — the tales of a pure man whose danger in pursuit of a noble cause brings him into communion with nature through the beasts he kills. This nature is a worthy brother of man, a worthy foil for his manhood." The making of masculinity through this ennobling of man the hunter informs Akeley's exploits in the field of photography. "Now it was time to hunt with the camera." As the "naked eye" of science came to dominate the ideological determinations motivating the collection and display of exoticized foreign animals in the American Museum of Natural History, the camera became more perfectly suited to this mode of containment, "ultimately so superior to the gun for the possession, production, preservation, consumption, surveillance, appreciation, and control of nature. . . . To make an exact image is to insure against disappearance, to cannibalize life until it is safely and permanently a specular image, a ghost. The image arrested decay."[39] By blaming or scapegoating "Woman," the transparent woman of white, civilization, construction, man the hunter-turned-photographer preserves, or rather conserves, his moral and noble superiority as the true father and author of nature. The video camera and fashion photographer for the Lynx campaign take off where the gun can no longer reasonably follow: "When we are afraid, we shoot. But when we are nostalgic, we take pictures."[40]

The absence of attention in Brody's *Living Arctic* to indigenous women's specific labor as trappers and tanners of fur hides maintains a conventional gender hierarchy between the masculine and the feminine. To the degree that Inuit and Dene hunting practices are affected by the uneven forces of postindustrial technological interventions, it must be said that the effects of postindustrial ideologies can also be felt in the redistribution of gendered social relations. To retain the egalitarian gendered relations of Inuit culture, as Brody does, while acknowledging the uneven effects of postindustrial technological forms of exploitation on hunting cultures, is at best utopian and at worst mythic, for it turns indigenous women into cultural "equalizers" even though their confrontation with postindustrial society is clearly not equal.[41]

The social discourses of fur in the late twentieth century disclose multiple tensions and contradictions between competing conceptions of cultural value for fur, the representation of gender and sexual differences among women, and the First and Third "Worlding" of cultural practices that mask the transglobal circulation of capital in fur production. The competing social discourses of fur, however politically visible in our current moment, are not new to the late twentieth century. In medieval England legislation was enacted to regulate the use of fur. This legislation attempted to order multiple regimes of value, not only fur's material signification as a sign of wealth but also its value for instituting class, gender, and religious hierarchies by turning fur into a visual representation of social difference. As we will see, the social differences informing this legislation historically overdetermine the contradictions presently at work in the reception and circulation of fur.

2

The Sumptuous Details of History

Order is, at one and the same time, that which is given in things as their inner law, the hidden network that determines the way they confront one another, and also that which has no existence except in the grid created by a glance, an examination, a language; and it is only in the blank spaces of this grid that order manifests itself in depth as though already there, waiting in silence for the moment of its expression.

Michel Foucault, *The Order of Things*

ITEM, *It is accorded, That no Man nor Woman of the said Lands of England, Ireland, Wales, or Scotland within the King's Power, of what Estate or Condition that he be, the King, Queen, and their Children, the Prelates, Earls, Barons, Knights, and Ladies, and People of Holy Church, which may expend by Year an [100 livres] of their Benefices at the least, to the very Value, only except, shall wear no Fur in his Clothes, that shall be bought after the said Feast of Saint Michael, upon the Forfeiture of the said Fur, and further to be punished at the King's Will.*

The Statutes of the Realm, (11) Edward III, 1336–1337

The regulation of material consumption in Britain began in the Middle Ages and continued until the early seventeenth century. Laws were enacted to regulate what food could be eaten and what fabric (including fur) could be worn by the nobility, the clergy, and the peasantry. They were passed by parliamentary statute, royal proclamation, ecclesiastical legislation, and in some cases, although less notably so, ordinances by local governments. Most of the clothing laws were legislated through acts of Parliament beginning with Edward III (1327–1377). Almost all the kings and queens of England up to and including Charles II (1660–1685) implemented some form of legislation dealing with the consumption of clothing, food, or drink. Henry VIII (1509–1547), Elizabeth I (1558–1603), and Charles I (1625–1649) issued royal proclamations, and the local government of Coventry enacted a "sumptuary ordinance" in the early sixteenth century. Sumptuary legislation was not limited to Britain but extended throughout Europe during the medieval period.

This legislation was meant not so much to curb extravagance as to preserve certain commodities for the wealthy, ensuring that symbolic displays of wealth were reserved to the property-owning classes. Given their attention to the question of excessive consumption, however, these acts have come to be known as "sumptuary legislation" — hence the title of Frances Elizabeth Baldwin's classic book on the subject, *Sumptuary Legislation and Personal Regulation in England*.[1] Several orders of material value, economic wealth, and commodity and social status were inscribed by "sumptuary legislation." According to Baldwin, the motivation for such legislation was threefold:

> (1) the desire to preserve class distinctions, so that any stranger could tell by merely looking at a man's dress to what rank in society he belonged; (2) the desire to check practices which were regarded as deleterious in their effects, due to the feeling that luxury and extravagance were in themselves wicked and harmful to the morals of the people; (3) economic motives: (a) the endeavor to encourage home industries and to discourage the buying of foreign goods, and (b) the attempt on the part of the sovereign to induce his people to save their money, so that they might be able to help him out financially in time of need.[2]

In her assessment of the motives underlying the implementation of the sumptuary laws, Baldwin distinguishes between economic factors and libidinal interests, those desires that will preserve class differences and maintain a strict moral code of behavior. In other words, Baldwin's text discloses a tension between hedonistic consumption and ascetic restraint. The line that Baldwin draws between economic and libidinal motivations lends support to Chandra Mukerji's insightful analysis of the libidinal forces at work in the Christian assumptions underlying the economic practices of consumption and production in early modern Europe. In *From Graven Images: Patterns of Modern Materialism* Mukerji critiques the conventional opposition between the ascetic rationality of entrepreneurialism introduced through the Protestant ethic and viewed by Max Weber as the spirit motivating early modern capitalism and the hedonistic consumerism generally attributed to a later moment in capitalist development, the industrial revolution. As Mukerji says, hedonism has always played a role in capitalist expansion and in the earlier mercantile expansion where the idea of an ascetic entrepreneurialism has tended to dominate: "The very existence of a hedonistic consumerism in the early modern period raises questions about the traditional association of early capitalism with asceticism and late capitalism with hedonism. . . . It suggests that so-called Capitalist Man was not transformed overnight with the industrial revolution, suddenly losing self-control and developing a voracious appetite for goods, but rather has always displayed some mixture of asceticism and hedonism." Regardless of their apparent opposition to each other, the hedonistic consumer who spends and the ascetic entrepreneur who invests share a common feature: "an interest in material accumulation."[3] Sumptuary laws were designed to regulate who would ultimately profit from such accumulation.

Claire Sponsler criticizes the application of the term "sumptuary" to this body of legislative acts: "Clothing laws were clearly part of an ideological agenda — one involving the interests of specific social groups — but the way these laws have been codified and interpreted has obscured the forces at work behind them. The chief impediment has been the persistent classification of clothing laws as sumptuary laws, suggesting that their primary function was to enforce against luxury, vanity, and excess." Sponsler maintains that "sumptuary laws" are best viewed as a form of "social practice." In the design and makeup of these laws, which list social classes according to their rank in the social hierarchy, together with what fabrics and furs may be worn by which class of individuals, a narrative of the social order is constructed. Sponsler concentrates on three of the earliest clothing laws. In the first, the 1363 law (37 Edward III), she reads the list of classes as an index of social construction which begins with a particular group in the social strata and follows from there in ascending order of hierarchical status. Sponsler notes that this early law — legislating dress for grooms, servants, handicraftsmen, yeomen, esquires and gentlemen with incomes less than a hundred pounds ("livres") a year, merchants, citizens, burgesses and artificers with incomes up to five hundred pounds a year, and knights with incomes of two hundred marks as well as clerks and agricultural workers — focused primarily on the middle classes. Two subsequent laws, the 1463 petition (3 Edward IV) and the 1483 (22 Edward IV), index social groups "coherently down the social scale, from the king to the lowest groups." As Sponsler writes, "The clarity and orderliness of this hierarchy are immediately apparent. The petition [of 1483] begins with the king and the royal family, then moves in a descending pattern down through dukes, lords, knights, yeomen of the crown, esquires and gentlemen, servants of husbandry, common laborers, servants to artificers, and their wives."[4]

It is important to stress that English clothing laws of the late Middle

Ages did not describe what people actually wore or, indeed, what they were necessarily expected to wear; rather, in Sponsler's view, these laws "reveal competing interests at work in an on-going negotiation of social relations." Clothing laws constituted a form of social practice tied "to what was perceived in late medieval England as the 'problem' of status and social mobility. By the end of the fourteenth century, status had come to be based less on the traditional standard of birth than on visible and acquirable markers of social identity, such as civic offices, land holdings, houses, household furnishings, coats of arms, seals, and apparel. As a result, the regulation of these material status signifiers came under increasingly greater scrutiny." Sponsler's notion of material status signifiers usefully dramatizes the relationship between material wealth and the acquisition of status through the outward appearance of things. Status for a rising urban merchant middle-class had become more fluid, as in more accessible, by the end of the Middle Ages; therefore, Sponsler suggests, "as an overt sign of an individual's status, clothing was an obvious target for those attempting to define or control such status. For this reason clothing laws are crucial texts in the dynamics of social change and social control in late medieval England."[5]

Although it could be argued that the juridical discourse on material regulation attempted to establish a symbolic system for determining class affiliation and social rank, it also inscribed symbolic and material values on the very commodities listed. In Edward III's 1363 act, "A Statute Concerning Diet and Apparel," fur is mentioned only in those items related to the apparel of knights and clergy. Presumably, it was altogether denied to the lower classes:

> ITEM, That Knights, which have Land or Rent within the Value of ii. C. [livres] shall take and wear Cloth of vi. Marks the whole Cloth, for their Vesture, and of none higher Price: And that they wear not Cloth of Gold, nor [Cloths], Mantle, nor Gown furred with Miniver nor [sleeves] of Ermins, nor no Apparel broidered of Stone, nor otherwise; and that their Wives, Daughters, and Children be of the same Condition; and that they wear no turning up of Ermins, nor of Letuses, nor no Manner of Apparel of Stone, but only for their Heads. But that all Knights and Ladies, which have Land or Rent over the Value of iv. C. Mark by Year, to the Sum of M. [livres by the year] shall wear at their Pleasure, except Ermins and Letuses, and Apparel of Pearls and Stone, but only for their Heads.[6]

Miniver, ermine, and lettice clearly represented the most exclusive of furs and were reserved for the aristocracy and higher nobility. Books on the history of fashion, or fashion discourse in general, confirm the hierarchical values attributed to fur. J. Anderson Black comments:

> One of the great luxuries in costume was the use of fur. Furs played an important part in the costume of the previous two centuries, but in the thirteenth century they were even more widely used throughout Europe and a wider variety of skins was adopted. The furs of sable, fox, beaver, cat and lamb were all common in the twelfth century, but to these were now added the skins of marten, squirrel, ermine and rabbit. The demand for skins increased rapidly and they were used not only for warmth but also for decoration. The necks, cuffs and hems of many garments were now trimmed with precious furs. A definite hierarchy emerged in the use of furs: sheepskin, badger, muskrat, cat and other coarse furs were used by the lower classes while, as today, the pelts of finer, rare and smaller creatures were only within reach of the very wealthy.[7]

Similarly, the fashion historian François Boucher narrates the hierarchy of fur's material value: "The furs most commonly worn were the back-fur of the grey squirrel, fox, marten, beaver and lettice, which was white and imitated ermine. Marten, *gris*, *vair* . . . and ermine were generally reserved for princely or court garments, while beaver, otter, hare and fox were worn among the lesser nobility and the middle classes, and lambskin, wolf, goat and sheepskin were left for the common people."[8]

"To be exclusive is the hallmark of fashion," writes Elspeth M. Veale. In her study of the English fur trade in the later Middle Ages, Veale notes that furs obtained from Russia and the Baltic lands, such as Baltic squirrel, were deemed valuable in part because they originated afar and could only be acquired through the exigencies of trade. More to the point, however, was that these furs initially appeared in small quantities. "As Hanseatic trade expanded in the thirteenth and fourteenth centuries, bringing squirrel skins in vast quantities to Western Europe, the circle of those for whom they were available grew steadily wider." Exclusivity no doubt created degrees of value for fur, but Veale maintains that the vagaries of fashion may have played a larger role: "Possibly of more significance were changes in the fabrics and styles which became fashionable, so that the fuller and darker furs of marten and sable were preferred to the soft, silken squirrel skins with their subtle colours. . . . Often the fur, like the subtlety of the weave of some Persian silks, would only show in movement, but we can be certain that its texture and colour were of great importance."[9] Here Veale evokes both style and sensuousness as predetermined factors in assigning value to fur commodities. The aesthetics of taste, however, is as much a social construction as the social order of consumers, inseparable from economic transactions and the availability or exclusivity of commodities. Juridical discursive practices that legislated the wearing of furs may also have contributed to the process of producing aesthetic, as well as economic, values for furs. Economic considerations, however, also determined the style of fur fashions. For example, Laura Hodges notes the practice of "purfling," in which more expensive furs were used as trim and less expensive furs completed the lining.[10] The desire to demonstrate excessive expenditure, however, could just as easily determine the mode of presentation, especially for the aristocracy. Boucher notes that "*Vair*, which was widely used during the Middle Ages, referred to the skin of the northern squirrel: the back (*petit gris*) and the white belly, arranged in a checkerboard pattern, gave *menu vair*; *gros vair* was marked by coarser quality. The consumption of *vair* was enormous: in eighteen months Charles VI [of France] used 20,000 bellies and Isabeau of Bavaria 15,000 for the linings of their garments."[11]

The discourse on material "excess" in relation to fur demands further elaboration. Baldwin's emphasis on ascetic restraint as the underlying motivation for "sumptuary legislation" signifies excess as a problem of morality and not material value. Sponsler, as we have seen, dismisses the discourse on excess, along with luxury and vanity, as codes that mimic and yet displace the more pressing question of social class hierarchies. But the fact remains that excess is affirmed by the legislation. Moreover, Baldwin and Sponsler's dismissive assessments of its significance suggests that "excess" is a complex, if not contradictory, ideological code.

In recounting the history of the discursive construction of so-called sumptuary legislation, Sponsler cites William Blackstone's authoritative eighteenth-century commentary on English law as "perhaps most responsible for the modern classification of clothing laws as a form of sumptuary legislation. . . . Like the *Parliamentary History*, Blackstone assumes that the essential issue involved in clothing laws is excess. He shifts the focus, however, from excess in the *appearance* of the apparel to excess in its *cost*. Blackstone implies that the motivation behind clothing laws was a desire to control extravagant spending, or what we would call conspicuous consumption; interestingly, he also recognizes that there is something about conspicuous consumption that is troubling to the social order, especially if that order is based on a vertical hierarchy, as Blackstone assumes it to be."[12] The shift from *appearance* to *cost* is not surprising if we consider the economic basis of symbolic power. Stated directly, excess in appearance is the symbolic construction of excessive material expenditure; indeed the space between the materiality of appearance and that of expenditure as the standard by which material wealth or lack thereof could be measured is very slight — merely a question of displacement.

The acts themselves clearly inscribe this discourse of excess. The 1363 law (37 Edward III) contains the following item: "For the Outragious and Excessive Apparel of divers People, against their Estate and Degree, to the great Destruction and Impoverishment of all the Land."[13] During Henry VIII's reign, the law of 1532–1533 (24 Henry VIII), titled "An ACTE for Reformacyon of Excesse in Apparayle" began with a lengthy coda condemning the vices of outrageous excess in clothing:

> Where before this tyme dyvers lawes ordyn'nces and statutes have ben with greate delibacion and advyse p[ro]vided establisshed and devised, for the necessarie rep[re]ssing avoydyng and expelling of the inordynate excesse dailye more and more used in the sumptuous and costly araye and apparell accustomablye worne in this Realme, wherof hath ensued and dailie do chaunce suche sundrie high and notable inconveniences as be to the greate manifest and notorious detryment of the cōmon Weale, the subv[er]cion of good and politike ordre in knowelege and distinc-cion of people according to their estates p[re]emynences dignities and degrees, and to the utter impov[er]ysshement and undoyng of many in-expert and light p[er]sones inclyned to pride moder of all vices; which good Lawes notwithstanding, the oulteragious excesse therin is rather frome tyme to tyme increased than diminysshed, eyther by the occacion of the p[er]verse and frowarde maners and usage of people, or for that errours and abuses ones rooted and taken into longe custome be not facilie and at ones without sōme moderacion for a tyme relinquisshed and reformed.[14]

The designation of these laws as "sumptuary legislation" in the juridical discourse of the eighteenth century, as well as in early twentieth-century academic discourse such as Baldwin's, reiterates a rationale already con-tained in the discursive codes of the laws themselves. Not only did these discursive practices set in motion an empirical order of ranks and classes; they also inscribed in the very codes of knowledge that would order the reception of these laws, the principal agents of excess — kings, queens, and the higher nobility — all of whom are already exempted from the critique of such excess. For "excess," rather, was carefully graded by social rank. For each rank, the law identified the fixed threshold of excess. In the case of kings, queens, and higher nobility, excess was no excess at all.

Pierre Bourdieu, writing on the aristocracy of culture, captures the "es-sence" of this contradiction between the aristocracy's introduction of a cri-tique of excess and their practice of excessive expenditure:

> Aristocracies are essentialist. Regarding existence as an emanation of essence, they set no intrinsic value on the deeds and misdeeds enrolled

in the records and registries of bureaucratic memory. They prize them only insofar as they clearly manifest, in the nuances of their manner, that their one inspiration is the perpetuating and celebrating of the essence by virtue of which they are accomplished. The same essentialism requires them to impose on themselves what their essence imposes on them — noblesse oblige — to ask of themselves what no one else could ask, to "live up" to their own essence. . . . The essence in which they see themselves refuses to be contained in any definition. Escaping petty rules and regulations, it is, by nature, freedom.[15]

The aristocracy is in excess of the laws it implements, yet morally obliged, in the case of "sumptuary legislation," to restrict excessive expenditure for the good of the crown. Thus, encoded in the very laws is a scale that distinguishes the aristocracy from everyone else. Clothing, furs, silks constitute the codes of this mode of distinction, introducing a system of coherences and resemblances between bodies and between bodies and their representation of symbolic power.

Notions of excess and its opposite, asceticism, were clearly important to the codification of sumptuary legislation, and they are particularly relevant to fur's material signification as a luxury good. The problem with "excess" appears to be its ability to disclose the realities of economic valuation. To dismiss the symbolic power invested in the codes of material excess, then, might contribute to the mystification of economic questions as well as the relationship of symbolic power to political power. The political power vested in the monarchy, the church, and the state is itself a form of symbolic power. If, however, political power becomes recognizable as simply "symbolic," then it can no longer hold its ground as a discreet and legitimate entity unto itself. Those who held political power during the Middle Ages in Britain wanted not only to preserve that power but also to control those whose emerging symbolic power, acquired through commodity wealth, threatened to overrun political power based in property ownership. One way to view sumptuary legislation is as a mode of discursive practice that represents struggles not only between competing class and social relations and competing ideologies of excess and asceticism but between political and symbolic modes of representation as to which ideology of power would politically dominate the value of economic wealth, in the competing forms of commodity wealth and land ownership.

The social and political realities of religion also provide analytical insights into the construction of social antagonisms in so-called sumptuary legislation. Locating Chaucer's "Monk's Tale" within the social text of clothing laws and religious ordinances against extravagance, Laura Hodges repositions the monk's attire between the poles of asceticism and *luxuria*.

The implications of this study are threefold: first, it acknowledges the variety of dress actually worn during the Middle Ages by those in religious orders. Secondly, it illustrates the degree to which such variety was either tolerated or embraced by many church authorities, while recognizing the humble practices of more ascetic monks. And, finally, it sheds light on Chaucer's appeal to costume associations in the minds of his fourteenth-century audience made through the complex pattern of costume rhetoric in the *General Prologue*.[16]

Fellini's Roma (1972) also deploys the complex rhetoric of religious vestments in order to comment on a late twentieth-century fascist-bourgeois nostalgia for the power of symbolic display.[17] In a memorable scene that includes the Ecclesiastical Fashion Show, the notable exclusion of monk's vestments underscores the division between asceticism and excess among the ecclesiastical orders. As the unwritten discourse of excess, especially linked to religious clothing, asceticism is, not surprisingly, altogether banished from the visual field.

The Ecclesiastical Fashion Show

Fellini's Roma begins with a voice-over in which "the film director" tells us that this film will not be a conventional story, a narrative with a beginning, middle, and end, but a story about a city, a portrait of the city of Rome based on the narrator's memory of "strange contradictory images," slices of life that move from the narrator's childhood in northern Italy to modern-day Rome, from before the war to after the war, covering a time period from the 1930s to the early 1970s. The film pays attention to Roman mythologies and, more important, the technologies and machines of representation that produce and reproduce the myths of the city. Slides of Rome's architectural monuments internally frame a scene of the narrator's childhood in school; a radio broadcast of the pope's blessing recenters a family's dinnertime; movies for entertainment and for Mussolini's fascist propaganda produce a cineographic sense of wonder, terror, and amusement; trains transport the young man from the country to the city; bullets ring out at night, echoing among the city's densely constructed and ornate buildings; the narrator's film crew replete with cameras and cranes; highways of overturned cars; an underground adventure into the unfinished subway system, blocked by archaeological problems: how to avoid destroying a subterranean layer of history like an acropolis of skeletons? But the machines push on, breaking down walls, exposing the time-hidden frescoes to the destructive outside air until they wash away to nothing. A mixture of memory and nostalgia for what was prewar, premachine, pretechnological, prefascist — Vaudeville and Roman ruins that are no longer ruins but present day structures. And a sexuality that was furtive and transgressive, confessional and "artistic" — the prostitute, the hetaerae, the exotic, the dominatrix. And after all these contradictory scenes comes the Ecclesiastical Fashion Show and a story about Princess Donatella and her bourgeois fascist English-speaking nostalgia for a time when Rome was different: "So much time has gone by. It is so painful to end my days in a city which is no longer mine. My Rome was not like this one. We all knew each other — bishops, cardinals, the pope. We were all friends, we were all related to each other. But now those close ties with the church have gone. The receptions we used to give. Enough villas, palaces. . . . It was as though life were a work of art."

In this scene, Princess Donatella sits beside His Eminence the Cardinal surrounded by her bourgeois friends and fellow nobility. The audience is assembled, along with rows of nuns and priests, to watch the Ecclesiastical Fashion Show. Like sumptuary legislation, which did concern itself with the attire of the clergy, the fashion show structures the hierarchy of its "orders," inscribing a technology of symbolic power in its procession. The fashion show proceeds as follows supplemented by the emcee's commentary delivered in English.

Model 1 [two female novices]: Fashions in a classical new line of black satin for novices. This model can also be executed in other types of fabrics such as silk or wool to suit different seasons. The boots are made of fine-quality leather and come in two tones, black and aquamarine, and are suitable for very cold climates.

Model 2 [two nuns]: Immaculate Turtle Doves. Starched bugle [headdress] and free-flapping wings invaluable for convents where ventilation leaves something to be desired.

Model 3 [two senior nuns]: Little Sisters of the Temptations in Purgatory.

Commentary from an elderly woman in the audience: "The world must learn to follow the church, not the other way around."

Let us now move on to sports models. They move faster to paradise. [Two young priests in red silk cassocks roller-skate around the proscenium to a cheering audience of nuns.]

Model 5 [two somewhat nervous-looking priests, dressed in white top and black pants with country-style hats, bicycle around the stage]: Specially designed for country priests.

Model 6 [three men in intricate lace ensembles]: Vestry Elegance. Three deluxe models for sacristan and high-class ceremonials.

We will now show you how ecclesiastical ornaments have also undergone a carefully concealed evolution: amices, copes, surplices, chasubles, and stoles are today manufactured in materials of gossamer lightness and a wide range of vivid colors guaranteed not to run.

The next part of the procession includes vestments for bishops and cardinals. Statues and moving automatons appear covered with plush red-silk vestments trimmed with fur or ostrich feathers, headdresses and cloaks made from tiny squares of mirror and papier-mâché, and neon lights cover these models that are empty of human bodies as if the radiance that shines off the surface of the mirrors empties these vestments of their mere human flesh. This display is followed by a wedding-gown-like dress for the Virgin Mary, her face an androgynous death mask veiled by layers of white gauze. Then follows the procession of cardinals and bishops elaborately adorned with headdresses and stoles studded with jewels. Their bodies covered by elaborate plates and carrying staffs, they move like soldiers with shields and spears. Next is a strange installation of skeletons draped with fine gauze: an aestheticization of the damned? Hell with a silver lining? At the finale mirrors and a golden arch drop from the ceiling. Princess Donatella falls to her knees, His Eminence dons his sunglasses, women stretch out their arms begging in supplication, reaching out in ecstasy. The pope appears on a raised platform, his head surrounded by rays of glowing white light. He is like a sun-god, a Dantesque figure, blinding Princess Donatella and her bourgeois friends with his brilliance, his radiance, his symbolic power.

The Ecclesiastical Fashion Show can be read as a commentary on Italian fashion as a form of religious devotion. It can also be read as a biting satire on the power of symbolic display used by the clergy to invest itself with luxury, wealth, and political power. As a device for structuring social order, the fashion show is as powerful a technology of symbolic production in the twentieth century as sumptuary legislation was for the Middle Ages in England.

The hierarchy of furs and social positions created by these regulatory acts does indeed tell us something about the *dominant narrative* informing the construction of a British medieval social order and its codes of symbolic power. There is, however, a subordinate narrative that weaves its way through the legislation, informing the construction of feminine and masculine genders, sexual differences between men and women, and class differences among women. Legislation forbade prostitutes to wear fur. Baldwin describes the regulation: "The next statute which is of interest to us is one which was enacted in 1355. 'After the Epiphany,' to quote Stowe, 'a Parliament was holden at Westminister, wherein an ordinance was made at the instance of the Londoners, that no known whore should weare from thenceforth any hood, except reyed or striped of divers colors, nor furre, but garments reversed or turned the wrong side outward upon paine to forfeit the same.' At first glance this ordinance seems to fall under the head of sumptuary legislation, but its fundamental purpose is evidently not to check extravagance, but to protect the morals of the community by forcing prostitutes to wear distinctive clothing, so that everyone might be able, on sight, to distinguish them from respectable women citizens. It must have been extremely difficult, however, to force the women affected by this law to wear the garments prescribed for them." The identity of the prostitute, the need to make her presence "known," turned on a reversal not only of her clothes but also of her sociosexual and economic position relative to the so-called respectable woman. Baldwin also notes that "in the sixteenth or seventeenth year of Henry's reign (apparently in the latter, though there seems to be some doubt about the date) 'it was ordeyned,' says the Short English Chronicle, 'that all the comyn strompetes sholde were raye hodis and white roddis in her hondes.' This is practically a repetition of the ordinance passed during the reign of Edward III, to which reference has already been made. This ordinance was not really sumptuary in character, but was intended to provide a means of distinguishing prostitutes from respectable women." [18]

Baldwin considers those aspects of the sumptuary legislation meant to distinguish between prostitutes and respectable women as attempts to regulate morality rather than sartorial excess, and therefore not proper sumptuary legislation at all. She does note the occasional reference to women dressing like men and examples of male cross-dressing including the "problem" of effeminate behavior on the part of men, especially with reference to Richard II.[19] The threat of a blurring of class boundaries among women is also addressed in the sumptuary legislation, largely in terms of protecting the privileges of higher-ranking women over the wives and servants of laborers. Under Edward IV the statute of 1483 declared that all "the penalties and forfeitures, except those within the county palatine of Chester, Exhamshire and the bishopric of Durham, for which special provision was made, were to go towards the expenses of the king's household, 'provided alwey that thys acte extende not nor be in any wise prejudiciall to or for any woman except the wifes and servaunts of laborers.'" Baldwin notes that in "the two acts immediately preceding the act of 1483, the wives of the persons mentioned in the statutes had been included with their husbands and placed on a plane of equality with them in the matter of dress, so that this exemption of women was a distinct change in policy. The reason for it is not clear, unless the legislators had come to believe that it was hopeless to attempt to put a curb on the feminine love of dress." Of course, singling out women and their attire also made it possible not simply to focus on women, heretofore "neglected," but to regulate their clothing consumption more easily. One unusual example of sumptuary legislation passed during the reign of Henry VIII instituted a distinction between the clothing of married and unmarried women; more unusual still, it referred to women's dress alone. As Baldwin observes, "The statutes of apparel usually regulated both men's and women's dress, though more stress was generally laid on the subject of male attire than that of female attire. Judging from contemporary pictures and descriptions of the costumes worn by the great ladies of the time, this neglect of women's dress can hardly have been caused by a conviction that the women were less extravagant than the men." [20]

The implementation of a juridical discourse on sartorial display suggests, among other things, that knowledge about the codes of sartorial display or, more urgent, about how to decipher the relationships between clothing styles and types of fabrics and furs worn, were entirely necessary to an individual's skill at "reading" and acting upon the social text. Diane Owen Hughes provides a excellent example of noblewomen reading their social text in her study of women's fashions and sumptuary legislation in Europe's Middle Ages. She notes that women's use of fashion could be a strategy for making their social and economic dependency on men less precarious:

Women were especially vulnerable to the social fashioning that costume allowed, for its visible marks helped to fix and solidify a social identity necessarily more fluid than that of the men who shaped it. A change that occurred almost simultaneously with the rise of cloth production in the twelfth and thirteenth centuries accentuated the ambiguity of their social position and contributed to their dependence on costume's distinctions and definitions: the development of a patrilineal ideology of descent through the male line. Designed to conserve the wealth and social position of families by limiting claims on their resources, patrilineal organization made the wife an outsider, lineally distinct not only from her husband but even, in a sense, from the children she bore him and his line. Her visual incorporation thus became more necessary as a way of blurring that distinction for the duration of the marriage in order to create an illusion of complete marital union. An unusual list of dresses, registered in Florence in 1343 so that they might continue to be worn in contravention of a recently promulgated sumptuary law, gives us a rare glimpse of such a process, as the matching costumes of wives of the Albizzi family form a clear patrilineal design in a riot of urban color. Shimmering white mantles embroidered with ivy and red grapes cloaked their natal identity and made wives from various parts of the city visual representatives of the Albizzi clan.[21]

Hughes links the display of symbolic power by the Albizzi wives to their legal dispossession. With no access to the political process that would ensure their access to material resources and security, the wives of the Albizzi clan made use of the symbolic powers open to them, in contravention of the contemporary sumptuary laws of Florence. They countered their legalized dispossession with an ideology of "marital union" achieved through the symbolic display of visual fashion signs that represented them as members of the Albizzi clan.

Clearly, noblewomen did not possess the same privileges as the men of their class and were able to secure only a re-presentation of such privileges through the ideological power of symbolic display. Thus, these noble/bourgeois women participated in creating a symbolic code of female economic power that could be *misread* as identical with the economic and political realities of their husband's material wealth and social power. In effect, what Hughes has done is to read the Albizzi wives reading their social "text" and devising strategies and tactics meant to secure, by whatever means possible, their access to material resources.

The increasing link between monarchial excess and women's attire and the further link between material and sexual excess with reference to women's bodies came into full force with the rise of Puritanism in the late sixteenth century, which directed its attention toward women, adornment, and sexuality, including cross-dressing, sodomitry, "ladies," and "whores." Texts such as Phillip Stubbes's Puritan rant, *The Anatomie of Abuses* (1583), in which he railed against *luxuria* in the clergy and women especially, and John Evelyn's *Tyrannus, or The Mode; In a Discourse of Sumptuary Lawes* (1661), a later seventeenth-century text that reintroduces sumptuary legislation as a metaphor for regulating the "problem" of effeminacy and fashion consumption for Britain's national interests, participated in reading this world of appearances as a taxonomy of identifiable differences of social rank, class, and genders.[22] In other words, these texts contributed to circumscribing a sartorial episteme. Whereas the official discourses of "sumptuary legislation" set in motion a whole series of discursive acts designed to regulate social class distinctions primarily by establishing clothing styles, fabrics, and furs as ideological codes of symbolic status, these supplementary discourses are arguably more important. They determined what acts of sartorial display were considered "normal," proper, legitimate, or transgressive in everyday practices.

The Allurements of Puritanism

The anatomy of fashion is clearly male (see Figure 8), with women occupying the conventional position of imitator; Thomas Dekker likens them to apes:

For as man is Gods ape, striuing to make artificiall flowers, birdes, &c. like to the natural: So for the same reason are women, Mens *Shee Apes*, for they will not bee behind them the bredth of a Taylors yard (which is nothing to speake of) in anie new-fangled vpstart fashion. If men get vp French standing collers, women will haue the French standing coller too: if Dublets with little thick skirts, (so short that none are able to sit vpon them), womens foreparts are thick skirted too: by surfetting vpon which kinde of phantasticall *Apishnesse*, in a short time they fall into the disease of pride: Pride is infectious, and breedes prodigalitie: Prodigalitie, after it has runne a little, closes vp and festers, and then turnes to *Beggerie*. Wittie was that Painter therefore, that when hee had limned, one of euery Nation in their proper attyres, and beeing at his wittes endes howe to drawe an *Englishman*, At the last (to giue him a quippe for his follie in apparell) drewe him starke naked, with Sheeres in his hand, and cloth on his arme, because none could cut out his fashions but himselfe.

For an English-mans suite is like a traitors bodie that hath beene hanged, drawne, and quartered, and is set vp in seuerall places: his Codpeece is in *Denmarke*, the collor of his Duble[t], and the belly in *France*: the wing and narrowe sleeue in *Italy*; the short waste hangs ouer a *Dutch* Botchers stall in *Vtrich*: his huge floppes [slops] speakes *Spanish*: *Polonia* giues him the Boates: the blocke for his heade alters faster than the Feltmaker can fitte him, and thereupon we are called in scorne *Blockheades*. And thus we that mocke euery Nation, for keeping one fashion, yet steale patches from euery one of them, to peece out our pride, are now laughing-stocks to them, because their cut so scuruily becomes vs.[23]

Women of fashion in the sixteenth century could only imitate men or distinguish themselves from improper women such as prostitutes. It is these two themes — women imitating men in their desire for luxurious dress and in their desire to look like men and wear men's clothing, and the class and sociosexual differences among women — that this Puritan discourse on adornment sought to order and regulate.

¶ The fyrst chapter treateth of the naturall dysposicion
of an Englysshman, and of the noble realms of
England, & of the money that there is vsed.

¶ I am an English man, and naked I stand here
Musyng in my mynde, what rayment I shal were
For now I wyll were thys and now I wyl were that
Now I wyl were I cannot tel what
All new fashyons, be plesaunt to me
I wyl haue them, whether I thryue or thee
Now I am a kryster, all men doth on me looke
What should I do, but set cocke on the hoope
what do I care, yf all the worlde me fayle
I wyll get a garment, shal reche to my tayle
Than I am a minion, for I were the new gyse

The

FIGURE 8. Englishman with scissors, woodcut (1542).
Reproduced from Andrew Boorde, *The Fyrst Boke of the Introduction of Knowledge*,
by permission of the British Library (c 71b29).

Stubbes's discourse on the sinful coupling of "apparell and Pride (the Mother and Daughter of mischiefe)" interweaves gender and national differences, especially as they relate to foreign trade and the preservation of symbolic powers among the nobility and religious hierarchies.[24] Stubbes develops similar rationales for the existence of sumptuary legislation: the problem of money leaving the country in the trade for luxurious fabrics such as silks, velvets, satins, and damasks; the blurring of class differences and the threat of social dis-order; and the display of material wealth by those who do not properly own the correlative symbolic powers of monarchial or religious status.

The problem of trade with foreign countries is largely traced to the Orient and, to a lesser extent, the New World. A persistent ideological subtext throughout Stubbes's discourse targets the Turkish empire. Stubbes both demonizes the Orient for its cruelty and "barbarity" and idealizes its riches. On the one hand, the Orient exemplifies an appropriate national economy for its fashionable attire: "Moreouer, those Cuntreyes are rich and welthie of them selues, abounding with all kinde of preciouse ornaments and riche attyre, as silks, veluets, Satens, damasks, farcenet, taffetie, chamlet, and such like (for al these are made in those foraine cuntreyes), and therfore if they weare them they are not muche to bee blamed, as not hauing anie other kind of cloathing to cover themselves withal. So if wee would contente our selues with such kinde of attire as our owne Countrey doeth minister vnto vs, it were much tollerable." And on the other hand, Stubbes locates in the Orient self-mutilation as an excess in the desire to display beauty: "There is a certen kinde of People in the Orientall parte of the World (as Writers affirme), that are such *Philautoi*, louers of them selues, and so prowde with all, that, hauing plentie of precious Stones and Margarits amongest them, they cut and launce their skinnes and fleshe, setting therin these precious Stones, to the end they maye glister and shine to the eye." Stubbes constructs his ideology of artifice by juxtaposing the conflicting ideals of an Orient depicted in terms of material excess and a New World that represents a primitive simplicity. He idealizes the simplicity of "women of the former age" — African and Brazilian — for their utilitarian approach to wearing "beasts skinnes, furres, and such like." He resituates England's superiority, however, in terms of a condemnation of its excessive pride: "Thus, you see, euery Nation, how barbarous soeuer, are much inferiour to *the* people of *Ailgna* in pride & excesse of apparell."[25]

Stubbes criticizes the blurring of distinctions between the middle and lower classes and among those who possess material wealth, such as the merchant class, but do not belong to the legitimate classes of symbolic power. While he supports the classes to whom he designates a justifiable mode of symbolic power, he is nevertheless critical of how the poor suffer because of the gross expenditure on luxurious fabrics and clothing:

> I doubt not but it is lawfull for *the* potestates, the nobilitie, the gentrie, yeomanrie, and for euerye priuate subiecte els to weare attyre euery one in his degree. . . . The maiestrats also & Officers in the weale publique, by what tytle soeuer they be called (accordinge to their abylities), may were (if the Prince or Superintendent do Godly commaund) costlie ornaments and riche attyre, to dignifie their callings, and to demonstrat and shewe forth the excelency and worthines of their offices and functions, therby to strike a terroure & feare into the harts of the people to offend against the maiesty of their callings: but yet would I wish that what so is superfluous or ouermuche, either in the one or in the other, shold be distributed to the helpe of the pore members of Christ Iesus, of whom an infynite number of daylie do perish thorowe wante of necessarie reflection and due sustentation to their bodies. . . . But now there is such a confuse mingle mangle of apparell in [England], and such preposterous excesse therof, as euery one is permitted to flaunt it out in what apparell he lust himselfe, or can get by anie kind of meanes. So that it is verie hard to knowe who is noble, who is worshipfull, who is a gentleman, who is not: for you shall haue those which are neither of the nobylitie, gentilitie, nor yeomanry; no, nor yet anie Magistrat, or Officer in the common welth, go daylie in silkes, veluets, satins, damasks, taffeties, and such like, notwithstanding that they be both base by byrthe, meane by estate, & [servile] by calling. This is a great confusion, & a general disorder: God be mercyfull vnto vs! [26]

Whereas Stubbes is ambivalent toward the spectacle of material wealth among the aristocracy and magistrates, he remains unambivalent toward such forms of display in those who "[show] forth *the* power, welth, dignity, riches, and glorie of the Lord, the Author of all goodnesse [i.e., 'thynges']." [27]

Religious social power constitutes for Stubbes the only legitimate realm of symbolic power, and the greatest threat to the symbolic power invested in God, is women who paint their faces, dye their hair, and wear richly adorned clothing. Women sin by competing with God as the makers and unmakers of their own bodies:

> The Women of [England] vse to colour their faces with certain oyles, liquors, vnguents and waters made to that end, whereby they think their beautie is greatly decored: but who seethe not that their soules are thereby deformed, and they brought deeper into the displeasure and indignation of the Almighty, at whose voice the earth dooth tremble, and

at whose presence the heauens shall liquifie and melt away. Doo they think thus to adulterate the Lord his woorkmanship, and to be without offence? Doo they not know that he is *Zelotipus,* a ielous God, and cannot abide any alteration of his woorkes, other wise then he hath commaunded?

Yf an Artificer or Craftsman shoulde make any-thing belonging to his art or science, & a cobler should presume to correct the same, would not the other think him self abused, and iudge him woorthy of reprehension?

And thinkest thou (oh Woman!) to escape the Iudgement of God, who hath fashioned thee to his glory, when thy great, and more then presumptuous, audacitie dareth to alter, & chaunge his woorkmanship in thee?

Thinkest thou that thou canst make thy self fairer then God, who made vs all?[28]

Woman's makeup and self-adornment would appear to threaten the creative privilege of God and man (at least by analogy the artificer or the craftsman). The virulence of Stubbes's objections suggests that female artifice constitutes a form of resistance to religious purity and control over "artistic, bodily, creativity" — women making themselves rather than being made "in God's image." The discourse on skin color and "fairness" which preoccupies Stubbes is also suggestive of racial superiority. As God's gender is clearly "masculine," so is his image racialized as "fair" or white. The image of God in which man's body is created, is itself textualized by Stubbes's discourse as masculine in gender and white in skin color.

In his critique of men's apparel, Stubbes declares that the anatomy of man is the likeness of God but man tries to exceed God, his creator, with his luxurious attire. God's masculinity is further threatened by the effeminacy of fine clothing on men: "Men weare stronger than we, helthfuller, fayrer complectioned, longer lyuinge, and finallye, ten tymes harder than we, and able to beare out any sorowe or paynes whatsoeuer. For be sure, this pampering of our bodies makes them weker, tenderer. . . . But now, through our fond toyes and nice inuentions, we haue brought our selues into suche pusillanimitie and effeminat condition, as we may seeme rather nice dames and yonge gyrles than [valorous and hardy] agents or manlie men, as our Forefathers haue bene." Ironically, whereas men sin by abandoning masculinity in adopting fine clothing, woman sin by appropriating "a kinde of attire appropriate onely to man, yet they blush not to wear it; and if they could as wel chaunge their sex, & put on the kinde of man, as they can weare apparel assigned onely to man, I think they would as verely become men indeed, as now they degenerat from godly, sober women, in wearing this wanton lewd kinde of attire, proper onely to man. . . . Our Apparell was giuen vs as a signe distinctiue to discern betwixt sex and sex, & therfore one to weare the Apparel of another sex is to participate with the same, and to adulterate the veritie of his owne kinde. Wherefore these Women may not improperly be called *Hermaphroditi*, that is, Monsters of bothe kindes, half women, half men."[29]

This cybernetic creature is also described as chameleonlike, ever changing, subject to metamorphosis, and a cross-dresser. Women, it would appear, are always "other" or double to themselves. Their anatomy of fashion is secondary, imitative, unstable, dissimulative, breaking the order of male/female sexuality through unrecognizable gender dress codes. These acts of deception or dissimulation in women's dress constitute what Stubbes sees as a "whorish" mode of sexuality. The woman, "painting and dying of her face, sheweth her self to be more then whorish. For she hath corrupted and defaced (like a filthie strumpet or brothel) the woorkmanship of God in her." The "variable fantasies of [women's] serpentine minds" threaten the creative legitimacy of God, confuse gender codes of identity and violate sexual controls. That Stubbes perceives great threat in the power of women's symbolic display is also evident in his description of women's hat styles, which appear to mock religious dress by imitating the horns of Satan: "And some [women] weare Lattice cappes with three hornes, three corners I should saie, like the forked cappes of Popishe Pristes, with their perriwincles, chitterlynges, and the like apishe toyes of infinite varietie."[30] During the fifteenth century, the same debate took place over female headdresses, and bishops denounced those that were Turkish in origin such as turbans and those with horns like the devil's.[31]

Not only did women mock God's power to create "man's image," but their extravagant attire was also thought to mock church vestments. The artificial woman threatened the social order of both material wealth and sexual/gender symmetry: "So that when they haue all these goodly robes vppon them, women seeme to be the smallest part of themselues, not naturall women, but artificiall Women; not Women of flesh and blod, but rather puppits or mawmets [consistyng] of rags and clowtes compact together."[32] Deception is akin to adultery and whoring. In the construction of Stubbes's text, the chapter that follows his critique of women's apparel concerns whoring in England: its crime and sin reside in its "deception."

As Stubbes contradictorily rails against middle-class extravagance in the name of the poor while lamenting the threat to recognizably entrenched class divisions, so he scrutinizes class divisions among women: "One can scarsly know who is a noble woman, who is an honorable or worshipfull Woman, from them of the meaner sorte."[33]

The last royal proclamation on sumptuary matters was in June 1643, under the reign of Charles I. There was an attempt in 1650, during the Puritan rule, to introduce sumptuary regulation of women's clothing, but the bill did not pass. Stubbes's critique of women and dress in the *Anatomie of Abuses* would seem to support Baldwin's supposition that

> once the Puritans had gotten the upper hand, they, who were so fond of regulating every detail in other people's lives in accordance with their own peculiarly strict moral code, would have regarded some sort of sumptuary legislation as absolutely indispensable. On the contrary, however, not a single law of this sort seems to have been passed in the interregnum between the death of Charles I and the restoration of his son. Further investigations in sources not at present available may perhaps unearth some such regulations, but as yet none have come to light. It is true that, in June, 1650, a bill was ordered to be read in Parliament "against the vice of painting, wearing black patches and immodest dresses of women." However, as the "Parliamentary History" says, it seems that "the ladies had interest enough to nip this project in the bud." Whether the defeat of the bill was due to the influence of the women of England or not, the records do not show, but it seems clear that it was defeated, and, as it is not mentioned in the journals of Parliament or elsewhere, no details of its provisions have survived.[34]

The attack on women could be interpreted as a displacement of the real object of critique, the aristocracy. Having brought the aristocracy down, the Puritans found that attention to women, especially aristocratic women, was no longer so important. Nevertheless the woman of artifice posed a threat to the social regulation of women's chastity and virtue, to the religious providence of God-made, as opposed to self-made, creativity, and to the legitimate domains of symbolic power in the aristocracy and the Puritan text of God.

Stubbes's discourse on clothing and excess represented its own special mode of artifice and deception. It served to ingrain a patriarchal superiority toward women by figuring them as imitators and deceivers, both in terms of appearance and with reference to their sexuality. Aside from attempting to discipline the desire for luxury goods, Stubbes also contributed to the production of a British nationalism that would protect and supposedly defend its domestic economy in the production of clothing, especially wool.[35] Class distinctions and the social order were to remain intact in the name of defending the poor, and the ideologies of religious Puritanism and Christianity in general were upheld in the name of defending them against the threat of the Turkish empire.

The discourse of Puritanism, represented in the *Anatomie of Abuses*, attempts to contain and order a burgeoning social, cultural, sexual, and political diversity through a hierarchy of differentiation. Stubbes repeatedly refers to the diversity of fabrics and clothing styles as if diversity itself were the problem. Trade with North America and the Orient had increased Britain's wealth and also introduced a multiplicity and diversity of materials, commodities, and styles, the effects of which Stubbes felt must be contained at an ideological level through Christian definitions of sinfulness. The sin of pride in apparel is one of dissimulation, located primarily in the figure of Woman, who is always other to herself, an artificial woman, a chameleon, manlike, a hermaphrodite. As England became other to "herself" in the context of an expanding European empire, the feminine became the site of an internal dissimulation that seemed susceptible to control and containment, even if international relations were not.

Engendering the Fabric of the Nation

During the seventeenth century, trade with the New World brought new pressures to bear on the political need to contain and rank the diversity of social relations and commodifications. John Evelyn's *Tyrannus* transforms the by now defunct laws into a discursive model for a satire on the influence of French clothing styles in England. But Evelyn's book is more a debate on nationalism, economics, gender, and religion than a discussion of the follies and foibles of fashion. The justifications for sumptuary legislation, the need to control the flow of money out of the realm, and the domestic economy of class relations provide Evelyn with a foil for expressions of anxiety and fear over the reversal of England's political power over France: "For my own part, though I love the *French* well (and have many reasons for it) yet I would be glad to pay my respects in any thing rather than my Clothes, because I conceive it so great a diminution to our native Country, and to the discretion of it. His *Majesty* speaks *French*, not so much to gratify the *Nation*, as because he has *Title* to it: For though *Lewis the Fourteenth* be the *French King*, *Charles* the II is *King* of *France*; and I shall not despair to see the day when he shall give his Vassals there the Edict for their Apparel, and not suffer his Subjects here to receive the Law from them." The symbolic powers sumptuary legislation sought to regulate become in Evelyn's discourse a rhetorical device with which to dissimulate the regulatory force of political powers: "*Mode* is a Tyrant, and we may cast off his Government without impeachment to our Loyalty." [36]

Clothing, like language, represents in Evelyn's discourse the cultural marks of a potential domination that lies elsewhere: "'Tis not a triviall Remark . . . that when a Nation is able to impose and give laws to the habits of another . . . it has (like that of Language) prov'd a Foreruner of the spreading of their conquests there; because, as it has something of Magisterial; as it gives them a boldnesse, and an assurance which easily introduces them, without being taken notice of for Strangers where they come; so as by degrees, they insinuate themselves into all those Places where the *Mode* is taken up, and so much in credit."[37] In the constantly changing theater of fashion, things appear to be that which they are not. *La Mode de France,* which seems a trivial intervention on the stage of cultural representation, Evelyn reads as a sign of inconstancy that threatens the political order of national loyalty.

The constancy of political power is also masculine in gender: "Doubtless, would the great Persons of *England* but owne their Nation, and assert themselves as they ought to do, by making choice of virile, and comely Fashion, which should incline to neither extream, and be constant to it, 'twould prove of infinite more reputation to us, then now that there is nothing fixt, and the Liberty so exorbitant. . . . What have we to do with these foreign Butterflies?" Clothing expenditures are referred to as "promiscuous Bravery," emptying the nation's coffers.[38] The masculinity of the nation is at stake: "But we in this Nation can plead neither of these of our Fantastical and often changes: the very frequency of altering the *Mode,* contradicts the Custom of being addicted to *One,* and so we are constant only by being inconstant, which if allowable in the weaker, becomes not the Viriler Sex; 'twas yet not ill observ'd of Sr. *Philip Sidney,* that Ladies though they were Naturally affraid of a Sword, were yet soonest in love with the men of Iron, whose shape is the most unalterable in all the Metals, and he noblest emblem of constancy."[39] The masculinity of the nation is also threatened by blurring of gender differences in fashion: "Behold we one of Silken *Camelions,* and aery Gallants, making his addresses to his Mistress, and you would sometimes think your self in the country of the Amazons, for it is not possible to say which is the more Woman of the two Coated *Sardanapaulas.* But how may we remedy this? Shall we descend to some particulars. I would choose the loose Riding Coat, which is now the *Mode,* and the Hose which his *Majesty* often wears, or some fashion, not so pinching as to need a Shooing-horn with the *Dons,* nor exorbitant as the *Pantaloons,* which are a kind of *Hermaphrodite* and of neither Sex: Me thinks we should make water sitting [i.e., like a woman], and since we deny our Sex, learn to handle the distaffe too."[40] Foreign trade is also perceived to undermine the unity of one nation, one father, one producer:

> Or, that there were a general prohibition, that persons beneath such a degree, should wear either Silk, Forreign stuffs, or Cloth, with a reasonable *Tassa* impos'd by the Magistrate upon the price of our own manifacture amongst us; How would this bring down the rates of those exotick

impertinencies, how many thousands hands imploy? how glorious to our Prince, when he should behold all his subjects clad with the Production of his own Country, and the people Universally inrich'd, whilst the *Species* that we now consume in Lace, or export for forreign Silks, and more unserviceable Stuffs would by this means be all fav'd, and the whole Nation knit as one to the heart of their Soveraign, as to a Provident and Indulgent father?"[41]

Fashion and fashionableness were once defined as an indicator of rank, "above the vulgar, and below nobility."[42] To be fashionable, then, meant to be a member of the middle classes with pretensions to nobility through the symbolic display of material wealth. Class cross-dressing disrupted the social order: "How many times have I saluted the fine *Man* for the *Master*, and stood with my hat off to the gay Feather, when I found the Bird to be all this while but a Daw?" Fashion not only transgressed class differences, it also upset racial hierarchies. Evelyn refers to an unacceptable *"Negro's* collar," as straight and scanty, a sign of poverty. He also satirizes an orientalized effeminacy in the figure of pinched waists among men: "This Gallant goes so pinched in the Waist. As if he were prepared for the Question of the Fiery Plate in *Turkey*."[43] Poverty is racialized and middle-class upward mobility feminized and orientalized with the explicit objective on Evelyn's part of ensuring the noble constancy of the virile nation. Evelyn's plea for the return to sumptuary legislation in the cause of protecting Charles II's virile nation is nothing short of ironic given that his reign is considered one of the most decadent, competing with the Renaissance in its lavishness and extravagance of dress.[44]

The King, the French, Their Adventurers, and His Company

As sumptuary legislation declined toward the end of the sixteenth century, so too did the availability of fur-bearing animals, especially beaver. The North American fur trade was to become the principal supplier of beaver from the seventeenth century onward. It was not so much the pelt that was in demand as the fur-wool, the layer of short, downy hairs found close to the skin. This fur-wool was used in the technologically innovative process of felting, to produce a whole set of capital goods ranging from fur-wool caps worn by the Spanish and Dutch immigrant and lower classes in England to broad-brimmed beaver hats worn by Puritans and Cavaliers alike.[45] Stubbes remarks on the variety and styles of hats worn by men and notes the new trend in beaver hats acquired through foreign trade: "And as the faſhions bee rare and ſtrange, ſo are the thinges wherof their Hattes be made . . . & which is more curious, ſome of a certaine kind of fine haire." A footnote explains, "These thei call Beuer hattes of xx, xxx, or xl shillinges price fetched from beyond the seas, from whence a greate sorte of other varieties doe come besides."[46] Despite Stubbes's dismissal of this new-fangled commodity, it was equally popular among upper-class Puritans and nobles, although hat styles certainly conveyed an ideology of political and religious preferences — for simplicity on the part of Puritans and ostentation on the part of Cavaliers, as J. Anderson Black and Madge Garland outline:

> Nowhere was there a more obvious difference in dress between the Puritans and the Cavaliers than in their choice of headgear. The Puritans preferred a high-domed, stiff-brimmed hat decorated with a simple hatband and silver buckle. The Cavaliers, however, adopted low-crowned hats with wide brims, decorated with jewelled hatbands and flowing ostrich plumes. . . . These two styles survived for some considerable time, but by the 1670s it was fashionable to wear the Cavalier style with a rather higher crown and with the brim cocked — that is, with the brim turned up on one or two sides. . . . Whatever the station or beliefs of the wearer, hats were invariably black and made from felt [of] beaver. But while the wide uncocked brim remained, courtiers embellished their hats with ostrich plumes or bunches of ribbons, whereas Puritans and the lower classes left their hats unadorned.[47]

With the restoration of Charles II in 1660, a figure who promoted the cavalier style of beaver hat, it is not surprising that this style came to dominate. The reign of Charles II is highly significant to the history of the fur trade with North America. Under his reign, Prince Rupert sponsored the first fur-trading expedition to the Hudson's Bay in 1668. Two French adventurers, Pierre Esprit Radisson and Médart Chouart des Groseilliers, persuaded Prince Rupert to sponsor their expedition after the confiscation of their licenses and furs (in an earlier trip to Chequamegon Bay) by the French governor of Canada with whom they refused to share the proceeds. Radisson captained the vessel named *Eaglet* and Groseilliers the *Nonsuch*. Only Groseilliers made it to Rupert River in James Bay on 29 September 1668. His cargo was sold privately in 1669, and on 2 May 1670 Charles II incorporated the Hudson's Bay Company by royal charter. The first public sale took place at Garraway's Coffee House in London in January 1672. To celebrate its 325 year transnational monopoly, the HBC held an anniversary tribute to itself in 1995, replete with storefront exhibits and marketable souvenirs to mark the occasion, not to mention to educate the public about its glorious imprint on the history of transportation, communications, and commodities.

In the center of its 1994 annual report, the HBC included a commemorative foldout. The cover shows a magnificent photograph (see Figure 9) of

FIGURE 9. Cosmetics counter in the Toronto Queen Street Bay store, Hudson's Bay Company 1994 annual report, anniversary insert, cover. © Hudson's Bay Company, 1994. Reproduced with the permission and cooperation of Hudson's Bay Company.

the cosmetics and perfume counters on the first floor of the downtown Toronto Bay store (at the corner of Queen and Yonge streets). The composition of this high-gloss image signifies a hyper reality effect with its rich texture of commodities and colors. The image falls on two divided pages that open out onto a four-page text/image montage (see Figure 10) of significant persons, objects, and events in the history of the company, pasted onto a seascape backdrop, presumably of the *Nonsuch* resting in calm waters under an expansive and cloudy sky. The four inner pages read chronologically from left to right, from the granting of the HBC charter on 2 May 1670 to the signing of the Canadian Charter in Ottawa in 1970, the most recent date given, although its historical significance to the HBC is not visibly apparent. The political economy of these images exchanges a set of meanings conventionally attributed to the history of Canada: an emphasis on technological advances in trade and navigation, from canoes, dogsleds, and early modern trading ships to twentieth-century industrial ships and delivery vans; extraction of resources and commodity exchange at a primary level in furs and gold (the "Edmonton store in 1898, the last supply stop to the Klondike"), as well as advanced commodity exchange in beaver hats ("The D'Orsay, 1820"), domestic items such as the "Western Treasure Range, 1910," "Ladies' Fashion, 1910," and "Former Hudson's Bay Liquor Brands." The avenues of communication opened up by trading routes and commodity exchange include the "telephone order board in Winnipeg," and "the *Beaver Magazine* celebrates it's [*sic*] 75th anniversary this year." Pictures of HBC stores and fashion images also connote status and wealth. In one of the window displays in the downtown Toronto store, which was part of an exhibit for the anniversary, a small sign in the corner of a display of various contemporary commodities reads: "Fashions on 3, Electronics on 5, Fragrances on main." The odd syntax of items mimics the discontinuous history of commodities and communications contained in the foldout and the window displays which exhibit dioramas of voyageurs and First Nations in the fur trade. Reading the signs and dioramas is almost like reading a history book.[48]

The story of the HBC, as told by an in-house publication, *Canada's Fur Bearers; containing Notes on the Principal Fur Bearing Animals of Canada, Trapping, and the Preparation of Furs for the Market*, relates not simply the success of this original monopolistic transnational corporation, but also the national victory of the English over the French (the Treaty of Utrecht, 1713, Wolfe's victory at Quebec, 1760) and the making of Canada as a nation-state (Lord Selkirk and the colonization of Manitoba, 1811, and the colonization of Vancouver Island, 1849), culminating in the British North America Act of 1867, when the "Company surrendered a large part of its [surface] rights to the Dominion and control of territory which had been governed by the Company for almost 200 years."[49] One of the more telling omissions from this HBC-style history is the Riel Rebellions and the problem — for the HBC — of métis trading with the United States in the latter half of the nineteenth century.

An origin story of fur styles and the mercantile expansion of the fur trade which led to the formation of the Hudson's Bay Company would not be complete if it failed to mention First Nations, those always already representative figures of the origins of Western civilization's evolutionary advance. "All products of old world civilization may not be suited to primitive races, but the aim of the company has always been to carry to the Indians as many as possible of the benefits of white man's civilization, with as few as possible of its drawbacks."[50] All the technological advances in trade and communication, along with the production of domestic and fashionable commodities would appear to constitute "the benefits of white man's civilization." In the insert, images of First Nations appear at the beginning, on the first leaf of the four-page display, (note "Indians visiting Fort Charles, 1673," "Indians trading with Pierre Esprit Radisson and Médart Chouart

FIGURE 10. Pictorial history collage,
Hudson's Bay Company 1994 annual report, anniversary insert.
© Hudson's Bay Company, 1994. Reproduced with the permission
and cooperation of Hudson's Bay Company.

at Charles Fort, 1671," and "The trading-store"). They are represented
as part of an archaic past that has all but vanished in the narrative of progress from fur trade to nation to the "signing of the Canadian Charter in
Ottawa, 1970."

The cover design of the insert — the image of the cosmetics and perfume counters — is, appropriately enough, a cover-girl's dreamscape of
femininity. As a powerful display of female commodity status, it is invested
with a kind of trivialized symbolic power that stands in marked contrast to
the real masculinized political power of the HBC's mercantile past. Famous
men are encoded in portraits: Prince Rupert (first governor, 1670–1682),
Samuel Hearne (famous eighteenth-century HBC explorer), and George
Simpson (overseas governor, dominated HBC for nearly forty years from
1820), Donald A. Smith (Later Lord Strathcona, resident governor, 1889–
1914), and Philip A. Chester (managing director, modernized the HBC
between 1930 and 1959). All these men acquire a legitimate mode of sym-

FIGURE 10. Continued.

bolic power through the aesthetic value attached to their portraits. If symbolic value can be amassed in images with a high degree of reality effect, as in the photograph of the cosmetics and perfume counters in the HBC store, it can also be produced with codes of aesthetic legitimacy, such as fine-art portrait paintings.

The cover of the HBC insert masters the preaesthetic ideology of feminine artifice, in turn acting as a cover for the mercantile and imperialist history of the early modern fur trade. That history is legitimated through the use of properly recognized aesthetic codes that valorize European masculinity in the political and economic domains.

The history of symbolic powers contained in the juridical discursive practices of sumptuary legislation primarily distinguish class and religious differences. The aristocracy and the ruling clergy were the principal bearers of social, economic, political, and symbolic powers. With the rise of British mercantile trade to new worlds in the sixteenth century and especially throughout the seventeenth century, gender, sexual, racial, and oriental differences served as the ideological front on which to resolve material disparities in what people (i.e., which class) and what country would gain access to luxury trade items such as fur. Texts such as those of Stubbes and Evelyn dramatize the contest between political and symbolic powers, heavily circumscribed by ideas about femininity, masculinity, and nationalism. The production of libidinal as well as political economies of exchange value was historically linked to the construction of sexual difference in the moral debates around material and sexual excess. Throughout the modern history of fur's symbolic power, sexual and material excess have run a similar and, at times, interchangeable course. The next chapter discusses one of the most spectacular narratives of sexual, textual, and material excess to emerge in the late nineteenth century: Leopold von Sacher-Masoch's *Venus in Furs*.

3

The Masochist's Gift

"Fur suits women because it's liquid," the photographer was saying.
"Women are liquid?"
"Yes, they move that way."

If liquid women wear soft umbrellas what good does it do them?
The climate is inside the garment.

If the fur coat is liquid and the woman is liquid then it's nothing
but a long rain.

Elizabeth Hay, *Crossing the Snow Line*

The mind is a metaphor of the world of objects which is itself but an
endless circle of mutually reflecting metaphors.

Pierre Bourdieu, *Outline of a Theory of Practice*

The centrality of desire and power to the symbolic economy of fur is most
dramatically represented in the figure of fur as sexual fetish in Leopold
von Sacher-Masoch's late nineteenth-century novel *Venus in Furs*. Masoch
virtually reinvents feminine despotism in the guise of a fur-clad, whip-
wielding woman in black velvet knee-breeches with high leather boots. The
Venus of the novel, Wanda, figures as an elaborate sexual metaphor for
cruelty and violence:

> I went on avidly reading tales of the most fearful cruelty; I gazed with
> particular relish at paintings and engravings depicting such practices,
> and I noticed that in every scene furs were the attribute of the torturer.
> The most bloodthirsty tyrants that ever sat upon a throne, and murder-
> ous inquisitors who had heretics persecuted and burned, and all the
> women whom the great book of history has placed under the sign of

FIGURE 11. "Man licking the shoe of a woman in a fur coat" (ca. 1937).
Reproduced by permission of the Kinsey Institute for Research in Sex, Gender,
and Reproduction.

beauty, lust and violence: Libussa, Lucretia Borgia, Agnes of Hungary, Queen Margot, Isabeau, the Sultana Roxelana and the Russian Tsarinas of the last century, all wore fur garments and ermine robes.[1]

Venus in Furs enacts a drama of surrogate mastery where power is willingly shifted by a man to his mistress. In a willful act of disempowerment, Severin, the male antihero, places himself in the role of sexual slave (see Figure 11). In *Psychopathia Sexualis* (1886), Richard von Krafft-Ebing reads Masoch's representation of masculine disempowerment as an exploration of sexual perversity to which he gave the name "masochism."[2] Masoch protested the categorization of his life and writings as sexually perverse; nevertheless *Venus in Furs* came to set the stage for what was commonly recognized, in the late nineteenth century and throughout the twentieth, as a psychosexual dramatization of masochism and sadism replete with sexual fetishes such as whips, masks, high leather boots, and of course, fur. The fur fetish is a central prop in this masochistic drama of self-willed masculine disempowerment. We might well ask why fur, in particular, comes to figure so prominently in Masoch's "masochistic" scenario?

Masoch attributes his fur fetishism and desire to be whipped to a single originary event in his childhood. One Sunday afternoon, he recounts:

> I had come to play with the children of my aunt-in-law — as we called her — and we were left alone with the maid. Suddenly the countess, proud and resplendent in her great sable cloak, entered the room, greeted us, kissed me (which always sent me into raptures) and then exclaimed: "Come, Leopold, I want you to help me off with my furs." She did not have to ask me twice. I followed her into the bedroom, took off the heavy furs that I could barely lift, and helped her into the magnificent green velvet jacket trimmed with squirrel that she wore about the house. I then knelt to put on her gold-embroidered slippers. On feeling her tiny feet in my hands I forgot myself and kissed them passionately. At first my aunt stared at me in surprise, then she burst out laughing and gave me a little kick.[3]

Even if Masoch forgets himself for a moment in his story, his reconstruction of an event of originary violence which follows is one he "shall never forget." While playing a game of hide-and-seek, Masoch finds himself hiding in his aunt's room behind a clothes rack when his aunt and her lover come in. True to narrative form, the husband suddenly appears to discover his wife in the act of adultery. The usual narrative sequence of punishment and admonishment is forestalled when Masoch's aunt anticipates her husband's moves and punches him in the nose, then brandishes a whip to send the other male voyeurs packing. At this point, the clothes rack falls to the ground, Masoch is exposed, and he finds himself at the stinging end of the whip:

> I tried in vain to explain my presence, but in a trice she had seized me by the hair and thrown me on the carpet; she then placed her knee on my shoulder and began to whip me vigorously. I clenched my teeth but could not prevent the tears from springing to my eyes. And yet I must admit that while I writhed under my aunt's cruel blows, I experienced acute pleasure. No doubt her husband had more than once enjoyed a similar sensation, for soon he returned to her room, not as an avenger but as a humble slave; it was he who fell down at the feet of the treacherous woman and begged her pardon, while she pushed him away with her foot.[4]

Masoch's origin story confirms for Krafft-Ebing that "in the life of every fetishist there may be assumed to have been some event which determined the association of lustful feeling with the single impression. This event must be sought for in the time of early youth, and, as a rule, occurs in connection with the first awakening of the *vita sexualis*." Masoch's novels in general functioned for Krafft-Ebing as explicit instances of "symbolic masochism," which exists at the level of fantasy rather than actuality.[5] If psychoanalysis regulated sexuality, as Foucault argues in *The History of Sexuality*, in Krafft-Ebing's study of symbolic masochism, the imagination is also subjected to the regulatory rigors of a psychoanalytical analysis of perversion — hence justifying for Krafft-Ebing his reading of Masoch's fiction under the rubric of the psychoanalytical case study.

Krafft-Ebing argues that certain materials, such as fur, velvet, and silks, take on the character of the fetish because of the tactile sensations associated with them; the fetishist displays a hypersensitivity to physiological stimulation. Krafft-Ebing dismisses what he interprets as Masoch's explanation that "fur (ermine) is the symbol of sovereignty, and therefore the fetish of the men described in these novels seems unsatisfactory and far-fetched."[6] For Masoch, fur fetishism is intimately linked to fur's history as a sign of absolute power and mastery. Although Krafft-Ebing's theory of fetishism dismisses this particularlity of fur's symbolic value in favor of its sensuous, tactile pleasures, Freud's theory of fur fetishism returns to the issue of mastery from the point of view of the male subject's experience of the visual sensorium. From Freud's perspective, dominated as it is by his theory of the oedipal complex and castration anxiety, the fetish is unambiguously "a substitute for the penis." In his view, "Fur and velvet — as has long been suspected — are a fixation of the sight of the pubic hair, which should have been followed by the longed-for sight of the female member."[7]

The emphasis for Freud is on the pleasures of a compensatory or supplementary visual potency, devoid of any tactile convergence. Fur fetishism functions as a surrogate, a substitute for the penis, the relative distance to which ensures mastery over visual pleasure and control over the fear of castration. As Kaja Silverman explains in the context of Freud's value for film theory and studies of the cinematic gaze: "Freud attempts to increase the distance between the male subject and castration by associating the fetishist's look with 'will,' i.e., with volitional creativity, and thus with mastery."[8] The dual bind expressed in the opposition between a close proximity and tactile experience of the fetish (Krafft-Ebing), on the one hand, and, on the other, the distance to the fetish produced through visual mastery (Freud), suggests that the general experience of pleasure is mediated though a concern for a hyperreduction in alienation from the "natural object" (such as fur or, indeed, parts of one's own body) through either tactile sensation or a dissimulation of alienation through visual surrogacy. In either case, the experience of alienation between the male subject and the natural world must be mediated for that subject through one or the other types of sensory (over)compensation in order to reduce or master the unpleasant effects of alienation.

What is the link within the Freudian drama between sexual fetishism and masochism? In "The Economic Problem of Masochism," Freud identifies three main types of masochism, of which the "most accessible to our observation and least problematical, and it can be surveyed in all its relations" is "feminine masochism" in the male subject: "But if one has an opportunity of studying cases in which the masochistic phantasies have been especially richly elaborated, one quickly discovers that they place the subject in a characteristically female situation; they signify, that is, being castrated, or copulated with, or giving birth to a baby."[9] In the Freudian masochistic drama, sexual fetishism represents a defensive strategy against the fears and fantasies of castration, a sort of compensatory mechanism where the sexual fetish exists as a projection by the masochist in order to relieve his anxiety over an impending disempowerment and impotence, especially in relation to feminine subjectivity or the anatomical threat posed by the female subject, who lacks a penis. While the masochist introjects, or internalizes, the experience of castration and "becomes woman," he also projects the effect of his loss onto an external object, the sexual fetish, a fetishized woman. Lest we mistakenly think that the feminine, and therefore passified, masochist represents failure to achieve an active masculine male identity, we should note that, on the contrary, masochism is, ironically, self-inflicted, an act of reverse mastery. What better way to beat the fear of a supposedly inevitable castration than to will one's own, to become the "feminine masochist," as Freud puts it, by will, rather than be forced by a female despot? Masoch, like the narrator of the *Confessions of a Supersensualist* in *Venus in Furs*, wills his own mastery over reality in his fictional creation of the whip-wielding feminine despot: "Whether she is a princess or a peasant girl, whether she is clad in ermine or sheepskin, she is always the same woman: she wears furs, she wields a whip, she treats men as slaves and she is both my creation and the true Sarmatian woman." [10]

Kaja Silverman observes that Freud exhibits a notable maliciousness toward to the female subject. Freud's contempt for woman, what he calls a "mutilated creature," bears the sense that she has somehow committed a crime for which she has to be punished. An investigation must follow that moves from "woman's 'outside' to her 'inside.'" Silverman elaborates: "That transfer is effected through an investigation, which 'reveals' that the female subject has either committed a crime for which she has to be punished, or suffered from a crippling illness. Since in either case woman's castration can be traced back to her own interiority, this resolution of the male viewer's anxiety permits him to place a maximum distance between himself and the spectacle of lack — to indulge in an attitude of 'triumphant contempt' for the 'mutilated creature' who is his sexual other." We might pause here to reflect on the Lynx images discussed in Chapter 1. In particular, my observation of the bourgeois woman in "Fur coat with matching accessories" as a figure who embodies an accessory to the crime of animal [read: man's] torture, demonstrated by the mutilated bleeding foot of an animal falling limp from her ear. Furthermore, the Lynx image that displays a trail of blood from the coat of the "dumb woman" suggests woman's wound, her menstruation, is being visibly enacted as a site, if not *the sight*, of castration. The silence of the decapitated woman in this image and the question of the bloody earring in the other further support Silverman's thesis that acoustic as well as visual regimes of displacement are at work in the oedipal-castration matrix. Silverman concludes that the idea of woman as a mutilated creature "attests to nothing so much as a successfully engineered projection, to the externalizing displacement onto the female subject of what the male subject cannot tolerate in himself: castration or lack." The fetish exists then, "not so much to conceal woman's castration as to deny man's." [11]

Interestingly, Krafft-Ebing is evidently surprised when a subject denies that he is a feminine masochist; he inserts a question mark after the disavowal of this subject position:

My masochistic tendencies have nothing feminine or effeminate about them (?). To be sure, in these, the inclination to be sought and desired by the woman is dominant; but the general relation desired with her is not that in which a woman stands to a man, but that of the slave to the master, the domestic animal to its owner. If one regards the ultimate aim of masochism without prejudice, it must be acknowledged that its ideal is the position of a dog or horse. Both are owned by masters and punished by them, and the masters are responsible to no one. Just this unlimited power of life and death, as exercised over slaves and domestic animals, is the aim and end of all masochistic ideas.[12]

This negation of feminine masochism suggests many things, not least of which is the difficulty for the male subject of even imagining a woman in the role of master. Significantly, however, it suggests that at the heart of masochistic/fetishistic relations lies not sexual difference but power. The threat of disempowerment and the need for a compensatory projection implicate other contestatory social relations and other sites in which to invest a desire for mastery not only over women but also over the colonized (i.e., slavery) and nature, more specifically, animals. A becoming-slave and a becoming-animal represent, along with a "becoming-woman," different modes of masochistic misrecognition in the social construction of a masculine-sexed identity. In all these examples, however, the question of power over other human or "natural" subjects is central.

Elizabeth Grosz elaborates the psychic defenses manifested in sexual fetishism, one of which is disavowal. Grosz explains the logic of the final prognosis in Sandor Lorand's famous study of the fetishist Little Harry: "He knows that [his mother's] sexual organ is not the same as his own. Yet he disavows any knowledge of genital differences in order to stave off the castration threat which he perceives being directed to his own organ." It is possible to appropriate the concept of disavowal as an explanatory vehicle for putting in motion the problem of man's inability to accept his domination of other men because of the identificatory regulations of male homosociality. In this critical scenario, the fur-clad woman would act the role of the fetish, "a substitute for, a talisman of, the phallus, but not just any old phallus. For the pre-Oedipal boy, the most valued of all phalluses is not his own (for his pre-Oedipal, imaginary penis is not yet elevated to the function of the phallus) but his mother's — the phallus, that is, that endows her with power and authority. . . . He must disavow maternal castration if he is to protect himself against the possibility of his own castration. . . . The fetish cannot simply be equivalent to the maternal or female penis because it *both* affirms *and* denies women's castration."[13] If castration anxiety can be likened to anxiety over a loss of power and authority consumed through the phallus, as I think Grosz's analysis affirms, then the investment of power and authority in the fur-clad woman can be read as a displaced fantasy of the European — white — man's fear of a loss of power and authority over himself and, by an identificatory logic of *sexed* biological essentialism, other men. Racially oriented biological essentialism will leave a very different mark in the case of ethnographic fetishism.

A second psychic defense Grosz describes is negation:

> In negation, there is an affirmation of what is repressed: to negate or deny something one must have previously affirmed it. *Affirmation* is the process of registering or fixing a drive to an ideational content, signifying the former by the latter. Affirmation is both the condition of signification and of repression — something must be signified before it can be relegated to the unconscious — and the return of the repressed. By simply adding a "no" to the affirmation, negation allows a conscious registration of the repressed content and avoids censorship.[14]

To the extent that the fur-clad white woman fetishizes the fear of a masculine loss of power and authority, femininity functions as a negative correlation. As the principle construction for femininity, the figure of the fur-clad woman, Masoch's Wanda, embodies this negativity precisely in her status as an agent of violence and brutality, which Severin creates for her and desires in her. Wanda's violence toward Severin is a materialization of the affirmation of her subjection as a woman and the return of her repression as the guardian of despotic domination.

Krafft-Ebing's and Freud's psychoanalytical explanations emphasize the representation of masculine dis/empowerment. Inadvertently, in the shift from power assumed to power disclaimed another meaning of masochism emerges. I mean the obverse side to which the term's attribution of significance to the male figure as both subject and object of masochistic inquiry is the norm. If in its conventional definition masochism signals a drastic *syndrome* of willful male impotence, a desire to give power over to those already imagined as disempowered, then it follows that to derive its proper meaning the definition of masochism itself must be given over to this originally conceived disempowered woman.[15] With all the falsity of agency masochism permits, then, let us imagine Venus as the subject of the masochistic bind and the object of an inquiry into the sexual politics of masochism. This is not to say that the female figure can necessarily be named a masochist; rather, she is the subject — or perhaps object — without whom there would be no such condition as "feminine masochism."

The female subject as disempowered woman is recontained in terms of an imaginary other, the female sadist.[16] Her initial loss of symbolic power and privilege within the oedipal matrix is rewritten in an act of dissimulation, the artifice of the feminine despot. Krafft-Ebing writes that "masochism is the opposite of sadism." Implicit in his oppositional presuppositions is that man is the opposite of woman, male feminine masochism the opposite of female masculine sadism.[17] A psychoanalytical reading of *Venus in Furs* might then analyze it as a case study of the sadistic/masochistic (s/m) bind: the fur-clad woman, whose "normal" state is passive feminine powerlessness, metamorphoses into a sadistic and despotic figure, an agent of power and domination. Angela Carter observes with reference to Sade that "sexual relations between men and women always render explicit the nature of social relations in the society in which they take place and, if described explicitly, will form a critique of those relations, even if that is not and never has been the intention of the pornographer."[18] Similarly, *Venus in Furs* can also be read as a text that opens up a different perception of social and sexual disempowerment. Masoch's sexualized version of the master/slave dialectic provides an interesting and complex representation of relations of power, femininity, and violence. Krafft-Ebing's and Freud's psychoanalytical readings of sadomasochism and fetishism, combined with Masoch's emphasis on sociosexual relations of power, allow for the possibility of reading his late nineteenth-century novel as a ruse of political violence represented in terms of a sexualized terrorism.

In the historical context of late nineteenth-century Wilhelminian Germany, Biddy Martin notes, "debates over sexuality and sexual difference were at the heart of the development and legitimation of a range of knowledge and social practices. . . . Definitions of sexual difference were central to racist and imperialist national politics, as well as to the various forms of opposition to official Wilhelminian culture."[19] Viewing the figure of the fur-clad feminine despot through the lens of imperial and patriarchal modes of political power opens up fur's fetishistic status to "race" and gender social relations. Metaphors of oriental eroticism and exoticism represented by the Ottoman Empire pervade the novel. African slavery is also recalled in a rather conventional portrait of Wanda's female slaves in terms of a European fantasy of so-called primitive religious fetishism. White fetishism, ethnographic fetishism, specular fetishism, anthropomorphic fetishism — all come into play in *Venus in Furs*, as if to freeze the action of historical change and social transformation. Refusing to give in to the fetishism of the very discourse of fetishism — to defetishize the fetish as a trope in psychoanalytical and economic discourses where the symbolic value of this metaphor has become inert and mute, its meanings contained and restricted by the very "thing-ification" it sets out to re-present — involves mobilizing the multiple meanings of this material signifier, this thing called a fetish. Such mobility in turn informs the movements and actions of social histories and actors. In the context of the emergence of commodity fetishisms, Arjun Appadurai coins the expression "methodological fetishism" to characterize a politics of reading and analysis of particular objects, notably the commodity, which tends to "excessively sociologize transactions in things." Appadurai guards against this tendency toward methodological fetishism. He recognizes that it cannot altogether be avoided in the study of commodities and the politics of value. Nevertheless, he attempts to counter this tendency with the following distinction: "Even though from a *theoretical* point of view human actors encode things with significance, from a *methodological* point of view it is the things-in-motion that illuminate their human and social context."[20] In other words, constitutive of the material organization of objects into commodities are intermittent, indeed somewhat aberrant sites of resistance and codification, sites in which objects have attributed to them meanings and values that belie the existing social order and its attendant human relations. The sexual fetish represents just such an aberrant moment in the circulation of meanings and values attributed to objects as commodities. As a thing-in-motion in the narrativity of a text, the sexual fetish comes to mark the socio-symbolic asymmetries between human and animal, man and woman, animate and inanimate. Extending Appadurai's analysis, then, I would argue not so much against methodological fetishism, as for a methodological de-fetishism that sets out precisely to mobilize the contradictory, and at times arbitrary, relations between "things" (or words) and "subjects," for it is in these relations that the contest between political and symbolic values — produced on gender, imperial, and "race" value differentials — is made and unmade.

Venus in Furs is one of those texts that, in Anne McClintock's words, opens the notion of fetishism to "more theoretically subtle and historically fruitful accounts" that "defy reduction to a single originary trauma or the psychopathology of the individual subject." The following reading of *Venus in Furs* attempts to bring to crisis a multiple field of social contradictions McClintock identifies "between imperialism and domesticity, desire and commodity fetishism, psychoanalysis and social history," contained by this impassioned object, fur.[21]

What's a Fetish between Men?

Masoch's feminized version of the master/slave dialectic begins with a dialogue between two men, Severin and the anonymous narrator. It is the anonymous narrator who brings Severin's manuscript *Confessions of a Super-sensualist* into the body of the text as its primary reader; thus, the "constructedness" of the narrative is foregrounded by the initial dialogue between the two men in a cozy living room, which introduces the actual story, the manuscript, which contains Severin's autobiographical account of his adventures in the libidinal jungle of sociosexual relations. Whereas the story itself dramatically destabilizes the regulatory expectations of heterosexu-

ality, sexual inequalities, and an essentialist ideology of gender/sex symmetries — masculine and feminine genders symmetrically mapped onto
biologically constructed male and female bodies — the textual frame in
which this story unfolds provides a controlling mechanism, as if the words
that pass between men could approximate by will or convention a secure
site of selfsame interests and identical ideological persuasions. The formal
design of *Venus in Furs*, in which Severin's manuscript is framed by a homosocial dialogue between himself and a friend, institutes an apparatus of normalization which contains and, finally, rejects the discourse of sexuality
constituted by the *Confessions*.

Severin's dismissal of his experiment into sexual "perversity" represents
a paradigmatic formulation of Foucault's insistence that the so-called Vic-
torian "repressive hypothesis" acted more as a strategy for the discursive
proliferation of discourses on sexuality than as a self-promoting mechanism
of suppression. Predictably, where Masoch would have us believe that Severin's momentary escape from the harsh repression of a protracted Christian asceticism represents a liberatory artistic gesture, Foucault would have
us recognize in Severin's sexual laboratory a discursive agent engineering
the very power mechanisms of sexuality which would establish heterosexual
difference as "normal" and "natural." The use of confessional and contractual methods for establishing this apparatus of normalization "construct[s]
an analytics of power that . . . takes law as a model and a code." [22]

If the manuscript can only serve as a conventional document through
which to will a homosocial controlling perspective on a radically unstable
reality, the legally binding contract Severin attempts to put into practice
between himself and Wanda exists to secure their heterosexual relations
through the force of law. The contract clearly sanctions the formal duties
of a master and a slave: "You can no longer lay claim to any rights, and
there are no limits to my power over you. Consider that you are little better
now than a dog or an object; you are my thing, the toy that I can break if it
gives me a moment of pleasure. You are nothing, I am everything; do you
understand?" (196). It is tempting to say that Masoch is only representing
in another form what is already legally codified by nineteenth-century
European marriage laws. [23] But there is a twist to this narrative certainty:
Masoch narrates a feminized version of the master/slave dialectic; furthermore, he inflects this feminized version of power with a European fantasy
of Oriental despotism. The radical instability of gender/sex symmetries
throughout the ironically framed *Confessions of a Supersensualist* can serve to
foreground the radical instabilities of imperialism that historically accom-
pany the libidinal ruptures of the domestic space of empire. In *Venus in Furs*
the web of power and desire is so tightly knit with the threads of an imperialist exoticism as to make such an analysis both pressing and necessary.

In the opening dialogue between Severin and the unknown narrator, which takes place by the fireside, the men surrounded by the objects of scientific discovery, biological imperialism, maps, and high culture — skeletons of exotic animals, stuffed birds, globes, plaster casts and paintings, not to mention skulls and leather-bound books (148, 175) — the conversation turns to a discussion of Titian's *Venus with the Mirror*:

> Later some connoisseur of the baroque dubbed the lady "Venus," and the despot's furs in which Titian's model wrapped herself (more out of fear of catching cold than from modesty) became the symbol of the tyranny and cruelty that are common to beautiful women. But what does it matter? As it stands, the painting is a biting satire on modern love: Venus must hide herself in a vast fur lest she catch cold in our abstract northern climate, in the icy realm of Christianity. (149)

The moment Severin recalls the origins of this symbol of the tyrannical cruelty of women's beauty, he dismisses it for a more promising satirical allegory on the condition of modern love: more promising for its bite, for its cool and critically distant perspective on the hypocrisies of social morality. While the critical perspective may have an icy edge, the intent is to defrost or liquefy the icy realm of Christian sexual deprivation, to fight ice with ice. If the symbol of the beautiful tyrannical woman is too static and conventional to combat the spread of a sexual ice age, she must be mobilized, unfrozen and deployed as an agent of power, as the satirical voice of Christianity's undoing. When she is made a fetishistic symbol of despotism, her power is contained and therefore weak and impotent; as an ambulatory fetish, she is free to put her despotic powers into practice: free to repaganize and resexualize the European world, but at a price. The cost is slavery.[24]

When Wanda becomes despondent over Severin's potentially unrealized enslavement to her whims and fancies in a European context where "slavery does not exist any longer," Severin "eagerly" suggests: "Then let us go to a country where it does, to the Orient or Turkey" (194). Wanda, however, decides not to go to Constantinople to sign the contract that will guarantee Severin's slavery. "What," she asks,

> is the point of having a slave in a country where slavery is common practice? I want to be the only one to own a slave. If we live in a cultivated, sensible, Philistine society, then you will belong to me, not by law, right or power, but purely on account of my beauty and of my whole being. The idea is most exciting. But let us go to a country where we are not known and where you can be my servant without embarrassment; Italy perhaps, Rome or Naples. (197)

To enact the master/slave dialectic, the Orient appears as a prop for the fantasy of its realization. But why leave Europe, when, after all, the fantasy is European? In a civilized country such as Italy, slavery need not be legalized but can be maintained as a fantasy simply through an aesthetics of domination. For it is Wanda's beauty and the totality of her being (the ontological supremacy of the autonomous and fully present subject) which will ensure Severin's position as a slave. If slavery figures as part of the European fantasy of a changeless and timeless despotism realized in the Orient or, perhaps more properly speaking, the Ottoman Empire, then to be within the realm of this supposed legally sanctioned slavery would create a situation in which Severin might never escape. He would be destined to remain — along with Europe's narrative containment of the inhabitants of the ruled colonial territories — like "creatures of European will."[25] Better to be the hammer and not the anvil. To secure his final authority, Severin opts for Rome, the symbolic embodiment of the twin signs of republicanism and European Christian hegemony.

While this reversal of the master/slave dialectic takes place within the narrative of the *Confessions*, during Severin's concluding dialogue with the narrator, he insists on the necessity of returning to a normal order of subordination:

> Goethe's words, "Be the anvil or be the hammer" are never more true than when applied to the relations between man and woman. Incidentally, the Lady Venus informed you of this in your dream. Woman's power lies in the passion she can arouse in man and which she will exploit to her own advantage unless he remains always on his guard. Man has only one choice: to be a slave or to be a tyrant. If he surrenders to her the yoke will begin to weigh on his neck and soon he will feel the touch of the whip. (150)

Woman is restored to her rightful place as a natural figure for slavery, and man is restored to his rightful place as a natural figure for mastery. In protest against Severin's brutal behavior toward his female servant — Severin's demonstration of his and her natural places — the narrator declares: "You may live like a pasha in your harem if you choose, but do not foist your theories on me" (150). Alain Grosrichard has noted that "above and beyond the anecdote which ornaments it, the 'harem connection' betrays its deep affinity with an Occident which is beginning to question the principles of its political institutions, the aims of education, the role of the family, the enigma of the relations between the sexes — all questions which involve, even more profoundly than may appear, the essence of its metaphysics."[26] Masoch's occidental fantasy of the fur-clad feminine oriental despot would indeed indicate that his critique of Christianity as the root of sexual inequality is filtered through a colonial gaze located elsewhere. The unknown narrator's admonishment of Severin's orientalism mimics the imperial voice of colonialism, which situates itself, as Malek Alloula observes, as "the final morality of Orientalism and exoticism." Alloula concludes his analysis of picture postcards of Algerian women produced and sent by the French in Algeria during the first three decades of the twentieth century with a critique: "Voyeurism turns into an obsessive neurosis. The great erotic dream, ebbing from the sad faces of the wage earners in the poses, lets appear, in the flotsam perpetuated by the postcard, another figure: that of *impotence*."[27] In the context of Masoch's particular brand of masculine disempowerment we might consider "masochism" an occidental syndrome of the radical instability colonialism renders in the European male fantasy of its fully autonomous subjectivity. Winifred Woodhull comments that "Alloula dislocates a set of colonialist male fantasies embodied in the haunting figure of the Algerian woman," but she notes that "Alloula's analysis is itself haunted by a kind of spectral presence, that of an undivided Algeria, an emerging nation in which the conflicting interests of men and women are first and foremost the product of the conqueror's sexual fantasies and administrative polices." He "repeats the gesture of the colonizer by making of the veiled woman the screen on which he projects *his* fantasy (an idealization fueled, perhaps, by his exile in France) — that of an Algerian nation untroubled by questions of women's oppression."[28] In both Masoch's European context and Alloula's Algerian context, woman's bodies exist as the site for resolving male homosocial disparities.

The willed impotence of the sovereign subject, a King Lear of modern times, characterizes masochism as, essentially, a study in the radical alterity required of masculinity by the imperatives of European imperialism, by which men must dominate other men. At the conclusion to Severin's narrative, he is "cured" by a brutal beating at the hands of "the Greek" the other "strong" man whom Wanda eventually takes as her husband in preference to Severin. "The first thing I felt after this," writes Severin,

> the most cruel disaster of my life, was the desire to live rough and experience danger and privation. I wanted to become a soldier and go to Asia or Algeria, but my father was old and sick and wanted me to stay near him. . . . Then my father died and quite naturally and without altering my way of life I became the master of the house. I donned my father's boots of Spanish leather and continued to lead a well-ordered life, as though he were still standing behind me, watching over my shoulder with his great wise eyes. (269–70)

If Severin cannot go to fight the imperial wars, battle it out man against man, he will stay at home and maintain the well-ordered life and the subordination of women which constitute the domestic supports of empire.

In the fantasy of the feminine despot, European bourgeois femininity is mapped onto the occidental fantasy of Oriental despotism. The European bourgeois woman is thus enlisted as a collaborator in the imperial enterprise. She is figured as capable of dominating the colonized man, and yet her femininity itself serves to feminize the Orient, to extend this stereotypical move in which the inferior and infantile attributes of femininity come to characterize colonized peoples, thus creating the necessary ideological support for colonial "penetration."[29] Another dimension of the feminization of the Orient involves the European conception of masculine subjectivity as stable, fixed, and most important, uncontested. Within the inscriptional space of the *Confessions* any pretense to a fully coherent masculine subject is radically undone when, for example, Masoch describes "the Greek," as possessed of a "fierce virility" and yet admits, "if his hips were less slender, he could be taken for a woman in disguise" (249, 246). "He has been seen in Paris dressed as a woman and men showered him with love letters" (250).[30] While the sexual play, gender ambiguity, and cross-dressing that constitute Severin's adventures into sexual deregulation are reintroduced into the regime of normality in the final dialogue between the two men, it is the feminization of the Orient in the figure of the fur-clad feminine despot and the ambiguous Greek who "fought the Turks at Candia and is said to have distinguished himself no less by his race-hatred and cruelty than by his bravery" (248), which ultimately serves to protect the fantasy of a stable European masculinity.

When the unknown narrator finishes reading the manuscript, he asks the moral of the story and is told:

> The moral is that woman, as Nature created her and as man up to now has found her attractive, is man's enemy; she can be his slave or his mistress but never his companion. This she can only be when she has the same rights as he and is his equal in education and work. For the time being there is only one alternative: to be the hammer or the anvil. I was fool enough to let a woman make a slave of me, do you understand? Hence the moral of the tale: whoever allows himself to be whipped deserves to be whipped. But as you see, I have taken the blows well; the rosy mist of supersensuality has lifted, and no one will ever make me believe that the sacred wenches of Benares or Plato's rooster are the images of God. (271)

What underlies the extraordinary subversion of traditional masculine and feminine gender symmetry in Masoch's sexual and asymmetrical reversals of power and eroticism is the European man's fear of coming to terms with his domination over other men. Domination of woman can easily be naturalized through an essential and biological determination of sexual difference. Domination of other men, however, within a homosocial nexus of patriarchal solidarity ruptures the very core of civility and the advance of civilization.

> In spite of all the advances of civilization, woman has remained as she was the day Nature's hands shaped her. She is like a wild animal, faithful or faithless, kindly or cruel, depending on the impulse that rules her. A profound and serious culture is needed to produce moral character. Man, even when he is selfish or wicked, lives by principles; woman only obeys her feelings. Never forget this, and never be sure of the woman you love. (192)

If woman remains in her proper place, man remains at the center of sovereignty and power. But if man does not remain in his sovereign place of power, if he is reduced to the condition of the woman, the beast, what of man's sense of himself as identical with power and control; how can man accept his domination of other men?

The figure of Wanda in *Venus in Furs* can be read as representative of the contradictory polarities of the times — the rise of a bourgeois feminist struggle for equal access to the established structures of power and the emergence of an ideological backlash in the shape of a moral and sexual monstrosity. But Wanda is more than a figure of feminine or feminist despotism. She can also be read as a charged characterization of a European fantasy of oriental despotism. To reconfigure the imperial fantasy of the oriental despot in the guise of a bourgeois European woman introduces into the picture a double gesture of feminine/female subordination; not only is the subordination of the bourgeois European woman ensured by this feminization, but the femininity attributed to the Orient works to supplant the mythical status of absolute political power with a far more ambiguous configuration of eroticized political power, captivating in its challenge to a European, predominantly Christian asceticism and, yet, suppressible and assailable in its feminine oriental guise. As a figure who embodies an ambiguous constellation of feminine and oriental despotism, Wanda is a receptacle into which pour those ideas and meanings that the imperial despot himself cannot absorb without facing the massive contradictoriness of his aggrandizement as the benevolent father and his practices of brutality, enslavement, greed, expropriation of territory, and so on and so forth. The mastery component of the imperial patriarch demands a reconfiguration elsewhere, perhaps in the form of a physical embodiment such as an animal or a woman or an inanimate object — a fetish? What could be a more compelling figure for the embodiment of the transference of desires and violence than the fur-clad woman, a material signifier whose essential properties are those of the animate and inanimate, the animal and the human?

The Libidinal Economy of Ethnographic Fetishism

If the identificatory relations between men are consolidated through their sexual symmetry, and the disturbance caused by dominating other men occurs at the level of this sexual symmetry, it is the designation of a racial difference that legitimates European bourgeois man's domination of "other" men. Masoch displaces subordinate masculine relations onto the feminine, in particular, the figure of woman. He resolves the contest between men ideologically through this displacement by inscribing a racial mark of difference in female relations, principally between the white bourgeois woman and the black African female slave.[31] Wanda's female African slaves materialize in the text in a rather conventional portrait of nineteenth-century European notions of a so-called primitive religious fetishism: "Three slender young Negresses appeared, like ebony carvings, all dressed in red satin and each with a rope in her hand" (222) and "To my misfortune I paid a little more attention than I should have done to Haydée who was serving the meal in my place. For the first time I noticed her noble, almost European features, her statuesque bust that seemed chiseled in black marble" (233).

In the beginning was the statue, an object made of stone, a graven image:

... my beloved is made of stone.

In the garden, or rather the small neglected park, there is a charming meadow where a few does graze peacefully. In its center stands a statue of Venus, the original of which I believe is in Florence. This Venus is the most beautiful woman I have ever seen; of course this does not mean much, for I have seen few beautiful women, in fact few women at all. (153)

William Pietz, in his study of the discursive and genealogical problem posed by the fetish, suggests that far from representing a continuation of Christianity's false other — the idol — the fetish constitutes a breakdown of the adequacy of this conventional view. Deleuze defines the fetish as "a frozen, arrested, two-dimensional image, a photograph to which one returns repeatedly to exorcise the dangerous consequences of movement, the harmful discoveries that result from exploration; it represents the last point at which it was still possible to believe."[32] The fetish signals a distinct reconfiguration of the relationship between words and things due to a cross-cultural clash of sign systems — religious or otherwise — brought on by mercantile expansion in the early modern period and, subsequently, by contesting modes of production among feudal, kinship, and capitalist social systems. Pietz argues that the meanings and values attributed to the fetish are an effect of European interaction with the West African coast after the fifteenth century, an interaction phantasmatically characterized by colonial records and descriptive texts, as an "abrupt encounter of radically heterogenous social systems."[33] The fetish signals, then, a categorical crisis in the order of things; neither graven image nor Christian symbol, the fetish is that which does not fit and, as such, signifies "difference" in the abstract. We could say that the fetish is the magical sign for an imaginary unassimilable difference, a radical alterity. In her poem *The Venus Hottentot*, Elizabeth Alexander represents the lure of fetishism in the service of the imperial master:

> I am called "Venus Hottentot."
> I left Capetown with a promise
> of revenue: half the profits
> and my passage home: A boon!
> Master's brother proposed the trip;
> the magistrate granted me leave.
> I would return to my family
> a duchess, with watered-silk
>
> dresses and money to grow food,
> rouge and powders in glass pots,
> silver scissors, a lorgnette,
> voile and tulle instead of flax,
> cerulean blue instead
> of indigo. My brother would
> devour sugar-studded non-
> pareils, pale taffy, damask plums.[34]

As Venus is the most beautiful woman for Severin, precisely because of his limited exposure to women, so too the Orient and Africa exist as radically different, exotic, and attractive places to the unknowing explorer. This is not to fetishize the real as a knowable entity but to insist that the imperial fetish constitutes a radical difference of the unknown, thereby creating the necessary conditions of "dehumanization" or "objectification" needed to legitimate imperial expansion and, on the home front, patriarchal domination.[35]

The historical conditions and social forces generated in the context of Pietz's perceptive genealogy of the fetish overlap and interconnect in various ways in *Venus in Furs*. For example, unleashing hedonistic desire from its lapidary domain, setting it free, as it were, to circulate in the intricate mediations of exchange, can induce anxiety. When Severin unleashes the graven image of a "White Venus" from its fetishistic stronghold, it sends him into paroxysms of panic and flight:

> But what is this? The goddess is draped in fur: a dark sable cloak flows from her marble shoulders down to her feet. I stand bewildered, transfixed; again I am gripped by an indescribable panic. I take flight. In my hurry I take the wrong path and just as I am about to turn off into one of the leafy avenues, there before me, seated on a bench — is Venus; not the marble beauty of a moment ago, but the goddess of Love in person, with warm blood and a beating heart! She has come to life for my benefit like Pygmalion's statue. The miracle is not quite compete, for her hair still seems made of marble and her white dress gleams like moonlight — or is it satin? The dark fur drapes her from shoulder to toe. But her lips are becoming redder, her cheeks are taking on color, suddenly her eyes shine with a wicked green glitter — she is laughing! (156–57)

The transformation from inanimate to animate object, from statue to ambulant fetish, mobilizes a narrative flow of defetishization. Entering White Venus into the circuitry of exchange constitutes a devolution of powers from the center to the margins, from man's self-centered autonomy to a dynamic of male-female relationality. Anne McClintock explains that "S/M performs the failure of the Enlightenment idea of individual autonomy, theatrically staging the dynamics of interdependency for personal pleasure."[36] Such "interdependency," however, becomes apparent only in the defetishization that takes place in the regime of a sexual circuitry of exchange, where the flows and intensities of sexed desire are set in motion: love is released from its lapidary state, the statue of Venus is freed, and Christianity's sexual deprivation is on the thaw. An ethnographic fetishism that denies relations of dependency remains fixed to the imperial anchors of an exoticized racial difference. The dark coat that gives definition to the white dress in Masoch's description suggests that the constitution of the White Venus can be consolidated only in relation to the dark fur. The "Black Venuses" remain engraved and frozen in the solid substance of black marble. But they too undergo a metamorphosis from inanimate to animate fetish when their facial features are described as "almost European."

In the context of a masochistic libidinal economy, as Masoch constructs its essential elements, fur is the liminal figure that crosses the threshold of male-female, black-white sexual relations. In mediating the hierarchical relationship between man-woman and European-African inscriptions of difference, fur realigns these dualities along an animal-human axis. The figure of fur displaces power from the realm of gendered and racialized relations

FIGURE 12. Nicole Brown Simpson as "White Venus" (1981).
Reproduced by permission of Photoreporters, New York.

onto the world of anthropomorphized relations (animal-human). In this
equation the figures of Black and White Venus are consigned to the animal's side (see Figure 12). We might ask here how fur serves to reinvest and
reinscribe white and black woman's status as Nature: Does woman-in-fur
become a doubly natured woman? "She treated him cruelly just as Nature

casts aside whatever has served her purpose as soon as she has no more need of it" (179). Or is fur the natural form that gives a specular shape to the matter of Woman as in the case of the dark fur that gives definition to a White Venus?

No writer has explored as graphically as Franz Kafka in *The Metamorphosis* the strained and alienated indifference of human relations in terms of an abject animalization. Like the phantom roach in Audre Lorde's account of her encounter with a fur-clad bourgeois white woman, Kafka's metamorphosis of human to animal, man to insect, succeeds because of the contempt, disgust, and filth this creature epitomizes in the urban imagination. Kafka's novella is particularly intriguing for its incorporation, at the beginning of the story, of an image of a fur-clad woman. She appears in a photographic display on Gregor Samsa's wall: "Above the table on which a collection of cloth samples was unpacked and spread out — Samsa was a commercial traveler — hung the picture which he had recently cut out of an illustrated magazine and put into a pretty gilt frame. It showed a lady, with a fur cap on and a fur stole, sitting upright and holding out to the spectator a huge fur muff into which the whole of her forearm had vanished!"[37] After Freud's classic account of the fur fetish as "the sight of the pubic hair, which should have been followed by the longed-for sight of the female member," such an image is overdetermined to the degree that its effect is comedic, an amplified version of "castration anxiety" blown up with the aid of photographic simulation — in Gilles Deleuze and Félix Guattari's words, "an exaggerated oedipus."[38] Not only does this image constitute an oedipal debt to Masoch's *Venus in Furs*, so, too, does the very name Kafka uses for his dispossessed hero. The name Gregor is taken by Severin when he occupies his contractual role as slave to Wanda. Samson appears many times, for example, in a description of a painting: "Delilah, an opulent creature with flaming red hair, reclines half-naked on a red ottoman, a sable cloak about her shoulders. She smiles and leans toward Samson, who has been bound and thrown at her feet by the Philistines. Her teasing, coquettish smile seems the very summit of cruelty; with half-closed eyes she gazes at Samson, while he regards her longingly, crazed with love. Already his enemy has laid a knee on his chest and is about to blind him with the white-hot sword" (221). Gregor Samsa is a composite figure taken from *Venus in Furs*. He actualizes a masculine, bestial version of oppression which Masoch could reproduce only in a feminine version of an almost-but-not-quite-sign-of-humanity, the fur-clad woman.

In their book on Kafka's animal stories, Deleuze and Guattari create a theoretical fabula of social transformation. A male "becoming animal" represents a model of unlimited divisibility in the deployment of revolutionary forces: "To become animal is to participate in movement, to stake out the path of escape in all its positivity, to cross a threshold, to reach a continuum of intensities that are valuable only in themselves, to find a world of pure intensities where all forms come undone, as do all the significations, signifiers, and signifieds, to the benefit of an unformed matter of deterritorialized flux, of nonsignifying signs." But becoming animal has its limits too, as Deleuze and Guattari note:

> We would say that the process of Gregor's deterritorialization through his becoming-animal finds itself blocked for a moment. Is it the fault of Gregor who doesn't dare go all the way? To please him, his sister wants to empty out the whole room. But Gregor refused to let go of the portrait of the lady in fur. He sticks to the portrait, as if to a last territorialized image. In fact, that's what the sister cannot tolerate. She accepted Gregor; like him, she wanted the schizo incest, an incest of strong connections, incest with the sister in opposition to Oedipal incest, incest that gives evidence of a nonhuman sexuality as in the becoming-animal.[39]

Perhaps the sister desires a schizo incest, or perhaps Gregor's clinging to this figure of the "lady in fur" is a final attempt to secure the territorialization of woman's bodies in the domestic space of empire and to remap her territorialization in the guise of an animal. Perhaps the sister is annoyed that Gregor did not consider her own desire to escape the becoming-animal that has been the naturalized state for women.

Becoming animal, becoming woman, becoming slave — these are the options by which social and political relations of imperial power, exchanged both materially and theoretically in the constitution of libidinous commodities and fetishes, are resolved and displaced. In the process of bringing about such temporary resolutions in the contest of imperial domination, dualities of masculine/feminine attributes of power, animate/inanimate flows of libidinal desire, and the black/white or smooth/hairy surface of animal or human skins emerge as affective sites where the values of economic exploitation and symbolic oppression are negotiated.

In Kafka's *Metamorphosis* I read the simulated image of the fur-clad woman as a metamorphosis of a psychically powerful "white fetish" into an empty signifier whose alienation from the psychic imaginary leaves a man facing himself without the benefit of a displaced fantasy to consume. The effects are, needless to say, horrific in terms of an internalization of masculine abjection and (d)emasculating self-hatred.

On Becoming "Human"

In *The Sadeian Woman*, Angela Carter contemplates the economic realities of many women's lives in contrast to the fantasy of their sexual power:

A male-dominated society produces a pornography of universal female acquiescence. Or, most delicious titillation, of compensatory but spurious female dominance. Miss Stern with her rods and whips, Our Lady of Pain in her leather visor and her boots with sharp, castratory heels, is a true fantasy. . . . She is most truly subservient when most apparently dominant; Miss Stern and her pretended victim have established a mutually degrading pact between them and she in her weird garb is mutilated more savagely by the erotic violence she perpetrates than he by the pain he undergoes, since his pain is in the nature of a holiday from his life, and her cruelty an economic fact of her real life, so much hard work. You can describe their complicity in a pornographic novel but to relate it to her mortgage, her maid's salary and her laundry bills is to use the propaganda technique of pornography to express a view of the world, which deviates from the notion that all this takes place in a kindergarten of soiled innocence. A kindergarten? Only small children, in our society, do not need to work.[40]

The Confessions of Wanda von Sacher-Masoch provides one opportunity to turn the tables on the normative field of inquiry into masochism, to study an autobiographical narrative whose author documents how Leopold's fantasy of "Wanda" impinged on her as his real-life wife. It must be remembered, however, that these autobiographical fragments, translated into English and published by the journal *Re/search*, are themselves a mediated dialogue, constructed to denounce and dethrone a man whose representative status as a great author and sexually liberated genius of Europe's late nineteenth century was, for Wanda, a historically engineered perversion. Notwithstanding the evaluative psychoanalytical importance given to masochistic sexual practices as perverse or otherwise, I read this sexual codification, whether as an avatar of a celebrated sexual excess or as a law designed to delimit the acceptable from the unacceptable, with a meaning that lies elsewhere. The editors of this first English translation imagine the difficult material circumstances that drove Wanda to record and sell her manuscript:

> In 1907, during a meeting at *Mercure de France*, Paris's foremost publisher, a little old lady in a ratty fur coat marched in and announced herself at the reception desk. . . . Decades earlier her pioneering, flamboyant "S&M" lifestyle had inspired numerous articles and several books, then she had fallen into poverty and obscurity. Out of a decrepit handbag she retrieved a thick manuscript, which *Mercure de France* would publish that year under the title *Confessions de ma vie*. (3)

The Confessions thematizes the oppressive conditions of middle-class women, their material dependency, especially in the case of property ownership, which they were denied, and their financially burdensome child-care responsibilities. When Wanda finally granted Leopold a divorce, he won custody of one of their children and was not responsible for any other child support or alimony. Wanda's class position created a particularly circumscribed set of oppressions, and not surprisingly her response to her oppressive existence, her attempt to write herself out of her material deprivation both symbolically through her characterization of her life with Leopold and financially with the publication of her confessions, was also circumscribed by her middle-class existence. In other words, her text reveals certain ideological contradictions that are fraught with tensions between the presumed illusoriness nature of symbolic power left open to middle-class and bourgeois women and the material and economic realities of political and juridical powers in the hands of a male ruling elite in late nineteenth-century Europe. Wanda's relative privilege as a middle-class woman offers limited solutions to the problem of material dispossession, inasmuch as a symbolic mode of agency will come to dominate, however ineffectually, over changes in political and economic power for the social class of middle-class women.

To consent to the rules of the masochist's game the reader must agree to a succession of reversals in sexual, religious, and material economies of exchange. In this world turned upside down, Old World commodities become New World gifts, Christian symbols become ritually personalized fetishes, and the discrete binary logic of human sexual-gender systems metamorphoses into bestial and carnal orders of the wild and the domestic, the animate and inanimate.

To play the masochist's game within the limits of the Christian middle-class family is to play "until death do us part," an interdiction that Leopold takes quite literally but Wanda finds repulsive and demeaning. Although Wanda at an early age disavows any affinity with the rituals of ecclesiastical flagellation, her confessions read as an ironic commentary on the lifestyles of the divinely decadent:

> And [the confessor] set about interrogating me — in sacrosanct tones, it is true, but using crude, explicit terms — all the while displaying a professional indifference. I was incapable of listening, so I simply looked him over — at his red peasant face, puffy and dripping with sweat, which he constantly wiped away with a blue handkerchief. I pitied the fate that had given me as Confessor a "Representative of God" so repulsive and vulgar. And when he questioned me about the Sixth Commandment in the same crude language I only partially understood, I rebelled within myself and, more stubborn than ever in my silence, vowed that *never again* would I return to confess myself! (6–7)

Why does the sixth commandment occupy such a memorable place as the occasion of Wanda's stubborn refusal? The purity of its meaning seems to Wanda so obvious as to be corrupted on the tongue of a red-faced peasant conducting a crude and vulgar interrogation. What could be more "crude," more direct and obvious, than that this law, "Thou shalt not commit adultery," must be repeatedly avowed, following its own temporal sequence within the text of the Ten Commandments, and that its crudity is what is most off-putting to the one who is above the law? This is the point of Wanda's stubborn refusal. In this moment of recognition that she is in no position to make the law, she yet sees herself as above the law. This is what the difference between being a "man" and being a "woman" means to Wanda: the prelegal right to assume the making of law. When Leopold does his best to grant Wanda a contractual right to commit adultery, to do violence to him, even to kill him if she so desires, she considers this reversal of the "natural order" beneath her: "Therefore, this was a matter not of any desire of *mine* but of *his*. It was because he wanted, in this way, to do violence to *my* nature that I revolted" (36). If Leopold's discourse of desire seeks pleasure in transgression and the breaking of the law, Wanda's discourse flies in the opposite direction, toward the sublime pleasures of transcendence: "Unceasingly my spirit reached out toward the supernatural and the sublime; I felt myself close to heaven, far from all evil. Until then love for my mother had filled my heart; now, bereft of my mother, I put God in her place" (4). The symbolic power invested in the figure of the mother increases throughout the confessional narrative. The mother comes to represent that which is "most sacred" (95), one who can make men serious and inspire fear, "Only the word 'mother' could make them serious. 'Mother' was for the child the equivalent of 'God.' Everything disappeared before mother. Mother — how his child's heart trembled with fear before her!" (109); and finally, the figure who holds the "highest and the noblest power: that of *mother* and *educator*, and if [women] have not found the happiness they hoped for at home, it is they alone who are at fault, because they have not been conscious of their *power* or have not known how to use it, because they have not realized that of their *sons* they must make future *husbands*" (119). The mother occupies an ideal position, above the vulgar and crude laws of man's mere making, laws that for Leopold are made to enforce his will and to be broken at will.[41] The mother transcends the machinations of man's law making and breaking through a spiritual dispensation embodied in the ideal of love. Profanity is not Wanda's strength, to be sure, although the conventional ironies of her situation rarely escape her: "And those who love the most will humiliate themselves the most" (99).

Wanda does not confess sins, rather her *Confessions*, her autobiographical narrative, represent sketches of the "truths" of her sorrowful existence with a man she truly believed had succumbed to an evil force. Wanda's trick is to not confess sin but its opposite, to confess that she is the ideal woman, the loving mother and wife, intelligent enough to know the disadvantaged position she occupies in a society that legally sanctions the subservience of women to men, and yet spiritual enough to transcend or "rise above" this degradation. The central device that motivates the narrative of *The Confessions* is the anticipation built up around the question of whether Wanda will succumb to Leopold's desire that she commit the crime of adultery.

> To avoid all misunderstanding, I pointed out to Leopold that Gross had nothing in him of the "Greek" in *Venus in Furs*, and that he could not expect to see him play this role to the fullest extent. Whereupon he assured me that he knew his will, and that for a long time he had renounced that part of the program; now all he desired was that I be unfaithful to him.
>
> "And then, when I have done it? Will you be satisfied and not ask me again?"
>
> "I have told you time and again that I would like to endure it *only once*. Such a thing *cannot* be repeated — you should understand that." (93)

As successful as this oedipal literary device is for creating narrative suspense and keeping the reader hooked by deferred gratification, the moment of sexual infidelity fails to obtain its critical point of climax. Eventually Wanda is no longer able to endure Leopold's persistent pressure that she commit an act of infidelity simply to feed his own perverse desire to suffer anguish over her "betrayal." Wanda, having nowhere else to go, succumbs to the desire of an ambitious French journalist named Armand who has coveted her for some time. During her marriage to Leopold, Wanda has received many fur-bearing gifts; yet, as if to mark her departure from Leopold and her arrival with Armand, her transition from the wild to the domestic, Wanda experiences a different kind of gift in the form of a living, rather than dead, fur-bearing animal. While in Armand's care, Wanda narrates a mode of gift exchange in which a dog is the object of trade.

DOG, the Dialectic of the Gift

Jeffrey Mehlman describes Walter Benjamin's view of the dog:

The dog, Benjamin goes on to say, is the only animal (with the possible exception of the horse) with whom humans have established bonds of intimacy. How so? "At the origin of it all lies the great victory, which man carried off, thousands of years ago, over dogs (in fact, over wolves and jackals). It was in becoming dependent on man and in allowing themselves to be tamed by him, that those wild animals became dogs." Dog, then, is another name for the master-slave relationship, an abbreviation, as such, for dialectic. . . . the wolf dormant within the dog would appear to afford a figure of the "unconscious." All that dialectic cannot encompass, all that might bring dialectic to a "standstill," stands poised for release in the very being of the dog.

For Mehlman, the psychoanalytical investment in the dog captures a further distinction "between (instinctual) aggressiveness and (sexual) sadism, which [Jean] Laplanche's reading of Freud, among others, has pinpointed as the very locus of the unconscious." Mehlman concludes that "ultimately, of course, in its median existence between lupine ferocity and human warmth, the dog straddles the line of demarcation between nature (or animality) and culture (humankind)."[42] In Wanda's narrative it is also the case that the dog straddles, to the point of breaking, forced lines of demarcation between the animate and inanimate properties attributed to female middle-class and male working-class existence. *The Confessions* provides material to explore further the undecidable "nature" framed by the various interpretations assigned to this culturally tame figure, the dog.

In the narrative segment dealing with Armand's gift of the dog, Wanda tells the story of a coachman who, having to wait long hours until he is called to Armand's service, spends his time joyfully playing with his little brown dog. When Wanda remarks to Armand on how attached the dog seemed to his master, "immediately he went and negotiated with the coachman to buy the dog for me" (117). For the price of two gold pieces, the coachman reluctantly relinquishes the dog, but the dog spends his time staring out the window at his master: "Days passed in the incessant fear that the dog would run away. He would accept from us neither food nor love. The little animal caused me much anxiety, and finally I decided to return him to his owner" (118). On the brink of this return, the little brown dog is anthropomorphized: "The dog, who until then lay quietly at my feet, had jumped up noiselessly onto the sofa and nestled up against me — but so gently, with such an evident intention not to disturb the music, that a *human being*, knowing that such an interruption might make a listener suffer, could not have shown more consideration. . . . After that moment the dog never left me" (118).

Contrary to the modern Cartesian anthropocentric tradition with its hierarchical differentiation between human souls and animal bodies, Wanda's religiophilosophical sensibility borders on a profane subversion of this mark of superiority when she concludes:

There is more in the souls of animals than we think. I have seen in the eyes of dying dogs the same tears that are shed by men, and the same terrible anguish that men have before death. Is this instinct? Instinct leads the child to love the mother; sexual desire leads the man to love the woman; why does the dog love the master who hits him and who kicks him away? Why is he ready to die defending him, in case of attack? The love of a dog! Why not, if it is worth *more than the love of a man*? (118)

To have a soul is to love while enduring the anguish of physical pain. The register of pain in the animal body metaphorically transports the martyrdom of Wanda's past suffering in her relationship with Leopold into a realm of concrete experience. The blows of physical violence become the scars of mental and emotional abuse. Analogously, the dog's abandonment of his master for the ties of love to Wanda consolidates the master-slave relationship in its gendered configuration between man and woman and also concretely expresses a transcendence of that hierarchical dynamic of power in the superiority Wanda accords in "love" as the female gender-preferred meaning of social relations between living beings. That sexual desire is absent from such "love," as it is between Armand and Wanda, receives its own profane expression through a description of the dog's physical expression of affection for her. I read the following passage, perversely, as a return of the absence of sexual relations in the form of a slavish gesture between Wanda and her pet: "Something moved at my feet; my dog stood up and looked at me. He gently pawed my hand as if to caress it, and tenderly put his head between my knees" (121).

Love becomes the gift between Wanda and her dog — a gift that was initially bought at the cost of humiliating the coachman into exchanging his beloved pet for material sustenance. Armand found his own poverty to be "a dog's life" (111), and his gift to Wanda of the coachman's dog marks the dialectic of the gift within a class society as the lie the wealthy give to their responsibility in causing the impoverishment of the laboring classes. The gift circulates only between Armand and Wanda, while the coachman receives the hard cold coins of abstract mediation. He is reminded through the exchange of gold pieces who can induce or alleviate, however momentarily, his own poverty and experience of love. In her reproduction of "love" bought at the cost of these slavish material relations of human exchange, Wanda also views her children through the filter of a dialectic of the gift in which the dog metaphorically rules supreme: "Timid and fearful, they clung to each other against some unknown peril, but did not dare to ask me direct questions, contenting themselves with ceaselessly following me with their eyes, like faithful dogs who fear to lose sight of their master" (108). Her eldest son is eventually "stolen" from her by Leopold. "How life is simplified, thus! I thought, in contrast to those of us who place so much value on the gift of ourselves, and who expect so many things from this, which it cannot give us!" (78).

Masoch's reinvention of the fur-clad feminine despot dramatizes the interrelatedness of fetishisms, sexualities, and European imperial practices. Wanda's refusal to play the role of the professional dominatrix opens the door onto another theater of cruelty crowded by props such as gifts, children, and dogs and motivated by a set of idealized values inverted from those created in Masoch's narrative of sexual liberation, namely, love and motherhood. The enemy here is domestic, not foreign. The social experience of a sentimentalized domestic sphere for a middle-class woman bears the marks of an internalized space of dominant/dominated relations. Animals, alive or dead, in disguise as fur-clad women or benevolent pets of undeserving masters, serve both as (inanimate) objects and (animate) subjects of displacement, depending on which side of the domestic/foreign configuration needs most immediately to be dominated, controlled, or contained.

The opening up of an ambiguously eroticized, hedonistic site of resistance to Christian repression constitutes the gift a text such as Masoch's *Venus in Furs* offers through its liberatory aesthetics of sexual excess, which must incorporate into its masochistic fantasy an exorbitant fear of the possibility of resistance to the European and patriarchal imperial project of mastery. What is particularly intriguing is that the political figure of totality and resistance in this narrative emerges in the shape of a fur-clad European woman. Wanda von Sacher-Masoch, however, refused to adorn herself with the falsity of fur's libidinal values in the name of a righteous and moral purity of domestic sanctity. The imaginary and real-life Wanda are both "feminist" and femininity incarnate, a figure of resistance to, as well as an embodiment of, a contradictory Euro-capitalist patriarchal fantasy of expansionist power.[43]

The fetishistic portrait of the fur-clad feminine despot is still with us today. She reemerged in the Lynx campaign in the poster captioned "Fur coat with matching accessories," a Lucretia Borgia of modern times. The conjunction of luxury goods, female sexuality, and despotic powers inscribed in *Venus in Furs* owes a visual debt to fine art paintings, especially those of Titian. While earlier texts such as Stubbes's *Anatomie of Abuses* and Evelyn's *Tyrannus* sought to regulate the visual field, to contain the circulation of signs and images as the principal site of social antagonism, all the while delegitimating their symbolic powers through their association with fashion, style, and femininity, Masoch's novel employs the aesthetic values of fine art to enhance such forms of symbolic power, only to emphasize symbolic power as the only "legitimate" — but of course despotic and therefore unacceptable — mode of political power open to women. The next chapter explores the use of aesthetic values in fashion history texts to relegitimate fashion as a meaningful site of scholarly analysis. In finding new ways to legitimate the social history of fashion through the aesthetic values attributed to fine art portraiture of the sixteenth and seventeenth centuries, these texts reveal the relationships among fashion, the political economies of global trade, and the domestic commodification of women's bodies through the mechanics of visual reproduction.

4

The Fecundity of Fur

The great painters, Raphael, Titian, Holbein, Georgione, Tintoretto,
Peter Porbus and Rembrandt, devoted themselves in a particular
manner to the art of reproducing with the brush the beautiful
varieties of furs included in the noble costume of the period.
Everybody remembers, who has once visited Rome, the wonderful
picture of the "Violinist," by Raphael, who is depicted as wearing
a fur tippet, so marvellously painted that one can examine it
with a magnifying glass. Equally well rendered is the tiger skin in
the grand portrait of his mistress, the Fornarina. All know how dear
to the artistic eye of Rembrandt was a handsome fur coat or cap, and
how tenderly he elaborated the shading of every undulation of the
surface of his sables. In France fur was always greatly esteemed,
and at a very early date the lower orders ornamented their gowns
with the skins of cats, lambs, squirrels and foxes, not forgetting, by
the way, the wolf, always a favourite skin on account of its beauty,
and in former times this ferocious animal was only too common in
every part of the country. As elsewhere, the nobility favoured those
costly furs, which have been noticed in the account of the English
costumes of the Tudor period.

Richard Davey, *Furs and Fur Garments* (1895)

In *Ways of Seeing*, John Berger discusses a painting by Rubens (1577–1640)
titled *Hélène Fourment in a Fur Coat* as an illustration of the representation
of women in modern Western art as objects of male sexual fantasy.[1] For
Berger, the Rubens painting holds a contradictory place in this long history
of the female nude, because while it is clearly constitutive of this larger
history of the fetishization of the female form, this image is dynamic and

animate in ways that run against the grain of the static portraiture of the female body as sexual fetish. In the previous chapter I found in Masoch's sexual fetishism of the female body a tension between the freezing and liquefying of the image of fur-clad woman, a tension that implicates fetishism in a larger discourse on female immobility and the threat of its undoing through the perceived power of feminine sexuality (149). Fur would seem to have a unique capacity for mobilizing the female nude from, in Berger's words, a "chilling" state of sexual inactivity and banality. Although Berger does not attribute the dynamic element of the Rubens painting to fur per se, it is the formal position the fur coat occupies in the painting which produces this visual effect:

> Her body confronts us, not as an immediate sight, but as experience —
> the painter's experience. Why? . . . the profound reason is a formal one.
> Her appearance has been literally re-cast by the painter's subjectivity.
> Beneath the fur that she holds across herself, the upper part of her body
> and her legs can never meet. There is a displacement sideways of about
> nine inches: her thighs, in order to join on to her hips, are at least nine
> inches too far to the left.
>
> Rubens probably did not plan this: the spectator may not consciously
> notice it. In itself it is unimportant. What matters is what it permits.
> It permits the body to become impossibly dynamic. Its coherence is
> no longer within itself but within the experience of the painter. More
> precisely, it permits the upper and lower halves of the body to rotate
> separately, and in opposite directions, round the sexual centre which is
> hidden: the torso turning to the right, the legs to the left. At the same
> time this hidden sexual centre is connected by means of the dark fur
> coat to all the surrounding darkness in the picture, so that she is turning
> both around and within the dark which has been made a metaphor for
> her sex.[2]

In Berger's interpretative frame the male gaze dominates as the visual structuring device with which to contain the female form. Berger's reference to the dark fur coat "which has been made a metaphor for her sex" conforms to a Freudian conception of fur's sexual fetishism. No doubt it would not come as a surprise to Berger that there are other ways of seeing how objects of material culture, notably clothing, shape the historical and cultural specificities of what constitutes the "natural" and the "real" in representations of the female form.

Anne Hollander, for example, argues for a shift in the object of the critical gaze from "the female nude" to the importance of clothing as a formal device for constructing our very ideas about what constitutes female nudity. In other words, nudity is complicit for its meanings with the oppositional values of adornment, artifice, covering, or clothing. "At any time, the un-adorned self has more kinship with its own usual *dressed* aspect than it has with any undressed human selves in other times and places, who have learned a different visual sense of the clothed body. It can be shown that the rendering of the nude in art usually derives from the current form in which the clothed figure is conceived. This correlation in turn dem-onstrates that both the perception and the self-perception of nudity are dependent on a sense of clothing — and of clothing understood through the medium of a visual convention."[3] In Berger's interpretation of *Hélène Fourment in a Fur Coat* it is the fur coat that divides the woman from her-self. A cyborg figure, she is half torso and half legs, turned in opposite di-rections, her "sex" supposedly the point of rotation, or the dividing line between the real and imaginary. The draped fur in the image sets up the incoherences of this formal design that "permits" Berger to read the "im-possibly dynamic" visual sensation of the image of the "nude female." In contrast to "Ruben's compulsive painting of the fat softness of Hélène Fourment's flesh" — flesh being the sign of nudity of which clothing is its opposition — the fur coat is painted in all its detailed complexity, the flow of the grain, color, and fine texture of fur.[4] The too frequent association of adornment with femininity or the assimilation of adornment to an essential aspect of female experience blinds Berger to the specificity of these differ-ent textures — flesh and fur, skins and hides — in constructing an ideology of what constitutes the "natural" in female sexual nudity.

Hollander, on the other hand, is very clear about the influence of the representation of clothing on our ways of seeing figurative art: "Looking at a range of works of art with figures in them, from painted vases and frescos to magazine illustrations and movie stills, one can see at once how the construction of clothing itself has changed over time and differed among people at one time." It is not the differences in clothing styles that are im-portant, however. Rather, it is the formal properties of the work of art which "offer different but even more important evidence about changing assumptions and habits of actual seeing, and so of visual self-awareness. Such formal elements demonstrate not how clothes were made but how they and the bodies in them were supposed and believed to look. Even actual garments themselves, old or new, offer only technical evidence and not perceptual knowledge."[5]

In the summer of 1994 the Victoria and Albert Museum in London dis-played an actual article of clothing, an embroidered bodice, beside a por-trait painting in which the bodice was depicted (see Figures 13 and 14).[6] The contrast between the actual bodice and the portrait is remarkable for a study in the transformation of the clothing-object into an object of paint-erly representation. Ironically, I can only represent the actual article of

FIGURE 13. Embroidered bodice (ca. 1620).
Reproduced by permission of the Board of Trustees of the Victoria & Albert
Museum (GE 4947). © The Board of Trustees of the Victoria & Albert Museum.

clothing in the museum with the aid of photographic realism. The structural limitations of the museum display in creating its own aura of realist
authenticity is another matter altogether. The actual clothing article, while
clearly a piece of extraordinary workmanship, is unable to convey any significance other than as the real that gives legitimacy to the re-presentation
in the painting. The image of the bodice in the painting focuses the eye on

FIGURE 14. *Portrait of Margaret Laton*, Marcus Gheeraerts (ca. 1620).
Reproduced by permission of the Board of Trustees of the Victoria & Albert
Museum (GE 4946). © The Board of Trustees of the Victoria & Albert Museum.

the detail, as if the detail of this aestheticism of rich texture could give meaning to the symbolic power of wealth of the woman wearing the article. The detail in various etchings and paintings of fur not only challenges the skill of the artist — etchers such as Wenceslaus Hollar and painters such as Rubens, Titian, and Holbein — but also, by attention to detail, works to inscribe that particularity and singularity onto the social power of the upper classes and aristocracy.

Such detail constitutes a form of *measurement*, a quantifiable code of complexity against which, beside which, the viewer measures her or his social position. "Only," Hollander comments, "when [the spectators] are safe inside that visual matrix do they then measure themselves against other persons inside the same frame and feel that they look different or similar, natural or strange."[7] If the point is to produce an effect of the "natural," what could be a more natural subject for inscribing the ideological containment of the natural or even "savage" nobility of the aristocracy than fur?

For Hollander, it is the correspondence between nude bodies and draped clothing, beginning with works of art from Greek antiquity, which has set the standard for what constitutes the "natural" in subsequent images of the "natural beauty of clothes." Rubens's image of Hélène Fourment draped in a fur coat mimics this classical Greek influence in Western art, replacing the natural folds of simple cloth with the natural fibers of fur. If simple cloth such as cotton or linen appear "natural" in part because of their correspondence with plant life, fur, like wool, achieves its authenticity through its association with animal life. All are heavily processed to bring them into "wearable" and aesthetic form. "The 'natural' beauty of cloth and the 'natural' beauty of bodies have been taught to the eye by art, and the same has been the case with the natural beauty of clothes," Hollander remarks.[8] So too, then, the reader of the cultural codes of adornment has been taught the "natural beauty" of fur through etchings and fine art in at least two ways. One way is through the iteration of images of women in fur, not simply by art or, since the late nineteenth century, by fashion magazines but also by the very fashion historians who produce books that rely on such images as evidence for what people actually wore. A store of images amassed and reproduced over time creates a visual vocabulary of fur fashion. The etchings of Wenceslaus Hollar, to which I turn shortly, are notable in this regard. Another way that fur has achieved its specifically aesthetic dimension is in its very representation in fine art, a mode of representation that has instilled what Pierre Bourdieu aptly calls an "aesthetic disposition." Deeply ingrained in our reception of fur is the idea that it is equivalent in aesthetic value to the very art in which it is depicted. This perception, in turn, reifies the commodity status of fur and contributes to justifying both its economic value and its symbolic status as a luxury item.

While Berger and Hollander draw attention to the way figurative images work — that is, how they work on the viewer and how they elaborate the very business of perception itself — it is still important to attend to the social forces that shape our reception of fashion images and their "readability." In *Distinction* Pierre Bourdieu demonstrates the hierarchical classification of aesthetic objects with their consumption across class differences: "The 'eye' is a product of history reproduced by education. This is true of the mode of artistic perfection now accepted as legitimate, that is, the aesthetic disposition, the capacity to consider in and for themselves, as form rather than function, not only the works designated for such apprehension, i.e., legitimate works of art, but everything in the world, including cultural objects which are not yet consecrated — such as, at one time, primitive arts, or, nowadays, popular photography or kitsch — and *natural objects*." Although Bourdieu's primary interest is in the classification of aesthetic objects and their reception, his notion of the aesthetic disposition also applies, as he notes, to many areas of material accumulation: "And nothing is more distinctive, more distinguished, than the capacity to confer aesthetic status on objects that are banal or even 'common' (because the 'common' people make them their own, especially for aesthetic purposes), or the ability to apply the principles of a 'pure' aesthetic to the most everyday choices of everyday life, e.g., in cooking, clothing or decoration, completely reversing the popular disposition which annexes aesthetics to ethics."[9] With fur fashions, however, there is a historical continuity between "art" and the everyday which complicates the symbolic transaction between these "aesthetic" and "nonaesthetic" objects. Furthermore, regimes of taste and their relationship to class differences obviously differ historically. With sumptuary legislation — the transformation of clothing laws into laws about sumptuousness — it is not so much that an aesthetic disposition is conferred on banal or "common" objects as that the exclusive privilege given to fur by the aristocracy confers on it an aesthetic disposition that presumably, the "common people" desire for themselves. The aesthetic and class values conferred on fur by the dominant narrative of clothing laws classified a regime of taste and social status which the middle and lower classes desired for themselves.

Mechanical Reproduction in the Art of Fashion

Anyone who has ever picked up a comprehensive history of clothing will immediately grasp the significance of "pictorial evidence" to this enterprise. Prehistoric and archaeological discoveries, woodcuts, engravings, etchings, lithographs, paintings, and photographs constitute the body of pictorial evidence on which costume history depends for documentation of the changing techniques, styles, textures, and materials of sartorial adornment. Actual articles of clothing are few and far between. Rarely do they date from before the early seventeenth century.[10] Museums devoted exclusively to the preservation, collection, study, and display of clothing have existed only since the mid-nineteenth century. The formal study of costume history in the West dates from Cesare Vecellio's (ca. 1530–1600) publication in Venice (1590) of "a book illustrated with figures representing peoples of different lands."[11] In British costume history the first major source, including text and images, is Joseph Strutt's *Complete View of the Dress and Habits of the People of England, from the establishment of the Saxons in Britain to the present time, illustrated by engravings taken from the most authentic remains of antiquity; to which is prefixed an Introduction containing a general description of the ancient habits in use among mankind from the earliest period of time to the conclusion of the seventeenth century.* As the title indicates the text contains Strutt's own engravings taken from "the most authentic remains of antiquity."

Clothing histories have always been illustrated, but the innovation of photography in the late nineteenth-century utterly transformed the kind of images. One could easily say that the mechanical reproduction of fine art paintings created a new genre of fashion history books. Walter Benjamin's essay "The Work of Art in the Age of Mechanical Reproduction" provides important insight into the photographic reproduction of fine art paintings.[12] I will be discussing aspects of Benjamin's essay throughout the remainder of the chapter, but first I want to consider an earlier form of image reproduction, etching and engraving. Benjamin draws attention to the iterability of photography, noting that the ability to reproduce an image diffuses the singularity and uniqueness generally attributed to the work of art. William Ivins refers to "repeatable pictorial statements" in order to capture the essential difference between the print (i.e., the etching or engraving) and the work of art.[13] The work of the seventeenth-century Bohemian-English artist Wenceslaus Hollar provides an interesting case study in an earlier form of documentary-style reproduction. Not only is Hollar's work representative of the repeatable pictorial statement in its time, interestingly, his etchings have also been used repeatedly in twentieth-century fashion histories to illustrate women's attire across different classes and in a variety of countries. His images of fur are especially notable.

Hollar's work was to have a tremendous influence during the seventeenth century on the aesthetic standards applied to etchings and engravings in England. Katherine S. Van Eerde writes that Hollar's engravings, in particular, "helped form the taste and educate the eye of the well-to-do and cultivated people who were to become his most consistent patrons." [14] His two major works on women's costumes, *Ornatus Muliebris Anglicanus; or, The Several Habits of English Women from the Nobility to the Countrywoman as They Are in These Times* (1640) and *Theatrum mulierum* (The theater of women, 1643), no doubt played a significant role in shaping fashion "tastes."

Originally from Bohemia, Hollar left Prague in 1627, during the first decade of the Thirty Years' War, at the age of twenty. The conventional explanation for Hollar's departure is political. "His family," says Van Eerde, "were Protestant and so incurred the danger of reprisals when Catholics gained the upper hand in Bohemia." In his adopted country, England, Hollar secured the patronage of the earl of Arundel in 1636. Hollar's reproductions of the Arundel collection are, in some instances, the only copies now extant. By the time of Arundel's departure at the outbreak of civil war in 1642, Hollar had established himself as an independent artist in London. "By now," Van Eerde remarks, "his private copies of the Arundel collection were extensive, and he began engraving and publishing these. Through the rest of his life, but especially in the difficult 1640s, Hollar was to use these copies as his reserve capital. With the breakup and sale of parts of the Arundel collection, the copies became an important record not only of the collection but of the works themselves. Their issuance at intervals kept Hollar's name and reputation in the public mind, in England as well as on the Continent." Between 1638 and 1640, Hollar produced most of the twenty-six plates of the *Ornatus Muliebris Anglicanus*. Van Eerde notes that these images portray "the familiar lady of the Caroline court. The appurtenances of wealth and elegance appear: elaborately coifed hair, jewelry, lace, cuffed gloves, magnificently embroidered low-cut gowns. . . . For the social historian, however, he showed also the mirror or scissors attached to the lady's waist; the high-heeled shoe; unusual millinery; and, finally, the countrywoman in pattens, with carrots visible in her basket, her skirts simple, and her hair blowzy." Van Eerde credits Hollar with an "aesthetic advantage" for his meticulous delineation "of a transparent veil or feather fan." She attributes Hollar's "intense interest in women's finery" to his wife: "His choice of selected luxury items for representation were guided by his wife. Her expertise in the luxurious and numerous articles of clothing and adornment (furs, muffs, laces, gloves, jewels) with which a highborn lady of great wealth surrounded herself in the court of Charles I can hardly have failed to influence her clever and industrious husband." In 1643 Hollar published his *Theatrum mulierum*. This collection included a wide variety of costumes from women across Europe, obtained during his exile from England to the Continent. A sequel to the *Theatrum* was published in

1644 as *Aula veneris; sive, varietas foeminini sexus*. The title page, Van Eerde says, "bears one of Hollar's most charming works — an agglomeration of feminine finery piled together, reminiscent of a 'sweet disorder in the dress'" (see Figure 15 and other images of muffs in Figures 16, 17, and 18). After the Restoration of Charles II, Hollar's fame was well established. He was widely known as "a recorder of geography, of monuments, of heraldry, and of various finely detailed artifacts." [15]

Hollar's attention to the detail of fur is significant. According to Jacqueline Burgers, "Hollar's specialty was depicting fur. He is said to have been the first artist to promote fur and lace as independent subjects." Burgers's commentary includes a reference to the etching *Winter* from the 1641 series *The Four Seasons* (see Figure 19): "The muff worn by the woman is one of the two muffs that Hollar owned. Time and again this muff of two different types of fur is seen: as an accessory, and as a kind of still life, such as the small one of a fur collar and mask on the windowsill." In the poem Hollar appends to the image, the reference to fighting the cold with fire and not sword transposes military aggression onto the less than sufficient artifice of dress. In another version of *Winter* from *The Four Seasons* of 1644 (see Figure 20), the caption makes use of a racial codification of the body, and in particular, the face, covered with a mask, is similarly marked and erased by the heat/cold opposition. Burgers reads this image and the previous one as "literally" as possible: "A young woman wearing a hood stands

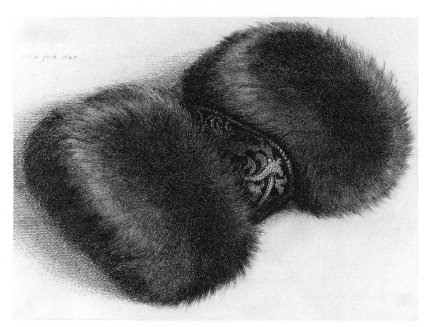

FIGURE 16. *Muffs*, Wenceslaus Hollar, etching (1647).
Reproduced by permission of the Trustees of the British Museum (P/P 1946).
© British Museum.

FIGURE 17. *Muffs*, Wenceslaus Hollar, etching (1645).
Reproduced by permission of the Trustees of the British Museum (P/P 19471).
© British Museum.

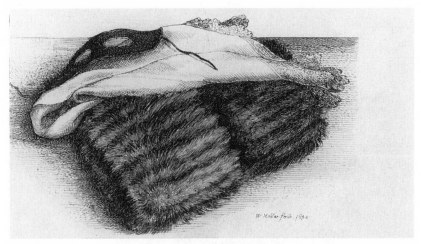

FIGURE 18. *Muffs*, Wenceslaus Hollar, etching (1642).
Reproduced by permission of the Trustees of the British Museum (P/P 1948).
© British Museum.

facing left. Her mask protects her face from the raw winter wind. Wearing such masks was originally a Florentine fashion that was introduced by Catherine de' Medici. Hollar still attracts many art lovers with this kind of print. His manner of reproducing fur and black velvet is inimitable."[16]

In his 1643–1644 version of *The Four Seasons*, done in full-length figures, Hollar produced a memorable *Winter* (with Cornhill in the background) (see Figure 21). As if the seductive pose of the woman, her masked face, and fur accessories were not enough to convey the figuration of woman as object of exchange in a seventeenth-century sexual economy, the inscription makes the point abundantly clear: "The cold, not cruelty makes her weare / In Winter, furrs and Wild Beastshaire / For a smother skinn at night / Embraceth her with more delight." In Hollar's text, fur appears to retain its utilitarian function; it is worn less for the sake of playing the cruel woman than from fear of catching cold. But the disavowal of an aesthetics of cruelty pointedly negates what the image actually depicts: the mythic figure of the fur-clad feminine despot. The poetic captions that underwrite all Hollar's allegorical figures of winter encode sexual fetishistic connotations, but neither Burgers nor Van Eerde comments on them. Their attention is focused on his work as pictorial evidence, and that exclusive focus repudiates the mythical trope of the fur-clad female white fetish altogether as it existed for Hollar in the seventeenth century. The attention to fashion details reduces Hollar's etchings to a functional demonstration of straightforward factual and formal components with no ideological import what-

HYEMS

Cum deformis Hyems gelidas constrinxerit undas
Pectore ne Sanguis torpeat hisce tegor
Pellibus Armenys, et relis, vincimus auras,
(non gladio) et claro MVLCIBER Igne tuo

WINTER.

Thus against winter wee our selues doe arm
and thinke you then the cold can doe us harm
but though it be to hard for this attire
yet wee'll orecome it not with sword but fire

FIGURE 19. *Winter*, Wenceslaus Hollar, etching (1641).
Reproduced by permission of the Trustees of the British Museum (P/P 613).
© British Museum.

WINTER

Cold as the Feete of Rocks so Winter stands,   Admit she coue'rd in warme habitt goe
With Masked face and Muff vpon her hands.   Though black without her skin is white as snow.

4.

FIGURE 20. *Winter*, Wenceslaus Hollar, etching (1644).
Reproduced by permission of the Trustees of the British Museum (P/P 617).
© British Museum.

The cold, not cruelty makes her weare *Winter* For a smoother skinn at night,
In Winter, furrs and Wild beasts haire   Embraceth her with more delight.

FIGURE 21. *Winter* (with Cornhill in the background), Wenceslaus Hollar, etching (1643–1644). Reproduced by permission of the Trustees of the British Museum (P/P 609). © British Museum.

soever. Burgers also reproduces an etching from 1644 which is not part of any series (see Figure 22), commenting, "While this print is not part of a series of seasons or costumes, all the accessories that Hollar used repeatedly in images of winter are here: the muff, feather fan, mask, cape, and stole. Hollar did a series of seasons with women shown full-length ... for which this may be a preliminary exercise. It is interesting to see how efficiently Hollar worked with the few 'props' he owned."[17] Hollar's work is praised for its "efficiency," for his expertise in rendering difficult objects realistically and truthfully.

I want to pause for a moment to consider the reception of Hollar's work by the discipline of fine arts in relation to Benjamin's critique of art history. One area in which film and photography were to have an enormous impact, according to Benjamin, was on the constitution of a public realm, in particular, the meaning of art in relation to the working-class or middle-class spectator. The history of art traditionally rests on certain concepts: uniqueness, authenticity, originality. To write a history of a work of art is to acknowledge its "unique existence" in a certain time and space.[18] Physical changes in its condition and changes in ownership are essential aspects of the historical narrative. The invention of a tradition for the work of art depends on a kind of patrilinearity, like a series of familial relations constituting a line of descent from an original birth, a first father, a primal scene, and a filial exchange. Without the proper sense of originality, the painting is a bastard child, a forgery, a copy, a replication. The work of art is a somewhat private affair, enjoyed by few in the privacy of an exclusive domain, the court or the drawing room of a wealthy man. Mechanical reproduction, however, makes art available to the public domain and alters access to private pleasures for working-class and middle-class consumers. Benjamin summarizes the dialectic: "That which withers in the age of mechanical reproduction is the aura of the work of art. This is a symptomatic process whose significance points beyond the realm of art. One might generalize by saying: the technique of reproduction detaches the reproduced object from the domain of tradition. By making many reproductions it substitutes a plurality of copies for a unique existence. And in permitting the reproduction to meet the beholder or listener in [her] own particular situation [i.e., 'The cathedral leaves its locale to be received in the studio of a lover of art; the choral production, performed in an auditorium or in the open air, resounds in the drawing room.'], it reactivates the object reproduced. These two processes lead to a tremendous shattering of tradition which is the obverse of the contemporary crisis and renewal of mankind."[19] Although mechanical reproduction liquidates "tradition," a tradition essential to establish the historical testimony that rests on concepts of originality, authenticity and a unique existence, it also creates new contexts for the

FIGURE 22. *English Lady in Winter Costume*, Wenceslaus Hollar, etching (1644).
Reproduced by permission of the Trustees of the British Museum (P/P 1999).
© British Museum.

reception and pleasure of art. The key word in Benjamin's discussion of the ideology that informs the history of art is "aura," which he defines negatively as that which goes missing when the mechanical reproduction of art comes into play. It is the mark of an absence that throws the positive aesthetics of art into crisis; it also opens up emancipatory possibilities by virtue of its disappearance.

The "decay of the aura" radically transforms human sense perception, our intellectual grasp of what constitutes reality. Benjamin registers one of the areas of this transformation in the spatial dimensions of distance and closeness. The "aura" generally contributes to distance, both socially through its inaccessibility and also through the activity of contemplation that the work of art supposedly demands for its reception. Reproduction, on the other hand, brings the object closer "by way of its likeness." "To pry an object from its shell, to destroy its aura, is the mark of a perception whose 'sense of the universal equality of things' has increased to such a degree that it extracts it even from a unique object by means of reproduction. . . . The adjustment of reality to the masses and of the masses to reality is a process of unlimited scope, as much for thinking as for perception."[20]

Burgers's and Van Eerde's assessments of the functional value of Hollar's work produces a certain distance between the image and its significance for social history. It is as if the contemplative detachment of the bourgeois consumer of art has been appropriated as a methodological approach by the art historian. The politicization of aesthetic values involves a relation of proximity which would destroy not only the "aura" of the work of art but the production and reproduction of that "aura" within the modes of perception or writing valued by the discipline of art history. Proximity to rather than detachment from Hollar's images involves not simply a physical closeness to the object but a way of approaching it which activates the relations of social difference in the reception of his work as much in its own time as in the present. My own reading of Hollar's images of winter as anticipatory codes of sexual fetishism dispenses with the containment of these images by their evidentiary claims on truth as well as their oppositional framing within art history as non–works of art. Non–works of art are as important to the history of fine art as their legitimate counterparts: works of art, the latter defined in relation to the former.

The mechanical reproduction of (non)works of art produces conditions of disinheritance, a rupture with the patrilineal descent of artistic influence. This break from tradition is potentially liberatory. Consider, for example, the use of Hollar's work in fashion history texts. Hollar is not always acknowledged in contemporary fashion sources as the artist who drew the store of images so important as historical evidence of women's costume —

unlike the portrait painters of the Renaissance such as Titian and Holbein. Nevertheless, the reproductive quality of his work has secured the image if not the signature. R. Turner Wilcox's *Mode in Furs* contains drawings done by the author, taken from various fine art and print sources. Several of Hollar's images, notably the full-length female figure in *Winter* from *The Four Seasons* (1643) appear in a rough copy of the original.[21]

In Black and Garland's *History of Fashion* the chapter on seventeenth-century fashions includes two images, however unacknowledged, from Hollar. The caption reads: "These two overgarments, using fur in a fashionable way, are long and voluminous. Such a size was necessary in order to cover the whole of the dress beneath, which was at this time becoming quite full despite the close tailoring over the shoulders." One of the images is from the *Theatrum mulierum* collection, "An Irish Woman (Mulier Hibernica)." The other is "The Winter habit of ane English Gentlewoman" (see Figure 22), also mentioned by Burgers. Two images from Hollar's *Theatrum mulierum*, "English Gentle Woman (Mulier Generosa Anglica)" and "Merchant's Daughter (Mercatoris Londinensis Filia)" also appear, again without acknowledgement to Hollar. The caption reads: "These mid-seventeenth century women show the new looseness of the female dress. An entirely new feature of fashion was the apron. Also typical was the carrying of either single articles such as a purse or fan, or the lifting of the skirt."[22]

Millia Davenport's *Book of Costume* does the reproduction of Hollar's work in fashion pictohistoriography the greatest justice. She devotes two full pages to Hollar's etchings, and gives a brief biography. She describes Hollar as one of "the world's great fashion artists." Whereas Van Eerde locates the women in *Ornatus Muliebris Anglicanus* with "the familiar lady of the Caroline court," Davenport states that these "are not great ladies in grand clothes, but the daily wear of the middle classes." She reproduces six etchings from the *Ornatus Muliebrus Anglicanus* and describes the clothing of each in detail, noting with reference to one that "muffs occur in late inventories of Elizabeth's wardrobe and rapidly increase in use, being carried by men as well as women, even by army and naval officers during latter half XVII-e.XVIIIc." On the following page Davenport reproduces the full-length female figures *Winter* (see Figure 21) and *Autumn* from *The Four Seasons* (1643) and the famous etching of the muffs (see Figure 15). She comments: "Scarcely a trace remains of the old rigidity of costume. There are black hoods and masks over loose curls; fichu-like collars; fur pieces and muffs; full, fashionable aprons; objects like fans, watches, mirrors or *nécessaires* of sewing or toilet articles hang from the waist; gloves lengthen as sleeves become short and wide. Background of the city views at which Hollar excelled." The fetishistic objects in the etching of the muffs produce commentary in which Davenport links these objects to questions of desire and sexuality: "Masks are fast coming into fashion all over Europe. Pepys mentions them first, June 13, 1663, when he sees Cromwell's daughter, the Countess of Falconberg, 'when the house began to fill . . . put on her vizard, and so kept it on all the play: which of late is become a great fashion among ladies, which hides their whole faces.' He stops to get his own wife a mask, at a milliner's (Jan. 27, 1663–4). . . . By 1712, masks have become the mark of prostitutes, and are worn by respectable women only at the first night of a play. . . . Muffs are coming into male use, also. On Nov. 30, 1662 Pepys 'first did weare a muffe, being my wife's last year's muffe; and now that I have bought her a new one, this serves me very well . . . in this month . . . of great frost.'"[23]

Davenport "reads" Hollar's images in the context of textual sources from the same period. Pepys's diary, for example, is a well-known source for the social practice of fashion, for observations of social decorum and the codes of sartorial conduct. Newspapers such as the *Tatler* and the *Spectator* are also important sources for Davenport. Reproducing sections from Hollar's *Coronation Procession of Charles II*, she notes the style of beaver hats: "The high-crowned hats, which we are inclined to think of as Puritan because they were the hats worn to America by our ancestors, were worn by both factions alike, as these Royalist illustrations show; Puritans differed only in an avoidance of extravagances. This hat, now ringed with feathers [for the Royalists or Cavaliers], will become low-crowned in a decade." In a discussion of women's hats, Davenport reproduces several etchings from *Aula Veneris* and from another collection *Runde Frauentracht*, which contains encircled portraits of female figures from the shoulders up. Davenport observes that "little hair shows below the fur hats of Swabian, Bavarian and Bohemian regional costume, since these hats, in a sense, replace hair." Davenport also notes that marital status was signified by hat wear: "The traditionally uncovered head of an unmarried woman has a little pill-box cap over the bun, while a married woman wears the characteristically conical fur hat of Prague."[24] Davenport not only documents fashion articles of the time but also attends to the sexual, gender, political, and social significance of fashion's ideological codification.

Pictorial Informatics

As etching and not "fine art," Hollar's work is aesthetically framed for its documentary and evidential value. He is a recorder, an important one mind you, but a "recorder" nevertheless. For Van Eerde, the value of his work lies in its contribution to print culture and its depiction of the costumes of women other than those belonging to the wealthy and landowning classes. Hollar is a "delineator of his times," in her view, and his etchings of women's dress served purposes of documentation similar to those of the photographic image now. Benjamin knows, however, that the "mechanical reproduction of a work of art . . . represents something new." The use of fine art portraits and paintings as documentary evidence is an entirely different matter. Such images are generally understood in terms of aesthetic criteria that, as Benjamin notes, are all but liquidated in photographic reproduction, where the "work of art" is made to serve other "functions," such as those of documentation or historical evidence.[25]

With mechanical reproduction the image-text relationship in fashion history books was dramatically altered. Although photographic reproduction was available to print culture in the early twentieth century, Dion Clayton Calthrop's four-volume study *English Costume* contains only drawings based on image-documents. At the conclusion to the third volume he reproduces a selection of thirty-six etchings from Hollar's two important collections, introducing this addendum with the following words: "These excellent drawings by Hollar need no explanation. They are included in this book because of their great value as accurate contemporary drawings of costume."[26] Whereas Calthrop clearly saw value in reproducing Hollar's work in the early twentieth century, by the later twentieth century, fashion texts include his work only marginally and in some cases, as I have noted, without any reference to Hollar himself. The value of the mechanical reproduction of the work of art as pictorial evidence in fashion historiography increases exponentially in relation to this earlier form of pictorial print culture.

Calthrop's belief that Hollar's etchings need no explanation stands in stark contrast to more recent fashion publications, where captions are obligatory. Roland Barthes observes a historical shift in the image-text relationship during the twentieth century: "This is an important historical reversal, the image no longer *illustrates* the words; it is now the words which, structurally, are parasitic on the image. The reversal is at a cost: in the traditional modes of illustration the image functioned as an episodic return to denotation from a principal message (the text) which was experienced as connoted since, precisely, it needed an illustration; in the relationship that now holds, it is not the image which comes to elucidate or 'realize' the text, but the latter which comes to sublimate, patheticize or rationalize the image. . . . Formerly, the image illustrated the text (made it clearer); today, the text loads the image, burdening it with a culture, a moral, an imagination. Formerly, there was reduction from text to image; today, there is amplification from the one to the other."[27]

The need for captions may also be the result of the kind of images that are subject to reproduction. Under the patronage of the earl of Arundel,

Hollar produced replicas of master works (by Leonardo da Vinci, for example). It was Hollar's job to produce copies for the purposes of documentation. But to the contemporary fashion historian with the ability to make full-page color reproductions of fine art paintings, Hollar's work appears mundane by comparison. In part, the mechanically reproduced work of art gains value through the use of color. The technological value of color reproduction can exploit the work of art in new ways, producing different conceptions of the real and correlative reality effects that overshadow the labor value contained by an earlier mode of reproduction, the black-and-white print.[28] Van Eerde describes Hollar as an "industrious worker," his images highly exploitable and appropriable against the work of art whose signature and copyright is always acknowledged.

François Boucher's expanded edition of *20,000 Years of Fashion* contains, according to the dust cover, "1,118 illustrations, including 356 plates in full colour." The book is without question beautifully illustrated with photographic reproductions of, among other things, canonical works of art, supplemented by a narrative construction of the text of fashion history. In Boucher's words, "All the reproductions collected here, representing a considerable and extremely varied body of documentation, have been chosen to form an integrated extension of the text." Boucher instructs the reader: "Beside the individual picture captions, the reader will find fuller general notes on groups of pictures, indicated by ruled lines above and below."[29] The photograph of the "work of art" supplements the printed text, provides evidence for historical changes in clothing styles, costume, fashion. Which metaphor is appropriate to this aestheticization of something so familiar or habitual as wearing clothes and adorning the body? As if such habits were merely a distraction of everyday life, so insignificant that only an aesthetic ordering over a long duration could convince us of its value for academic scholarship. But the aesthetic value of canonical works of art is not the primary "function" of their inclusion in fashion history books. It is as *evidence* of clothing styles, as conveyors of information, that they are used.[30] Hence, there is a need to supplement the image with further textual elaboration on the clothing depicted, with "general notes . . . indicated by ruled lines above and below." The obligatory captions are what Walter Benjamin calls signposts.[31] They are framed, and they point the way to concrete information. The ruled lines regulate our perception toward an understanding of these captions as discrete entities that can be accumulated like the very objects of material culture the words between lines seek to contain. Take the example of the full-page color reproduction of Jan van Eyck's *Jan Arnolfini and His Wife* (1434), which forms the frontpiece to chapter 7, "Costume in Europe from the Fourteenth to the Early Sixteenth Century (see Figure 23)." The caption reads:

FIGURE 23. *Jan Arnolfini and His Wife*, Jan van Eyck (1434).
Reproduced by permission of the National Gallery, London (NG 186).

BURGHER'S COSTUME

344 The man wears a *huque* in velvet lined with fur, over a black pourpoint with the cuffs embroidered in gold, and a hat of shaved felt, in the shape of an inverted truncated cone. Beside him are his wooden pattens [shoes] with wide straps and two heels. His wife wears a cloth gown

trimmed with fur; her wide, open sleeves are decorated with shell-shaped cut work. The fine linen *huve* rests on two *truffeaux* held inside a gilded hairnet. The high belt accentuates the prominent abdomen, which it was then fashionable to stress.

The credits for the image read: "344 Jan van Eyck: *Jan Arnolfini and his Wife*, 1435 [*sic*]. London, National Gallery (Photo Thames and Hudson Archives)."[32]

Compare Boucher's information-laden caption with H. W. Janson and Dora Jane Janson's analysis of the significance of this painting for the Italian Renaissance:

> The Flemish cities where the new style of painting flourished — Tournai, Ghent, Bruges — rivaled those of Italy as centers of international banking and trade. Their foreign residents included many Italian businessmen. For one of these Jan van Eyck produced what is not only his most remarkable portrait but a major masterpiece of the period, *Giovanni Arnolfini and His Bride*. The young couple is solemnly exchanging marriage vows in the privacy of the bridal chamber. They seem to be quite alone, but as we scrutinize the mirror, conspicuously placed behind them, we discover in the reflection that two other persons have entered the room. One of them must be the artist, since the words above the mirror, in florid legal lettering, tell us that "Johannes de eyck fuit hic" (Jan van Eyck was here) and the date, 1434. Jan's role, then, is that of a witness; the picture purports to show exactly what he saw and has the function of a pictorial marriage certificate. Yet the domestic setting, however persuasively realistic, is replete with disguised symbolism of the most subtle kind, conveying the sacramental nature of marriage. The single candle in the chandelier, burning in broad daylight, stands for the all-seeing Christ (note the Passion scenes of the mirror frame); the shoes which the couple has taken off remind us that they are standing on "holy ground" . . . ; even the little dog is an emblem of marital faith, and the furnishings of the room invite similar interpretation. The natural world, as in the *Merode Altarpiece*, is made to contain the world of the spirit in such a way that the two actually become one.[33]

The symbolic analysis of the shoes, "taken off [to] remind us that they are standing on 'holy ground'" appears as intrusive a remark as Boucher's description of the "wooden pattens with wide straps and two heels." Both the aesthetic and functional discourses are imposed by the regulatory demands of fine art and fashion historiography. And yet, the irony of this particular painting is that it too "functions" within the discourse of aesthetics as pictorial evidence, a "pictorial marriage certificate," where the artist is rendered as a surreptitious "witness" to the event, or perhaps the crime. But what crime? Something else that strikes me as odd in the aesthetic discourse is the lack of commentary on the "prominent abdomen" of the bride. Arnolfini's bride's protruding stomach may be such an obvious reference to marriage and human reproduction as to need no symbolic commentary whatsoever, although it is tempting to say something else about the pregnant symbolism of the birth of humanism or, more specifically, the birth of "man." Boucher, the fashion historian, writes of the stylistic innovation of the "prominent abdomen" that the "fashion for protuberant stomachs, which were achieved with small bags of padding under the costume, affected all aspects of the plastic arts in the fifteenth century." [34] The textual constructions of this image by the art historian or the fashion historian tell me little about what is the most remarkable, or outstanding, feature of this painting: the simulation of a pregnant woman. James Laver in his *Costume and Fashion: A Concise History* also includes van Eyck's painting, under yet another title, *The Marriage of Giovanni (?) Arnolfini and Giovanna Cenami (?)*. He notes that the "front formed a kind of stiffened stomacher known as a 'plackard.'" [35] Is this merely a fashion innovation? Or a symbol of patrilineal control and regulation? Or, as I think, does it tell us something else about the regulation of women's bodies, to adornment, and their sexuality? "Fashion," it is worth noting begins with humanism. Boucher traces the origins of "fashion" to a stylistic change in clothing between the sexes: "The great innovation in the development of costume in Europe after the mid-fourteenth century is the abandonment of the long flowing costume common to both sexes; costume then became short for men and long for women." [36] Sexual differentiation constitutes the origin of fashion during a time when, as Boucher writes, "the first symptoms of Humanism" (and I might add capitalism) were in evidence. Do we still doubt a complicity among the ideology of modernity, humanism, and the genealogical enforcement of patrilineal descent through the regulation of women's bodies, as if those bodies, too, could also be possessed like land? If women's bodies are not objects of artifice like other examples of material culture, then they are nature. In either case, they are mute, voiceless, possessable, and exploitable.

Let us look more closely at the kind of pictorial evidence used in the history of European fur fashions, especially for the sixteenth and seventeenth centuries. The works of famous sixteenth-century portrait painters such as Holbein and Titian regularly appear in fashion histories as examples of "very grand people in their very grandest clothes," to use the words of James Laver, who includes in his history Holbein's *Ambassadors* (1533) (see Figure 24) and Titian's *Emperor Charles V with His Dog* (1532). Laver's cap-

FIGURE 24. *The Ambassadors*, Hans Holbein (1533).
Reproduced by permission of the National Gallery, London (NG 1314).

tions, when they exist, are brief and deliver information less mechanically than Boucher's. The dialogue between image and text is also more integrated than Boucher's. *The Ambassadors* provides an example of men's clothing, specifically what the German's called a *Schaube*, which Laver describes as "an overcoat shaped like a cassock but generally without sleeves. If it had sleeves, they hung empty behind the visible sleeves of the garment worn underneath. The *Schaube*, often lined with fur, became the typical garment of the scholar. Luther wore one and thereby dictated the costume of the Lutheran clergy to the present day. In England Thomas Cranmer wore a similar garment, and this, with the chain round the neck, became the ancestor of the accepted costume of mayors. The vestigial sleeves of the sleeved variety can still be seen in academic dress."[37] In the discourse of the fine arts, Helen Langdon explicates another meaning:

> A very different work from this period, *The Ambassadors* of 1533, also showed foreigners in England. This ambitious painting is a life-size double portrait of Jean de Dinteville, French Ambassador to London, and Georges de Selve, the Bishop of Lavaur. Between them are two shelves covered with an array of objects, which indicate their knowledge of sciences, religion and the arts. At first sight the grand scale and superb realism of the painting make it appear an overwhelming statement about Man's potential and attainment; yet the heraldic symmetry of the composition is roughly broken into by the blurred shape that obscures part of the mosaic floor. This is a human skull, painted in a distorted perspective, which assumes its true shape when seen from the bottom right corner. This reminder of death is taken up in other details of the painting. There is a crucifix in the top left corner; the badge on de Dinteville's hat shows a human skull; and the string on the lute is broken. The painting thus celebrates Man's power whilst at the same time reminding us of the ultimate futility of human endeavour.[38]

The clothing depicted in *The Ambassadors* represents fine examples of men's attire. What I find interesting about the image is the display of objects on the two shelves. The upper shelf, on which these great men rest their arms, is filled with objects of scientific significance, especially instruments of measurement related to navigation, including a sturdy globe with navigational lines wrapped around it. These instruments of scientific discovery and navigational importance rest upon an oriental rug. On the lower shelf, sitting on plain, unadorned wood, are objects of cultural significance, a broken-stringed lute, Luther's translation of *Veni Creator Spritus*, bamboo scrolls and another globe, this one with a wooden handle attached to its bottom, presumably so it could be spun in the hand. On the floor is the surreal image of the skull, positioned rather oddly, for it appears to be floating in the bottom foreground, attached to nothing. The plethora of scientific instruments sit like special ornaments on the upper tier and are matched in their ornamental value only by the extraordinary rendering of clothing textures. The rich texture of clothing would appear equivalent in symbolic value to the hierarchically placed objects of science over religion and the arts. While we might assume that fashion belongs to the lowly arts, in *The Ambassadors* it is clearly a symbolic force in sixteenth-century portrait painting, requiring as much precision and skill as the scientific instruments were designed to measure. Of *The Ambassadors*, James Malpas notes, "Like Titian, Holbein was an assured painter of fur (a crucial ability for a court painter) and the contrast between the soft ermine and the glistening metal chain serves as a rich textual counterbalance. The intense realism Holbein achieved here was due to his prodigious visual memory and refusal to let either draughtsmanship or the application of paint alone dominate the execution." On Holbein's *Sir Thomas More* (1527) he also remarks, "The fine drawings made prior to the painting show a new delicacy of touch prevalent in the artist's manner after his visit to France; greater attention to the texture of material, fur and velvet was the painterly consequence."[39] The scientific instruments of navigation depicted in *The Ambassadors* made possible trade, such as the fur trade with North America, and the very accumulation of the objects that rest underneath the instruments of scientific discovery. This re-presentation of the methods of material accumulation, aided, of course, by mercantile capitalism or economic imperialism, in conjunction with the painterly "realism" of Holbein's work help to explain why this painting lends itself to "documentation" in fashion historiography. The painting documents not only the material objects of what constitutes masculine fashion but also the epistemological methods behind material accumulation.

In the case of Laver's reproduction of *The Ambassadors*, the photographic reproduction of this portrait painting does indeed, as Benjamin anticipates, shatter the history of its exclusive historical testimony as fine art and release its evidential potential, so that while we can learn from the art historian about the skill of Holbein's craft in reproducing the material effects of fur's luxuriousness, the shattering of that tradition in the context of fashion history, releases the objects of material culture that invade the painting so that they too come forward for analysis. It is as if the flattening-out effect of mechanical reproduction deprivileges the textual intentions of the artist to create an aura of symbolic power through costume, and allows for a homogeneity in the field of vision where multiple objects are reactivated, in this case, as instruments of fur and textile trade and mercantile expansion.

Identifying an earlier transition from the religious containment of the work of art as "magic" to its increasing exhibition value since the Renaissance (a value that gave art its decidedly "artistic function"), Benjamin argues that photography and film "are the most serviceable exemplifications of this new function."[40] But cult value does not give way without resistance. It reappears, according to Benjamin, in the "human countenance." Portrait painting, so important to the fashion history of fur, gives way to the photographic portrait. The disembodied image of the loved one or family member is suffused with the "aura" of the human countenance glorified in Renaissance portraits of wealthy merchants and nobles. One attempt to eliminate this persistent trace of authenticity was to produce photographs devoid of any human element. Benjamin's example is Eugene Atget, who photographed the empty street as if it were the scene of a crime and contained evidence. The evidentiary aspect of the photograph constitutes for Benjamin the most important sea change in the function of art brought about by the photograph. As demonstrated with the examples of Jan van Eyck's *Marriage of Giovanni (?) Arnolfini and Giovanna Cenami (?)* and Holbein's *Ambassadors*, the mechanical reproduction of Renaissance portrait painting for the pictorial documentation of fashion holds the residual aspects of the "aura" of the human countenance in combination with the evidentiary claims of mechanical reproduction. The obligatory captions in fashion texts often attempt to empty the image of its "aura" and reduce it to its minimal function as a strictly pictorial statement. This attempt is so mechanical as to place the exhibition value of the photographically reproduced work of art under discursive constraints and subjugate the image to the tyranny of empirical evidence.

"Exhibition value" nevertheless supersedes the "cult value" of traditional aesthetics, thereby reducing the "aura" in the photographic portrait to the status of an incident, which survives, if at all, as a trace of an earlier aesthetic dimension of art. The photographic image of the empty street that Benjamin likens to a crime scene, clarifies for him the evidentiary potential in any photographic image. The ideology of evidence that emerged with the photograph, combined with the supersession of exhibition value, suggests not only that a crime scene is represented but that crime constitutes a new context in which to receive the mechanically reproduced work of art. Is the mechanically reproduced work of art on trial, then? Is Benjamin implying that the photograph introduces a new ethical point of view? In the case of the fashion statements taken from Jan van Eyck's and Holbein's work, only the wealthy landowners, political figures, and merchants are represented. Symbolic power accrues through the collective containment of traditional aesthetics as much as through representation of the codes of wealth and power in clothes. The symbolic power of art is placed on trial by the agents of mechanical reproduction. The emancipatory narrative that emerges to contest the past injustice of traditional aesthetics is to be found in "modern man's legitimate claim to being reproduced," which, as Benjamin writes, is denied by the capitalist exploitation of film.[41] If I substitute woman for man in Benjamin's critical statement, the alteration is significant enough to warrant further comment. During the twentieth century, it is difficult not to notice that in fashion magazines, for example, white women could hardly be said to have been denied access to reproduction. But the reproduction of white women in various media in the twentieth century is such that the very concept of "woman" has come under scrutiny. What image of "woman" is being reproduced? "Woman" would appear to be an operative site of reproduction; the very definition of the image depends on construction of this figure as irrevocably linked to reproducibility. I will return to the question later on but note it here in order to underline an important point, which is that the legitimate claim to being reproduced is not a naive affair. Any form of reproduction raises questions of gender, race, and sexuality, as well as class, that must be attended to. For whereas the 1990s phenomena of talk shows such as *Oprah Winfrey* proclaim themselves an avenue to legitimate the reproduction of modern "man" and "woman," they not only contribute to the cult of the personality, as Benjamin would say, but, more specifically, mobilize assumptions about gender, sexuality, race, and class identities.

Feminist cultural critique has enabled, since Benjamin's writings, a critical process that attends to "woman" as an image constructed through these social relations. It has also demonstrated that the reception of film images of women by women varies considerably depending on the social knowledge and experience of the viewer. The marketplace of spectator-consumers is a contradictory field of reception. It is so, says Benjamin, because film, unlike paintings, provides a site where the "critical and the receptive attitudes of the public coincide." In other words, film and fashion constitute a marketplace, where consumers can exercise a mode of critical agency not possible with traditional aesthetic forms. It is the attention to detail and everyday which that nurtures this critical agency, what Benjamin calls a "deepening of apperception." The psychoanalytical focus of much feminist theorizing on the role of the spectator is also supported by Benjamin's borrowing from Freud's work on the everyday world of language games, where unconscious slips of the tongue reveal the contradictions of social, historical, and material forces. Benjamin writes: "The camera introduces us to *unconscious optics* as does psychoanalysis to unconscious impulses." Under the capitalist exploitation of film, the critical agency that emerges from the degree of control the consumer-spectator can exercise over film and the *unconscious optics* that underlies the contradictions and multiple points of view in the life of everyday practices, opens up an emancipatory potential to counteract the film industry's attempts to "spur the interest of the masses through illusion-promoting spectacles and dubious speculations." The quantitative change in the influx of image reception to the "masses" in the twentieth century brings about, for Benjamin, a qualitative difference in our mode of participation. Benjamin takes issue with the idea that the "spectacle . . . requires no concentration and presupposes no intelligence." Clearly, he counters, "this is at bottom the same ancient lament that the masses seek distraction whereas art demands concentration from the spectator." Benjamin interprets distraction not as something less than concentration but as a sign of habituation to the environment. In Benjamin's words, "The public is an examiner, but an absent-minded one."[42] As public examiners the collectivity of consumer-spectators habitually engages with an examination of society, such as the crimes of material wealth and decadence which pervade the images of fur fashion historiography. Such critical skills constitute for Benjamin the foundations of a politicization of aesthetics, which is itself open to the masses. Nowhere, I think, has this been better demonstrated than in feminist cultural critique, especially with regard to the question of pleasure in spectatorship.

Suzanna Danuta Walters maintains that "'pleasure' has become the new catchword of feminist cultural theory in an attempt to displace the emphasis on negative and oppressive images and construct instead a discourse that centers on the liberatory possibilities of female viewing practices and pleasures."[43] Valerie Steele's study of fashion, fetishism, and power acknowledges the shift in the reception of fashion fetish photography: "Fashion, especially fashion photography, has played an important part in the so-called sex wars or the sex/porn debates, which began in the 1970s and continue to rage today. The orthodox feminist view emphasized the aggressive aspects of the 'male gaze' and the way fashion objectified women. The most overtly erotic fashions and fashion photographs came in for the most criticism. But by the 1980s, some feminist scholars questioned whether fashion imagery could be decoded so simply. Do women necessarily respond to fashion images with a passive narcissism? Might not some viewers (such as lesbians) consume fashion images in a defiant or subversive way?"[44] The shift from the male gaze to female spectatorship is empowering not only because "defiant or subversive" readings become possible but because women do indeed read the world in multiple ways, depending on social and cultural contexts, experience, and political consciousness. In turn, feminist visual artists recreate images of women which highlight the playfulness of their own ways of reading and seeing the world, and subvert dominant and mainstream representations of women. The images of fur and especially fur-clad women in fine art and fashion historiography rarely move away from the equation of fur with decadence. Interestingly, this convergence of fur with decadence works to subsume the pleasure of the female spectator. Particular technologies of representation can function to regulate the reception of fur for middle-class women either by subsuming their experience of pleasure or by distancing them from it through the ideological representation of fur as decadent, an object of material excess and an elite commodity, especially in fine art images. The effect of distancing the female spectator from her experience of pleasure and pain is clearly overturned in Judy Olausen's parodic images of a 1950s-style representation of women in fur: *Mommy Deer* and *Mother in Camouflage* (see Figures 25 and 26).[45] These images bring us closer to the dialectics of pleasure in their re-presentation of the painful sterility of mass media images of white middle-class women depicted as agents of consumerism during the post-war period.

FIGURE 25. *Mommy Deer*, Judy Olausen (1996).
From *Mother* by Judy Olausen. © 1996 by Judy Olausen. Reproduced by
permission of Viking Penguin, a division of Penguin Books USA Inc.

In the next chapter I turn in another direction to glance at fur's relationship to modes of symbolic violence — economic, social, ideological, and
political. Twentieth-century wars and the "style wars" of late capitalist
postmodern parodies bring the realities and ironies of an irreducible prob-
lematic of political and symbolic violence into view. For what purposes is
the wealth of a nation to be used: to indulge bourgeois habits of conspicu-

FIGURE 26. *Mother in Camouflage*, Judy Olausen (1996).
From *Mother* by Judy Olausen. © 1996 by Judy Olausen. Reproduced by
permission of Viking Penguin, a division of Penguin Books USA Inc.

ous consumption with fluff, finery, and fashions or to make war, cover the
war debt, engage in the seemingly inconspicuous consumption of human
life and weaponry? The text of the bourgeois woman — and in the twentieth century the middle-class woman — serves as a convenient ruse with
which artfully to disguise those sites of political power where violence is
exercised which strikes most efficiently and surgically at women's bodies.

How to Misread Fashion

Perhaps it reveals too clearly that violence has always been the method by which institutions demonstrate their superiority. . . . male political dominance might be less a matter of moral superiority than of crude brute force and this would remove a degree of glamour from the dominance itself.

Angela Carter, *The Sadeian Woman*

I tell him I will let him have the passport in the afternoon and he gives my hat a gloomy, disapproving look. I don't blame him. It shouts "Anglaise," my hat. And my dress extinguishes me. And then this damned old fur coat slung on top of everything else — the last idiocy, the last incongruity.

Jean Rhys, *Good Morning, Midnight*

At the General Court of the Governor and Company of Adventurers of England trading into Hudson's Bay, held on Tuesday, 29 June 1926, in London, the presiding governor, Charles V. Sale, was compelled to defend the fur trade as a worthy capitalist venture against the socialist Mr. Barnes, who in the House of Commons on 10 February 1926 "used the fur trade as a weapon with which to attack 'Capitalism.' [Mr. Barnes] began with the doubtful assertion that the 'costlier an article, the less is the labour represented in the production of it.'"[1] An excerpt from Barnes's speech indicates that he used the fur coat as an example of the sort of luxurious commodities that contribute nothing to the general happiness and comfort of the majority:

Let me give a simple illustration to show what I mean. If you want increased production we can demonstrate how you can get it. It is well known that the costlier an article the less is the labour represented in the production of it. I have here an illustration of a fur coat, and similar illustrations can be seen in any newspaper. (An Hon. Member: "A Russian coat?") Very likely it is a Russian coat, but it is of the sort that we do not buy. I notice that it is advertised for 128 guineas. As a matter of fact, you could produce 42 three-guinea coats for the same money. The 42 coats would provide more work; they would represent the greater output, if hon. Members opposite are so much concerned about increased output. The production of 42 useful three-guinea coats means greater output, more employment, and certainly it means more happiness and comfort for 42 women to have a three-guinea coat each than for one woman to have a coat costing 128 guineas.[2]

In response to Barnes's suggestion to put into production a three-guinea coat, presumably for the benefit of the majority of female consumers, Sale makes the following argument, in which he, too, places the female consumer in a position of economic agency:

> The fur trade benefits a large number of people who do not, and could not, make cheap coats — the Eskimo, the Indian, and the white trapper, who have nothing to offer except skins in exchange for the goods they require; it also employs directly and indirectly hosts of workmen in almost every occupation — shipbuilders, seafaring men, engineers, weavers and artisans of every trade, producing blankets, guns and other necessaries for barter, the staffs at our posts and on the lines of communication, the warehousemen who sort out and handle the furs, and lastly the furrier and the shopkeeper.
>
> If ladies ceased to buy fur coats these communities of people would fall out of employment altogether, and the agitators who now seek to destroy the luxury trade would find it impossible to provide alternative work and wages. The lady who buys a fur coat merely completes the cycle, and enables the capitalist to commence another round of employment, and so provide to labour fresh wages for the purchase of three-guinea coats and all other necessaries of life. Mr. Barnes and his friends seem to lose sight of the truth that labour works for the present and capital for the future. If the people of this country really desire security for the future they must listen less to the loud voice of the Socialist and more to the still small voice of the Capitalist.[3]

For Sale-the-Capitalist, the female purchaser of the fur coat is a privileged entity. She occupies a pivotal place in the cycle of production. Indeed, in the whole linear process of fur production from the farthest reaches of the British colonies inhabited by the "Eskimo" to the most local site represented by the London shopkeeper, it is the bourgeois female consumer who keeps the wheels of capitalism oiled. For Barnes, the comfort and happiness of an expanded realm of female consumers would be met by the ability to purchase a cloth coat, for example, for a mere three guineas.

Judging from her theoreticofictive political work *Three Guineas*, published in 1938, it is not difficult to conclude that for Virginia Woolf, the symbolic agency that middle-class women would acquire from the erotic power and material wealth represented by a fur coat is no substitute for the economic agency that middle-class women would gain through entry into the professions and the right to earn a living from professional work. In Britain middle-class women were not legally allowed to enter the professions until the Sex Disqualification (Removal) Act was passed in 1919. It is financial independence from men that would enable middle-class women to work for prevention of war, the central problem of Woolf's feminist polemic. Interestingly, Barnes's argument for increased production was addressed specifically to the payment of the war debt from World War I. War and dress are as intimately connected for Barnes as for Virginia Woolf, but whereas Barnes is concerned with the material production of clothing, Woolf focuses her critique on the symbolic production of clothing, in particular, the clothes worn by educated men in the public realms of political, legal, and religious power: "Now you dress in violet; a jewelled crucifix swings on your breast; now your shoulders are covered with lace; now furred with ermine; now slung with many linked chains set with precious stones. Now you wear wigs on your heads; rows of graduated curls descend to your necks. Now your hats are boat-shaped, or cocked; now they mount in cones of black fur. . . . After the comparative simplicity of your dress at home, the splendour of your public attire is dazzling."[4] In her introduction to *Three Guineas* Michèle Barrett observes: "Men, Woolf argues, use distinctions of dress to symbolize rank and status; like the labels on things in a shop, they advertise the quality of the goods. . . . The function of the photographs in *Three Guineas* is, of course, to ridicule these patriarchal, hierarchical dress codes. But the point is closely drawn into Woolf's underlying theme when she argues that the symbolic function of dress is closely connected to war: 'your finest clothes are those you wear as soldiers.'"[5] It is strikingly apparent throughout the social history of fashion that symbolic display in the form of clothing has also represented for middle- to upper-class women a kind of weapon in the battle against female servitude, familial domestication, and economic dependency. Woolf makes her own contribution to the history of women's sartorial strategizing in the observation: "Since marriage until the year 1919 — less than twenty years ago — was the only profession open to us, the enormous importance of dress to a woman can hardly be exaggerated. It was to her what clients are to you — dress was her chief, perhaps her only, method of becoming Lord Chancellor."[6]

The interconnectedness of symbolic agency and access to economic capital for middle- and upper-class women in late nineteenth- and early twentieth-century Britain, Europe, and North America, is especially important to the representation of women in fur. It is particularly notable that the fur coat in the late nineteenth century and throughout the twentieth emerges as primarily an object of female apparel and hence comes to bear the mark of femininity itself.[7] The practice of putting the meanings and values ascribed to fur into circulation in the twentieth-century metropolis rests with the female consumer or cosmopolite. I do not mean to suggest that the female cosmopolite necessarily produces the value of a fur coat as a sign, for example, of wealth and social prestige. Rather it is as a reader of the signs of fashion that the woman adorned in fur produces and reproduces the symbolic and material interests of fur. As a reader of the signs of fur fashion, the female cosmopolite keeps the official meanings assigned to the fur coat in circulation both by the very act of buying such a luxury item and by wearing it in contexts in which others can reread its symbolic value. The bourgeois woman who purchases or acquires and wears the fur coat is herself a reader of the codes of prestige, wealth, and femininity. Such skill in "reading," however, must incorporate into its everyday practice a "misreading" of the relationships between and among symbolic, political, and economic values.[8] While it is apparently in the interest of bourgeois and, by and large, white women to seek, maintain, and reproduce their symbolic value through exhibition of symbolic agency, such acts not only create a dimension of power for relatively few women, but they can also disempower these women and the majority — hence, contributing to the repression and stifling of political agency. In other words, symbolic agency can be as debilitating as it is strategic. It is one of the contradictory aspects of symbolic agency that the price to be paid for symbolic power is continuing representation by cultural studies theorists and advertising agencies alike of the female bourgeois consumer as passive, stupid — and spectacularly so.

Roland Barthes, like many theorists of fashion, underestimates how much decoding consumers must do to maintain the meanings and values ascribed to articles such as the fur coat. In *The Fashion System* Barthes analyzes fashion as a linguistic structure, breaking it down into its constituent units, combinations, and bundles of relations, in much the same way as Lévi-Strauss isolated the elementary structures and relations of myth.[9] Like a myth, indeed like "literature," fashion unfolds its meaning in an oedipal narrative structure and can be reduced to a systematic rhetoric of ideological and social meanings. As a literature, fashion at best belongs to the popular; it is akin, in Barthes's words, to "a whole literature for young girls."

Lacking the rich textual play of "good" literature, fashion is a poor substitute, a simplistic system composed of *petits récits*, paradoxically "rich" only in the wealth it signifies.[10] The reader of fashion magazines, for Barthes, is always a woman or a girl. In keeping with Barthes's infantilization of the fashion system in general — displayed through a rigorous scientific approach that borders on the parodic at times and which he imposes in a rather sadistic fashion on his object(s) of analysis — so too the feminized reader of fashion magazines is infantilized by her (in)ability to "read" this poor literature:

> When the magazine speaks of *big brother's sweaters* (and not men's sweaters), or of the young girl who likes *surprise parties and Pascal, cool jazz and Mozart* all at once, the somewhat childish "homeliness" of the first utterance and the eclecticism of the second are signifieds whose very status is questionable since they are perceived in one place as the simple expression of a simple nature and in another with the distance of a critical regard which discerns the sign behind the index; we can assume that for the woman who reads Fashion there is no awareness here of a signification, yet she receives from the utterance a message structured enough for her to feel changed by it (for example, reassured and confirmed in a euphoric situation of "homeliness" or in the right to like very different genres which nonethelesss have subtle affinities). With the rhetorical or latent signified, we thus approach the essential paradox of connoted signification: it is, one might say, a signification which is *received*, but which is not *read*.[11]

In short, the passive female "reader" (who is not a reader but a spectacle and a spectator who cannot, of course, actually read but just stand still, frozen by the fixity of her narcissistic gaze) receives but does not "read." And yet, she is exemplary for Barthes as a demonstration that stupidity — as in the tendency to be easily duped — underlies the function of "connotation" in mid-twentieth-century theories of mass culture. The concept of connotation is decidedly marked by gender in Barthes's analysis, by the passive receptivity that characterizes femininity.

Fashion magazines not only play a major role in the larger symbolic apparatus producing the values and meanings attributed to fur fashions but also contribute to the creation of the singular figure of the passive and narcissistic female bourgeois consumer of fashion. To speak of the bourgeois female consumer in the singular is to mark the "singularity" typified by this figure in her configuration as a narcissist. Simone de Beauvoir captured the image of the female narcissist at midcentury: "All the future is concentrated in that sheet of light, a universe within the mirror's frame; outside these narrow limits, things are a disordered chaos; the world is reduced to this sheet of glass wherein stands resplendent an image: the Unique." As de Beauvoir characterizes the narcissistic woman, she stands immobile or resorts to false actions played in perpetuity to an imaginary audience receptive to the delusions and illusions of masquerade. "For lack of action, woman invents substitutes for action; to some the theater represents a favored substitute." [12] Applied to the female bourgeois consumer, de Beauvoir's stony image of the narcissistic woman denies the very mobility of her actions as a consumer and wearer of fashion. The bourgeois female consumer engages in an active production and reproduction of class ideologies such as elitism and cultural as well as racial superiority. In other words, she participates in the activities of symbolic agency. Socially constructed in the interstices of female narcissism and commodity fetishism, the female bourgeois consumer is a far more contradictory social subject than de Beauvoir's psychological explanation suggests. The subject in question is, in effect, the white bourgeois female consumer of Western European origins, but the singularity with which it is possible to identify this unique figure is entirely constitutive of the ideological interests of the fashion apparatus, which, in the final instance, would have the fashion article stand in for and give shape to a figure designated as "woman."

The apparent autonomy of the fashion system contributes to the seeming autonomy of the fur coat. In fact, the singularity of this fashion item, signifying the signs, meanings, and values of bourgeois class affiliation, has been produced by a history of commodity and sexual fetishisms. From the late nineteenth century on, the singularity of the fashion fur coat and its female bourgeois consumer has been maintained by a specifically cultural and racial ideology of gender difference, the effects of which are, first, to differentiate the regimes of consumption and production along the lines of a gender division of labor; second, to produce a symmetrical relationship between male and female bodies and corresponding material and symbolic interests such that the female figure constitutes a spectacle of symbolic value and the male figure embodies the material values of wage earner, laborer, and money maker; and third, to inscribe those asymmetrical symmetrical bodies with sexualized and gendered connotations of desire and power. The fur coat appears to have a life of its own, but like any prop in a theatrical play, it comes into view only as a support for the narrative or to fill out a character. The fur coat is nothing if not a prop giving shape to the matter of "Woman," central for the last century and especially since *Venus in Furs* to an oedipal drama of castrated desire.

There are two theoretical questions to be elaborated here. First, what does it mean that women figure as objects of exchange in a libidinal economy of desire constructed for the purposes of heterosexual and reproductive ideological containment? It is also equally important to figure women as subjects of exchange and as subjects and objects in exchange if the tensions between symbolic/economic and political forms of agency are to be differentiated, maximized, and particularized.[13] Second, how is it that femininity constitutes a form of cultural capital amassed by bourgeois women and, as a result, desired by lower- and middle-class women? What is its value or transvaluating significance in Western culture? Obviously, there are benefits to be gained in the accumulation of femininity which reside in part in its value as a negative corollary to masculinity.

During the early part of the twentieth century, when the fur coat began to circulate primarily as an object of female consumption, the figure of the fur-clad woman emerged as an exemplary token in the libidinal and political investments of the sexual exchange of women's bodies. G. W. Pabst's silent film *The Joyless Street* (*Die freudlose Gasse*, 1925) traces the significance of a fur coat as an object of credit in a restricted mode of sexual exchange. His film dramatizes an imaginary resolution of the material contradictions bourgeois women face as producers and reproducers of symbolic value — that is, their production of symbolic value as a substitute for their lack of access to material value, which, in turn, reproduces the condition of their dispossession. This is the basis, then, of the bourgeois female consumer's "misreading" of both her lack of access to material independence and the ideological power she accumulates imaginatively in investing femininity with symbolic value. "Femininity" is transposed into a "negative" image of female erotic power — negative because it is an image of power produced only in relation to the real positive power of ruling men.

Pabst's film constitutes one sort of inscriptional space, linked with the general fashion commodity apparatus of displays, spectacles, and other visual pleasures that inculcate the female bourgeois consumer with the techniques of misreading. Misreading here suggests that economic dispossession must be compensated for by a high degree of symbolic realization of the signs of wealth and prestige. And yet, "femininity" always marks or undercuts the radical difference between symbolic and material values. Nevertheless, in the interest of preserving a misreading of the lack of material valuation, the female bourgeois consumer negotiates this economic lack in the context of a desire for symbolic plentitude: to become a figure of power, she must deploy a powerful eroticism, already inscribed in the commodity and sexual fetishisms attributed to fur. Under the system of credit, she can draw on the bank of signifying practices at her disposal and achieve material gains through the circulation of their symbolic value. She pays the interest with the excess of libidinal energies accrued in her figuration as a "knowable" object of sexual pleasure: the prostitute, the dominatrix, the spectacle of luxury-commodity consumption. I want to explore these questions in detail through analysis of Pabst's film.

The Sex of the Credit and the Fetish of the Debt

In *The Joyless Street* the sexual exchange of women operates as the central metaphor with which to represent a general economic situation of deprivation and dispossession in post–World War I Vienna. At all levels of the social hierarchy, bourgeois, middle-class, and poor women, participate in an economy that places their capital, their cultural capital, in the sexual status of their bodies. A fur coat becomes a complex and contradictory sign by which the heroine of the story, Grete Rumfort (Greta Garbo), mediates her position between the decadence of the society woman and the deprivation of the impoverished woman. She occupies the middle ground. She is a middle-class woman, teetering on the precipice of a fall into sexual disgrace materially determined by the loss of her father's income. In the end she remains a figure of moral and emotional authenticity. The fur coat moves in and out of various systems of value, as a sign of women's sexual status, as an article of credit, as a mark of social prestige and wealth, and as an object of utility, simply a warm and protective article of clothing. The last meaning stands as the final image of the film, but not without bearing a trace of the sexual interest it has accrued by then, which must still be paid off.

The film comprises multiple narrative threads driven by lines of class division and woven into a tight net of sexual intrigue and innocence. The single most important frame for this tapestry of complex social and sexual relations is the binding quest for money. Spatial continuity is provided by the mise-en-scène: Melchiorstrasse, Melchior Street, which runs through a poor area of the city, a joyless street inhabited by impoverished, depraved, and sick individuals. The first shots of this melodrama contain images of anonymous and singular people, walking on the street, depressed, hungry, physically afflicted, and alienated from one another.[14] Action begins with the introduction of the villainous characters Josef Geringer (Werner Krauss) and Frau Greifer. Geringer is the local butcher, the "tyrant of Melchior Street." He hangs a sign outside his shop that reads "Tomorrow Morning: Frozen Meat from Argentina." Greifer is introduced with the following text: "The other influence of the neighbourhood, Frau Greifer, keeper of the Merkel Hotel, runs a clandestine joint under the cover of a fashion boutique." Both Geringer and Greifer traffic in flesh, one in the meat of dead animals, the other in women supplied to the wealthy clientele at Greifer's joint. The specificity of female sexuality located in the inanimate flesh of meat or a fur coat signals a particular metaphorical condensation linked to a pervasive sexual cynicism in Weimar society. Mary Ann Doane, in her analysis of Pabst's later film *Pandora's Box* (*Die Büchse der Pandora*, 1929), points out that the "cultural artifacts of the Weimar Republic evince a fascination with sexual transgression and the violation of traditional taboos through the exploration of pornography, prostitution, androgyny, homosexuality. . . . Weimar's strategic immoralism was an aspect of its pervasive sexual cyncism, a rejection of the romantic idealism and corresponding repression of an earlier era." Constitutive of the trangression of sexual identity was a boundary crossing between female human sexuality and a bestial, carnal, carnivorous, and carnival-like sexuality. The fur coat marks a particularly telling dissimulation of the embodiment of this primitive animal nature in the sexuality of women. Dissimulation, Doane maintains, is key to maintaining this sexual cynicism: "In Weimar Germany, exposure of the flesh became tantamount to a confrontation with the facts, with the real. The period cultivated a modern sophistication wherein not to be deceived meant to know that everything is deception — a knowledge which seemingly compensated for the losses effected by modernization." The "loss" dramatized by Weimar cynicism also helped to create "a crisis in male identity provoked by the defeat of World War I." [15] Compensating for these losses, masculine male subjectivity turned toward a sexual economy of desire and its exploitative potential to infuse the in/animate object with libidinal value for the purposes of an illicit trade in flesh, animal and female.

The centrality of feminine dissimulation to exposing the evils of symbolic decadence in the face of the economic devastation of the Weimar Republic finds its expression in *The Joyless Street* in the use of a fashion boutique as a cover for Greifer's decadent after-hours club. This spatial duplicity reenacts an essential meaning attributed to fashion — the masquerade that not only "covers over" but also protects the "undercover" operations of illicit sociosexual relations. As the primary article of fashion in the film, the fur coat functions as a cover for a clandestine ideological operation in which women's identity is constructed on the basis of their value as objects of sexual exchange, as indeed their bodies are made to circulate in the clandestine joint as objects of sexual pleasure for men. On another register the fur coat, once an animate cover of animal flesh but now an inanimate cover of female flesh, reinforces a series of parallel associations between male and female, human and animal, animate and inanimate, legal and clandestine.

Pabst re-presents the social hierarchy of his characters again through the strategic use of the mise-en-scène and the spatial dimensions of the living arrangements on Melchior Street. In a basement live the "miserable Lechners," a poor family. When the Lechners' daughter, Maria (Asta Nielsen), fails to bring food home, her wooden-legged father (here is a classic oedipal fracture) threatens her with physical violence. The first floor of the same house contains "a well-to-do home, Counsellor Rumfort's family." The counsellor is described as a "resigned victim to the events"; Grete Rumfort is his daughter. The top floor contains Frau Greifer's clandestine enterprise. If the basement represents the spatial equivalent of the lower classes, the poor, and the next floor up the precarious middle ground of the middle class, Frau Greifer's lofty establishment ironically twists the outward regulatory form of social distinctions by creating an aura of social transcendence where the rich and the poor, wealthy men and prostitute women, mingle. Frau Greifer's clandestine operation exists somewhere beyond the normative continuities of the social hierarchy.

Through the technique of montage Pabst juxtaposes Grete and Maria, their habitations and their social displacements, thus initiating the conditions for differentiating their respective class affiliations and sexual (im)-moralities. Patrice Petro, in noting the melodrama of the film, borrows from Peter Brooks the idea that melodrama is fundamentally constructed through "bipolar relations." In *The Joyless Street*, the juxtaposition of Grete and Maria represents one way in which the film instrumentally constructs this bipolar relation. According to Petro, however, *The Joyless Street* "structures polarization in a much more fundamental way, since the juxtaposition of two separate dramas becomes the very basis for the divided mode of perception which governs our response to the film. . . . Rather than establish an explicit relationship between the two characters, the narrative implies a connection between them by situating one story as the formal and, indeed, the dramatic counterpoint to the other."[16] The only point of convergence between Grete and Maria occurs in the line outside the butcher shop, where they stand together, side by side and without mutual recognition, waiting until morning to buy meat. Maria is the tragic figure of the film, and the events of Grete's life represent a frame of realist and emotional authenticity in relation to which Maria's life unfolds in a series of macabre, twisted, and pitifully bizarre events. Or to put it another way, the relatively privileged genre of filmic realism belongs to the morally strong character of Grete, and the world of fantasy, of filmic representation, which the film itself would appear to deny, belongs to the tragic and distorted figure of moral degeneracy, Maria.[17]

Maria's story links romantic fantasy and the quest for material wealth in a perilous series of tragic events. Maria's object of romantic love and material security is Egon Stirner, the private secretary to a wealthy Viennese speculator. Maria is shown fantasizing about Stirner, conjuring up a still photographic image of his face on the screen. The object of Stirner's sexual and material desires is Regina, the daughter of a rich man. His only problem is that he is not rich enough to convince Regina that his love is true and pure and not materially motivated. Maria's only problem is that she is not rich enough to fulfill Stirner's desire for social status and material wealth. Stirner finds himself ideally located to improve his financial situation. At the posh Hotel Carlton, Stirner meets his boss and a man called Don Alfonso Canez: "He's an international speculator . . . ten thousand dollars in his pocket and no scruples." Stirner listens attentively while Canez and his boss devise a scam to bring down shares in the Petrowitz mine, the only supplier of coal to Vienna. "We are going to spread the rumour of a strike. . . . It will drop the value of the shares and we'll buy them back for a mere song." "Then from the inflation that will follow we'll get a nice little profit." In order to capitalize on this surreptitious venture, Egon must play the gigolo to a married society woman, Lia Leid, who has romantic designs on him. If he meets her need for "romance," he hopes she will supply him with cash to invest in the scam. He arranges a clandestine meeting for the following evening at the Merkel Hotel on Melchior Street. They agree to disguise themselves so that they will not be recognized by "unwanted souls."[18]

That same evening the wealthy men from the Carlton arrive at the Merkel Hotel in a limousine. On the street, the line outside the butcher's shop has gotten longer and the police have been called in to keep everyone "in line." Scenes of the orgy that is taking place in the hotel are juxtaposed to scenes of the line, where Grete faints and has to be taken home. Maria, too terrified to go home after the butcher announces there will not be any meat tomorrow, decides with a friend to follow the lead of the sex workers, who appear to get what they want through the sexual display of their bodies. The two women allow themselves to be looked over by the butcher in exchange for some meat; Maria, however, can't go through with it and runs away. The butcher throws the meat to a dog, his relationship to meat and to women's bodies apparently one and the same.

Although Maria is not pursued as an object of desire, she is driven to seek a solution to her poverty, a man with material security. In the process she debases herself to the point of begging Egon to take her on as his servant to help her out of her misery. Even though he refuses her, Maria listens to his troubles, his need to acquire a hundred dollars by tomorrow in order to make five thousand dollars on the stock market. She is determined to get the money for him, but he laughs at her for thinking such an outrageous and fantastical idea was even possible.

Grete, for her part, must actively fend off those who desire her as an object of sexual pleasure. Although exhausted from lining up outside the butcher's shop most of the previous night, Grete dutifully goes off to her secretarial job the next morning. When she arrives in a tattered fur-lined coat, her coworkers laugh at her behind her back. Her boss, in an exemplary display of sexual harassment in the workplace, calls her into his office, makes advances which she pointedly rejects, but still gives Grete "an advance on her salary" in order to cement his sense of his power over her.

Meanwhile Grete's father decides to take action to get the Rumfort family out of its misery. He accepts an option to retire early which comes with a large cash incentive. On the advice of an investment broker, Rumfort invests all his money in Petrowitz shares. In the following scene, the unscrupulous speculators initiate their plan to bring the shares crashing down. Rumfort returns home with packages of food and wine for Grete and his younger daughter to celebrate their anticipated financial security. When he notices the shabbiness of Grete's coat he urges her to go and buy a proper coat. Grete heads off for Frau Greifer's "fashion boutique."

The scene in the supposed fashion boutique consolidates the relations among Grete, Maria, Frau Greifer, and a couple of her sex workers. In this central scene a different line of credit from the one Rumfort recently initiated will be extended, one that plays surreptitiously on an unspoken traffic in women's bodies as tokens in a sexual economy of exchange. Frau Greifer brings out the fur coat to Grete, rubbing it on her face to display its sensuality. Grete exclaims, "It's a beautiful coat, but too expensive." Frau Greifer replies, "Did I ever bother my customers with the payment?" Her question is directed toward two women who have come into the shop and are observing Frau Greifer at work. As the women smile knowingly among themselves, Grete puts the coat on. The shot of Greta Garbo in the fur coat is striking. She is narcissistic feminine woman incarnate, whose pose, like that of a model in a fashion magazine, captures the aesthetic disposition of the beautiful and sensual woman. The camera virtually transforms the image of Grete from a struggling middle-class female character in Pabst's filmic critique of corruption and disparity to the future star of Hollywood cinema. The cinematic voyeurism is right in focus. As in Stephen Heath's description of the fetish, the fantastic, hallucinatory quality of Garbo's image in this scene is "a brilliance, something lit up, heightened, depicted, as under an arc light, a point of (theatrical) representation; hence the glance: the subject is installed (as at the theatre or at the movies) *for* the representation." [19]

Maria enters the same scene like the dark shadow of Grete's rising star. Frau Greifer treats her brusquely and sends her off into a back room. Caught up in the illumination of her own image, Grete appears unaware of the system of exchange she has just entered. Her apparent ownership of the fur coat as an extension of her own aesthetic and symbolic value blinds her to the line of libidinal economic credit she has just taken on, which must be repaid at some point. Frau Greifer looks pleased with herself. She has speculated, economically and libidinally, on Grete's sensual appeal, on the value of her image, the function of her body as spectacle, and later she will attempt to capitalize on it. Grete leaves the store wearing her new fur coat; Frau Greifer walks away with her girls; and Maria is left alone to wait.

While she waits she hears the noise on the other side of the door. Curious, she opens the door on the orgy and quickly closes it, but not without catching the attention of the unscrupulous speculator Don Alfonso Canez. Canez follows her back into the empty room. Maria tells him she came to borrow a hundred dollars. Canez playfully hands it out to her and then withdraws the money making it clear that there is a condition attached. She must keep him company that evening. Maria resigns herself to the job.

Midnight. Maria is sitting beside Canez in a hotel room when she hears something in an adjoining room and hurries Canez out, telling him she will meet him later. Once he leaves, Maria opens the curtains to the window into the next room. She looks through and sees Egon disguised in a beard embracing Lia. Lia gives him her pearls, and he kisses her hand. Maria, in a jealous frenzy of shock and despair, goes into the room, and while Lia is preening herself in front of her hand mirror, strangles her.

The scene of Lia Leid's murder is disturbing from the point of view of visual continuity. Maria comes from behind, and yet Lia doesn't see her in the mirror. The murder is dramatized by a shot of Maria's hands only, creeping slowly toward Lia's bare neck. Fade to black. Why doesn't Lia see Maria in the mirror? Is she so enraptured by her own image that the view of another person eludes her, or is Maria such a shadow figure that she is not even reflected in the mirror? What matters are her hands, hands that are stretched out far from the body and manic in their desire to reach their destination. These hands take action only in the most destructive manner.[20]

During the investigation into Leid's death, the police suspect the man with the beard, for whom Canez is mistaken. In this scene of misrecognition, Canez is drunk and laughs off the accusations. Maria bears a peculiar smirk on her face, as if there were some kind of justice in accusing Canez of a criminal act, although one that is disguised by his wealth and status. The officer asks who Maria is, and Canez protects her, if not from charges of murder at least from a potential charge of prostitution, by claiming she is an employee of the consulate.

While the investigation takes place at the Merkel Hotel, the Hotel Carlton is the scene of Mr. Leid's discovery of his wife's murder, Stirner's successul financial deal, and the introduction of a new set of characters, "two members of the American Red Cross." Lieutenant Davy is the new man of the hour. When asked by his colonel what he thinks of Vienna, he replies, "I find her happy and dressed up to the hilt like a courtesan. And I wonder what our mission is doing at this big party?" Davy resolves to "look for a room in a poor neighbourhood so as to unmask the real face of this city."

The theme of cynicism, more developed in Pabst's later film, *Pandora's Box*, is anticipated in the tensions that emerge between Davy and his superior. Mary Ann Doane elaborates on how this theme of cynicism "attached to modernity is thus approached by its analysts as the symptom of a difficulty in male subjectivity, a lack in subjectivity which is then compensated for by a knowing wink which understands the emptiness of ideals and obtuseness of the real." [21] In *The Joyless Street*, however, Pabst posits countervalues to replace the fatalistic and cynical ones that pervade *Pandora's Box*, where the status quo, as Doane points out, is ultimately maintained. The "real face" of the city, which Davy's colonel would prefer that he dismissed rather than naively embraced, belongs to none other than the stunning and glamourous Grete. Unmasking the reality of the city's temptations and desires is the quest of the earnest social worker, the male counterpart to Grete's moral authenticity. Grete's fur coat, however, represents a temptation that may lead her past her staunch middle-class moral frontier to follow Maria into the abyss of sexual and moral degeneracy. The symbolic value of the fur coat as a sign of sexual and material decadence costs Grete her job. When she arrives at work, her boss reads her display of the coat as a sign that Grete has become an object of sexual pleasure: "What a beautiful coat. It wasn't necessary to get angry the other day. I would have bought it for you, my pretty one." Grete retorts, "Brute! I won't stay another minute longer in your house!" She must physically wrestle out of his grip to get away.

This scene is followed by the text "Things are going faster and faster." Indeed, the speed of Grete's disaster quickens like the speed of capital transactions. With the economic collapse of the Petrowitz shares Grete's father loses all his savings. Regina rejects Egon, who is arrested for murdering Lia Leid and robbing her in order to speculate on the stock market. Maria becomes Canez's mistress, a doll for him to dress in a new wardrobe of clothes and jewels. When he attempts to purchase a pearl necklace for her in the style of a "choker," her blank, sullen response sends him into a rage: "Your coldness is unbearable. What do you want? Tell me." She answers, "I want to go back to Frau Greifer's tonight."

Meanwhile Grete tries to cope with the loss of her father's money by renting out a room to Lieutenant Davy. Like Prince Charming, he shows up at the right moment, gallantly pays her more rent than she is asking, treats Grete with respect, and offers tins of food to the little girl. In other words, he brings money, friendship, and good will — all the ingredients of material and sexual security. This fairy-tale illusion of well-being bursts asunder over a couple of missing tins of food, initially offered to the little girl. Rumfort had felt insulted by this charity and had returned them. The little girl steals back the tins, and when Rumfort is confronted by the actions of his daughter, he is again insulted by the accusation and denies it.

The scene is prefigured by Davy's friend showing off to Grete. He shows her his sword and shatters the glass of a window in the process. It is Davy's friend who squeals on the little girl, as if he must compensate for his bumbled display of masculine prowess with the control he can ultimately gain over Grete's life by telling Davy about her little sister's thievery. When Grete discloses to her father the truth of the little girl's actions, Rumfort collapses. The last of Grete's money goes to the doctor. When the glazier stretches out his hand for payment, Grete sees a specter coming at her. "Facing the ghost of misery, Grete makes up her mind to go and see the Greifer woman."

Now it is time for Grete, although she is unaware of it, to pay back the debt she has incurred by accepting the fur coat. Patrice Petro remarks on the importance of "virtue" to Grete's charactization. The recognitions and misrecognitions that inform relations among spectator, character identification, and the visual logic of the film's narrative sequence are structured by the apparent misrecognition on the part of the film's characters of Grete's virtue and the ostensible recognition by the audience that Grete is virtuous and often wrongly maligned. From this point in the film on, Petro observes, "Grete's innocence is made even more apparent to the spectator, precisely because Grete remains unaware of the threat to her virtue. With her father's illness, Grete is left with no choice but to seek help from Frau Greifer. On Frau Greifer's suggestion, she agrees to meet a wealthy man, who turns out to be the butcher, now dressed in his Sunday best. The scene of their meetings is presented in a highly elliptical fashion, so that the spectator is made to experience the slow passage of time and the tense exchange of glances which render the seduction impossible." [22] When the butcher makes advances, Grete recoils and runs away. She begs Frau Greifer for money, and the procuress gives it to her to ensure that Grete will attend Greifer's birthday party that evening. Grete agrees. Meanwhile, before confessing her crime to the police, Maria returns to Melchior Street to say good-bye to her parents. She is dressed like a tart and obviously physically sick with a bad cough. She finally confesses her crime of passion to the police and through the technique of a flashback, Pabst repeats the dramatic scene image by image, thus reintroducing the trauma of Maria's state of mind at the time.[23] Egon is set free. On signing Egon's statement of release, the officer asks out of curiosity, "And the false beard?" Egon replies, "A romantic whim of a poor soul." The beard, like a woman's "muff," also figures in the oedipal mythology of sexual fetishism. False beards clearly belong to the unreality of masquerade and, like the undercover operations of the fashion apparatus, hide not only reality but its sordid, degenerate, and "feminized" configuration.

When Egon faced the possibility of imprisonment and death, Regina vowed her undying love for him. When Maria confesses that she acted out of madness and killed Lia Leid because of her love for Egon, she finally gets if not his love then at least his attention. Apparently confessions of love are easiest when the object of desire is about to go off to jail.

The final set of scenes deals with Grete's dramatic role in the Greifer party. The narrative strength of Maria's life, set in a dramatic and traumatic re-presentation of the gender dynamics of her lower-class affiliation, turns into a melodramatic farce of moral dilemmas and the restoration of middle-class values as the solution to the economic instabilities of the times. Grete is now called upon to circulate her body in a libidinal economy of exchange. Her resistance to playing that role is parallelled with a revolt in the street against the villainous butcher and Frau Greifer's decadent party.

"The elegant and cosmopolitan crowd is rushing to the Greifer party." Women are getting dressed up in the lady's change room, preparing to put on a show for the men in the audience. Frau Greifer brings Grete along, holding onto her tightly and moving her about the room. Grete watches in horror while the women smoke, brush their hair, put on makeup, black nylons, and garters. Grete looks through the curtain and is shocked to see Lieutenant Davy. When Davy left the Rumfort's rented room, he was taken away by his colonel, who is always opposed to Davy's benevolent attitude and encourages him to succumb to the temptations of Vienna, to be cynical rather than attempt to apply social welfare to its problems. When Grete tries to resist Greifer's insistence that she get dressed, Greifer pulls the fur coat off her and undresses her. It is time for Grete to pay back the loan she owes Greifer in accepting the fur coat.

Grete wears an extraordinarily revealing dress, it is clear that she is re-paying the loan with interest, since very little of her body is covered. A man comes at her, and in trying to escape from him, Grete stumbles onto the stage where Lieutenant Davy sees her. Davy goes after her: "You here! What a shame!" he says. "Yes, like many other young girls in Vienna, so that our parents don't starve," Grete replies. "Hunger!" says Davy incredulously. "What about the $60 I gave you for rent?" He throws money at her in disgust. Grete is distraught. "Don't leave me like this. . . . listen to me," she begs. "I don't want to listen. What I saw is enough." Rumfort shows up and explains to Davy with a letter as evidence that Grete used the sixty dollars to pay off his debt on the shares. Davy smiles to think that Grete is still "pure" and uncorrupted. Rumfort hugs Grete and picks up her fur coat and wraps it around her, ironically, to preserve her dignity and to clothe her in something more substantial. This display of parental exhibitionism is followed, as Petro notes, by "a shot of an audience [the audience for Frau Greifer's revue] composed of men who vigorously applaud."[24] Out on the street, the people are gathering in anger. They throw rocks at Frau Greifer's windows. They beg the butcher for meat. He says, "I have meat, but not for your child!" Geringer is murdered by a distraught woman, the police arrive, Frau Greifer runs away, and the party is over.

The ethics of middle-class heterosexual differentiation are upheld by the ethic of resistance to class exploitation and oppression. Pabst's metaphorical substitution for class affiliations of sexed modes of social differentiation operates because sociosexual relations appear as natural and filiative bonds and therefore, in the final instance, stronger than the affiliative bonds of class and revolutionary resistance. Sexual differentiation, although linked to class position, remains for Pabst a ground of authenticity, both economic and moral. The fur-clad middle-class woman played by Greta Garbo may not be able to transcend her economic dependency, but she will transcend the moral dilemma of her sexuality. She retains the fur coat lovingly wrapped around her by her father for warmth and protection. But the utilitarian value assigned to the fur coat in this final scene belies the libidinal economy in which it also circulates, if not as an object that connotes woman as object of sexual pleasure then in its utilitarian configuration, which reproduces the presumed certainties of heterosexual, reproductive exchange, Pabst's ground of economic and moral authenticity. The revolutionary subject for Pabst, then, is the distraught mother who kills the butcher for the sake of her child and not Maria, the lower-class woman who turns from beggar to prostitute, self-destroyed by her romantic fantasies. And yet, perhaps in spite of Pabst himself, Maria is also a revolutionary subject in the film who turns the mask of bourgeois self-deception into a mirror of blinding self-reflection. Her narrative runs through the film like a shadow text, turning the light out on the dazzling brilliance of sexual and commodity fetishism. Like Lia, unable to see the shadow creeping up from behind, like Grete, misreading the fur coat in Frau Greifer's mode of exchange, Maria waits in the shadows for her story to be told. In the meantime, fade to black.

Investments in Femininity and Cultural Capital

In the making of the female bourgeois consumer, her position as a known entity appears as singular, unique, and objective as the article of fashion itself. More often than not, a clothing style becomes the article by which an individual obtains a recognizable identity. Fashion and identity are inextricably intertwined; however, any knowable, visible, and recognizable identity achieved through the masquerade of fashion comes into existence as a result of several interrelated activities, which combine to create "identity-by-style." Those activities that constitute identity through the fashion apparatus may include designers (especially their "signature"), fashion photography, fashion magazines, fashion shows, fashion television, models and supermodels, spectators, readers, and consumers. Standing at the tail end of a long production line of meanings and values, the consumer is offered a field of possibilities with which to inscribe an identity. Not only can the female bourgeois consumer take up a given position within this field, she may also manipulate those position takings in order to further her "vested interests," to borrow from Marjorie Garber; those interests that symbolically and materially invest the codes of femininity and masculinity through sartorial display.[25]

The positions and position takings opened up by the field of possibilities in the fashion apparatus constitute for the consumer subject an "identity." The social production of that identity is part of a complex struggle produced in and by social modes of differentiation. In Barthes's *Fashion System* sartorial dispositions appear as the result of relations among clothing styles or fashion codes. For example, a feminine mode of dress may be said to constitute its identity as "feminine" in its relation to and differentiation from masculine clothing styles. Hence the woman in drag re-presents a heretical challenge to the socially regulated and instituted feminine attire deemed appropriate to women. More than an act of resistance to proper gendered sartorial display, social identity here already appears to conform, or not, to the corporeal identity of male and female bodies. This kind of analysis is often done at the expense of understanding the social modes of differentiation informing the symbolic dynamics of the fashion apparatus. When the social mode of differentiation in the gendering of sexed bodies is re-presented as identical or nonidentical with the aesthetic mode of differentiation in clothing styles, a symmetrical balance of identifications is created between socially constructed gender identities and biologically determined bodies. It is a mistake to view this homologous set of relations as a result of cause and effect. Rather, "identity" is compounded by vested interests, the products of differential oppositions within reinforcing and yet mutually discontinuous spheres of gender construction. As Pierre Bourdieu argues, the relational thinking in an analysis of the fashion system is a more or less transformed expression of *social relations*.[26]

In this example, I am speaking about socially regulated gender relations between men and women and among women themselves. Instead of seeking in the fashion system the principles of its dynamics, I suggest we turn to the social conditions of the production of meaning and value that create "fashion" as a site for which and by which "identities" and, in particular, gendered identities may be constituted. Two late twentieth-century "documentary" films, Jennie Livingston's *Paris Is Burning* (1991) and Douglas Keeve's *Unzipped* (1995) use "fashion" — notably fur fashions — to disrupt the early twentieth-century logic of feminine cultural capital as an identifiable position exclusive to female bodies. I want to focus first on Jennie Livingston's documentary on black and Chicano gay youth in New York during the late 1980s, and then, in the next section, on Keeve's documentary about the creative process of an American fashion designer, Isaac Mizrahi.

The Virtual Ontology of a Fur Femme Realness Queen

The title *Paris Is Burning* conjures up an apocalyptic image of a self-destructing city burning under the weight of its civilizing impulse: this isn't South Central L.A. in 1991, nor is this Ralph Ellison's Harlem in *Invisible Man*. This is Paris, a totalizing representation of the world of appearances, of high fashion, of class, of fame, fortune, stardom, and spotlights, a transplanted Hollywood that is even more mythical and more powerful in its mythology for its non-Americanness, for embracing black artists such as Josephine Baker and Charlie "Bird" Parker during the 1940s when America wouldn't. To make Paris burn is to make it sizzle with a consuming desire that plays to the many worlds of sexual, ethnographic, racialized, and commoditized fetishisms.

The film is about the "Balls," an event in which black and Chicano young gay men, representative of their respective "houses," gather to compete within specific "categories" in a display of cross-dressing — dressing across sexual, gender, class, and race boundaries.[27] As one commentator says, "You're crossing into the looking glass. . . . [It] feels 100 percent right . . . not what it's like in the real world. . . . Ball to us is as close to reality as we are going to get to all of that fame, fortune, stardom, and spotlights." The balls are for those who have gone through the looking glass and peer back, amazed at the faces of "self-reflection," those bourgeois individuals who are still staring at the mirror, expecting it to show them something about themselves they don't already know. The documentary dramatizes the condition of postmodernity as a state of disconnection between words and things, between people and images, between meaning and value. On the other side of the looking glass, meaning becomes mimicry, double plays and double-directed voicedness abound, comic and tragic ironies are the discourses of the day. Take the word "Balls" — a signifier that plays on the Queer reconfiguration of a disenfranchised black masculinity and an elite white heterosexual display of wealth and prestige. Or gems of discursive play between sexuality and clothing by Dorian Corey: "It's really a case of going back into the closet." And the exponential irony of such remarks as, "The REAL you look, means, you look like a real woman." The categories flash on the screen in capital letters. REALNESS is one of many categories created at the balls. Dorian Corey explains that realness is being "able to blend. . . . If you can pass the trained eye or un-trained eye and not give away the fact that you're gay that's when it's real. . . . The idea of realness is to look as much as possible like your straight counterpart. . . . The real you look means you look like a real woman or you look like a real man, a straight man. . . . It's not a takeoff or a satire. No, it's actually being able to *be*." On another category, EXECUTIVE REAL-NESS, Corey, a transvestite of the old school and one of the film's best social critics along with Pepper LaBeija, observes:

> In real life you can't get a job as an executive unless you have the educa-tional background and the opportunity. Now, the fact that you're not an executive is merely because of the social standing of life. That's just . . . pure thing. Black people have a hard time getting anywhere and those that do are usually straight. . . .
>
> In a ballroom you can be anything you want. You're not really an ex-ecutive but you're looking like an executive and therefore you're show-ing the straight world that I can be an executive. If I had the opportunity I could be one because I can look like one. And that is like a fulfillment. Your peers, your friends, are telling you, "Oh, you'd make a wonderful executive."

Those who do make it are straight, white, middle-class, physically healthy, and beautiful, and for many of these "LEGENDARY CHILDREN," female.

The test of being a FEMME REALNESS QUEEN, says Corey, is "when you're undetectable, when they can walk out of the ballroom, into the sun-light and onto the subway and get home and still have all their clothes and no blood running off their body. Those are the femme realness queens. And usually it's a category for young queens." A femme realness queen, Venus Xtravaganza, tells us why she wants to be a white, straight, bourgeois woman:

> I would like to be a spoiled rich white girl. They get what they want, whenever they want it. And they don't have to really struggle with fi-nances, and nice things, and nice clothes, and they don't have to have that as a problem. . . . I don't feel that there is anything mannish about me except maybe what I might have between . . . down there, which is my little personal thing. So, I guess, that's why I want my sex change to make myself complete.

That being like a real woman constitutes realness is an irony of expo-nential proportions. Are we to read this as naive biologism or essential-ism? After all, "woman" is a construct, and one whose constructedness is often demonstrated by her narcissism, her embodiment of the world of appearances. As in René Magritte's painting *The Philosophy of the Bedroom*,

FIGURE 27. *Presence through Absence*, Arinia Ailincai, detail of installation, Banff (1994).
Reproduced by permission of Arinia Ailincai.

women's bodies figure as costumes, appear as ephemeral, as trivial, as superficial as fashion itself. And as in Arina Ailincai's installation *Presence through Absence*, the re-presentation of the nothingness of woman — a nothingness aided by a sartorial disguise that interchangeably writes "woman" as "object-of-desire" — is emptied of its hollow meanings (see Figure 27).

Similarly, what is being mimicked, if not mocked, by Venus Xtravaganza?[28] Is her transgendering and transvestism a conjuring of the reality of "woman" or the reality of the condition of her virtual ontology as a simulated figure who re-presents, symbolically, the symbolic power of a virtual existence?[29] Pepper LaBeija, at least, has the presence of mind to note that "having a vagina doesn't mean you are going to have a fabulous life — it could be worse!"

VOGUE-ING is one means by which the virtual world of appearances receives artistic expression. Like break-dancing in the late seventies, vogue-ing is a performative mode of warfare done in dance.[30] Vogue-ing is a spin-off from giving SHADE, which is a takeoff from READING. Reading and giving shade involve finding a flaw in your opponent and exaggerating it. Dorian Corey explains that "vogue-ing came from shade, a dance two people did with each other because they didn't like each other. You would dance it out on the dance floor and whoever throws the better moves . . . " In his demonstration of VOGUE-ING, Willy Ninja performs "a pantomime form of a vogue," as he calls it. "This is what generally sometimes I do is I make my hand into a form like a compact or makeup kit and I'm beating my face with blush, shadow, or whatever to the music. Then, usually, I'll turn the compact around to face that person, meaning like — almost like — my hand is a mirror for them to get a look, and I'll start doing their face because what they have on their face right now needs a dramatic makeup job. . . . So, vogue-ing is like a safe form of throwing shade." The dance moves involve striking poses taken from fashion magazine photographs. The movement of the arms is angular as if the dancer is photographically framing his own face at the juncture of every still pose.[31] In vogue-ing the feminine fashion apparatus serves a function in the war of aesthetics. To make the style war work, however, you've just got to be a woman.

The link between femme and furs is an ongoing theme throughout the documentary, exploited for its powerful ideological strength as a "natural-ized" example of wealth, prestige, and femininity. At the beginning of the film, there is an image from a fashion magazine of a man embracing a woman dressed in a blue-dyed fur. In a final image, one of many that cuts through the text of the credits, there is a shot of a man leaving the ballroom in daylight, dressed in a fur and carrying a large trophy onto the street. Between the still frame and the moving image fur emerges in several con-texts as a symbol of the contested terrain of gender dissymmetry:

1. Following a discourse on the military theme, the commentator says, "The more natural you are the more credit your outfit is given." An image of a man in fur, looking, naturally, like a woman, appears, a disconnected scene between the categories of military wear and high-fashion evening wear in which a discussion on the evening bag as an essential accessory is

taking place. Here again we see an extraordinary juxtapostion of the symbolic dialectic between war and fashion. The image flashes across the scene as part of a montage series, its meaning constructed in the juxtaposition of the discourse on the natural and the essentials of evening wear.

2. Pepper LaBeija, mother of the House of LaBeija, tells an origin story about his mother and the painful birth of his own transvestism. In a parodic imitation of his mother's voice, which is only slightly perceptible in his own oral performance but present enough to throw the listener into a moment of dislocation, a reminder that his mimicry has its roots in someone else's domestication and dissimulation, Pepper recalls how "she burnt up a mink coat. . . . I stood there and cried like a baby. . . . She don't want me in no girl's clothes. She can't take it."

3. Dorian Corey describes the competitive spirit of the balls as a "war on the floor." Livingston juxtaposes Corey's discourse on the warlike spirit of the balls with an example of a style war. A man in fur is walking the ballroom floor as a man in fur. A heated dispute breaks out when someone tells the emcee that he's wearing a woman's fur coat. Corey explains: "He looked like he had on a man's fox coat. Someone came up to the emcee and told him it was woman's coat. I thought it was kind of silly. Nit-picky." We see the man in fur arguing that the clasp is on the right side. Being a man in fur is clearly risky business. Did the style war ensue from the man's incorrect use of a woman's fur coat or was it the very wearing of a fur coat by a man, and not a man looking like a woman, that was the problem? Did the naturalness of his representation produce an odd sort of backlash in that "naturalness" is "real" only when the fiction of creating the natural is clearly delineated. In other words, a black man in a fur coat cuts too close to the bone, conjuring up the stereotypical racist image of the black pimp in popular TV cop shows. If you are going to be natural, you had better create the necessary boundary between the parody and the stereotype, you had better engage a denaturalizing figure rather than one that reinscribes the ideological function of making natural, canonic, fixed and binding.[32]

4. Final words of the emcee: "Okay, WINTER SPORTS WEAR, preferably fur but if not, you know in error you can — natural fibers — if you choose the polyester, God help you, you know how the children are. . . . " Natural fibers, the threads of the wealthy, polyester, the threads of the poor, the working class, the dispossessed. Fur is the ultimate natural fiber. It's what, in the well-known slogan from *Blackgama*, "becomes a legend most."

That femininity is a source of symbolic agency worth the time, energy, and MOPPING (i.e., stealing) to acquire comes across clearly in the voices of Octavia St. Laurent and Willy Ninja. Octavia is a transsexual who wants to be a female model. She wants "to be wealthy, a somebody, a rich somebody." Willy Ninja works part time giving modeling lessons to the young women of Harlem. He wants "to bring femininity back and bring some grace and poise . . . to make women more attractive to men." This goal is especially important because "if she's in a man's world, she can still have her equal rights but be able to manipulate a man with her feminine wiles." What these remarks and the example of Venus Xtravaganza tell us is that femininity is a powerful symbolic tool in the hands of women. In the hands of women, that is, as READ by men. This READING operates as a kind of mis-reading. On the one hand, the competitive spirit of the dancing style wars functions as a critical misreading that can be directed toward denaturalizing the symbolic capital invested in haute couture. On the other hand, READING femininity reproduces the ideological blindness of the female gender as an immutable mystery that magically attracts fame, fortune, money, and wash-ing machines. The latter misreading is a function of ideological violence, and the former reproduces symbolic violence in order to disenfranchise the ideological of its power to control symbolically what is natural and, hence, unchangeable. And yet these men who become "woman" must undergo some extraordinary corporeal changes. The realness of the body stands as the final horizon of the self-made man-cum-woman.

Paris Is Burning brings its narrative to a close with knowledge of Venus Xtravaganza's murder, Willy Ninja's successful debut in a Malcolm Mac-Laren (of Sex Pistols fame) video, and a high-profile Love Ball to raise money for the homeless who have AIDS. The Love Ball is framed by Liv-ingston with television news broadcasts and sound bites of famous New Yorkers such as Fran Liebowitz praising the ball. The balls have reached the apex of their commoditization with Madonna's video, "Vogue," and the not-so-surprising-by-now ironic use of the ball as an act of social welfare.

There are at least two ways to MISREAD *Paris Is Burning*. One possibility is to see the competition of the balls as representing the unlimited free market of consumable identities. It is as if participants such as Willy Ninja and Venus Xtravaganza believe in the bourgeois ideology of the free market with its unrestricted flow of commodities, allowance for the free play of ideas, and the "unprincipled principle" of a truly open society of unlimited exchange of things.[33] The postmodern condition of late capitalism extends the possibilities of trade to the free play of identities and the unlimited exchange of libidinal interests circulating in the corporeal status of the body — the body, the key figure of transvaluation across the lines of iden-tifiable oppressions: race, gender, sexuality, and class. "Woman" comes to figure as the privileged site of exchange, her body easily transvaluated across the restricted boundaries of class, gender, sexuality, and race. And new forms of ideological containment appear in the "categories" and the "houses." In the competition for what constitutes the performance art of everyday life, in which are included the bourgeois arts of haute couture, the balls take up a position within this field of cultural production and success-fully expand it to include an artistic re-presentation of the bourgeois com-moditization of identity, of personal style, of virtual ontologies such as "executive realness" and the "femme realness queen." Symbolic capital is demystified and yet redirected and relocated from the realm of business to the realm of high-fashion aesthetics. In Harlem, then, the fetishisms of an alienated bourgeoisie become the virtual realities of dispossessed black and Chicano gay youth. This is their world, so disconnected from the so-called real one that its reality is alive with the intensities of a continual making, a becoming that has nothing left to lose but to create another world. In other words, we can see this phenomenon as only ever, in the final instance, compensatory.

The other possibility is to find the fleeting transformative power that bleeds from the filmic re-presentations of a fictional world more alive than the living. Another way to misread the documentary is to say we are left with something of a hoax couture, a body speaking in someone else's clothes. In contrast to the stylized aestheticism of haute couture, this pa-rodic hoax couture introduces into that signifying apparatus a semiotic in-tention that is directly opposed to the original one. Hoax couture, having made its house in the other's style, clashes violently with its primordial host and forces it to serve directly opposing aims. Couture becomes an arena of battle, a style war between two bodies differentiated by class, by gender, by race, and by sexuality. In other words, the balls are a grand stunt, a terrific hoax, that doesn't simply play to a mimetic fallacy of desire for the lives of the rich and famous, but underscores precisely the ideological modes of manipulation and control which ensure the lack of access to the free market and the unrestricted flow of commoditized identities. Being gay, being a woman, being black, being poor — these can only ever function as virtual ontologies in the world of REAL (as in restricted) ONTOLOGICAL LEGITI-MACY, the world of straight white upper-class men and women.

During the 1980s, the urban dispossessed represented in Livingston's documentary responded to the rise of symbolic powers invested under Reagan's government by both exposing and appropriating these "illegiti-mate" powers.[34] I want to compare Livingston's politics of symbolic appro-priation on the side of the "underclass" (much like the demonstration of anxiety in British medieval sumptuary legislation to control lower-class ap-propriation of the signs of power, prestige, and commodity wealth) with the symbolic appropriation by Isaac Mizrahi of the signs and symbols of the dispossessed.

Animals Who Control the Means of Producing Reality

Unzipped is a self-conscious documentary that in both its content and form recalls an originary moment in silent motion picture documentary film history, *Nanook of the North* (1922) (see Figures 28 and 29). *Unzipped* is shot largely in black and white, sometimes unfocused, with a highly grainy visual texture. A few scenes, most notably the fashion show sequence, are shot in color. As in the silent motion picture, captions appear on the screen to mark transitions in the narrative. The film opens with shots of Mizrahi on the street walking to the local newspaper stand to read reviews of his 1993 spring fashion show. The first three captions read: "Isaac Mizrahi is a fashion designer." "He has just shown his spring 1994 [*sic*] collection." "This is the story of how the next collection gets made." The reviews are devastatingly bad. Mizrahi appears as a tragic hero, gazing out on the street from the fire escape of his New York apartment, hating the mediocrity of the criticisms directed toward his show.

The film is about "process." Its educational component — if there is one — is to help the unknowing viewer gain a certain measure of cultural competence in how the fashion industry sews the creativity of the fashion designer into the larger fabric of fashion's industrial demands to produce a high-profile seasonal fashion show that will sell "the product." The fashion industry itself invested in the film, produced by Hachette Filipacchi Productions and *Elle*, the fashion magazine. Douglas Keeve directs the film. His recollection of the silent film documentary format is an inspired formal device that takes its point of departure from Mizrahi's own narrative of creative inspiration for his next fashion show. Under the caption "Nanook," Mizrahi is shown watching a video of *Nanook of the North* on his TV. To complete the picture, Mizrahi is talking into a telephone and explaining his viewing experience. Creativity flows on electromagnetic waves through the telephone wires, and camera recording, communication, and a sense of an industrial community are woven into a circular stream of particles and words.

It's so amazing, isn't it? So inspiring. I can't even believe how beautiful all these Eskimos are. And I love it . . . all those fur pants. And the thing is, all I want to do is fur pants. But I know if I do them I'll get stoned off of 7th Avenue. Like some kind of wanton heretic or something. So there won't be any fur pants coming down my runway. It's about women not wanting to look like cows I guess. You know and in fact, there is something very charming about cows, but, anyway, well you know what I mean, there is something very charming about a big fat fur pant. . . . Actually there was one thing I wanted to do which was a fur jumpsuit.

A wandering ice field drifts in from sea and locks up a hundred miles of coast. Though Nanook's band, already on the thin edge of starvation, is unable to move, Nanook, great hunter that he is, saves the day.

FIGURE 28. Photographic stills from *Nanook of the North* (1922). Reproduced by permission of International Film Seminars.

While the angered herd
snorts defiance, the
mate of the harpooned
walrus comes to the
rescue -- attempts to
lock horns and pull
the captive free.

FIGURE 29. Photographic stills from *Nanook of the North* (1922).
Reproduced by permission of International Film Seminars.

Like the Banana Splits. Those big. . . . I would love to have one of those in beast's fur. To walk the dog in. You don't have to think about anything. You just have your bra and panties on. You just put this giant fur jumpsuit on, head to toe, hood and little hush puppy boots. You're out walking the dog. And looking amazing. Surprising everyone in your neighborhood. Which in this case would be the Upper East Side or Alaska (laughs).

Mizrahi explains how he works: "Here's my process. I get inspired somehow, somewhere, from the ballet, from dance, from a movie. I get this gesture in my head and then I think, is this worthy of doing a whole collection. And usually it is, because it's the only thing I can think of. And from there I just do all these millions of sketches about that one gesture." For Mizrahi, the best part of this process is "creating a look" and not the "show" which gets to be irritating because it's like a giant jigsaw puzzle whose pieces must be fitted together. The expression — "to create a look" — is the textual equivalent of the epistemological game Mizrahi plays at; it's all about looking, about the fashion designer as a "cultural reader," observing her or his world and picking out pieces and fragments that are themselves acts of looking brought together to form "a look" in the colloquial language of fashion. A variety of cultural codes inform Mizrahi's narrative process: cultural tokens such as *Nanook of the North*, directed by Robert Flaherty and chosen by the American Academy of Film as one of the ten most important films to be preserved in perpetuity; mainstream Hollywood narrative cinema such as *Call of the Wild*, *The Red Shoes*, *Valley of the Dolls*, *Marnie*, and *What Ever Happened to Baby Jane?*; television serials such as *The Mary Tyler Moore Show* and *The Flintstones*; popular cultural references to Mick Jagger, Snow White; high-brow references to the romantic ballet *Giselle*, and a mixed bag of musical references including Debussy, Beethoven, Eartha Kitt, and theme songs from *That Girl* and *The Mary Tyler Moore Show*. The social context also shapes Mizrahi's "creative process," but as something that impinges upon his creativity and which is noted largely with contempt: "And the thing is, all I want to do is fur pants. But I know if I do them I'll get stoned off of 7th Avenue. Like some kind of wanton heretic or something. So there won't be any fur pants coming down my runway." Polly Mellon, creative director of *Allure* magazine comments on the "political correctness" of Mizrahi's fake sable coat; Mizrahi discusses with the vice-president of Mizrahi and Company, Nina Santisi, the difficulties of building a scrim for his show; a side comment is made about some "scary union thing" and fears of the press. The media, working conditions, political activism impress themselves on Mizrahi's "creative process," as do the symbolic brokers of the fashion industry, allegorized by figures such as

André Léon Talley, creative director of *Vogue*; Gilles Bensimon, creative director of *Elle*; Polly Mellon, creative director of *Allure*; Ingrid Sischy, fashion writer for the *New Yorker* and editor-in-chief of *Interview*; and the supermodels Kate Moss, Cindy Crawford, Naomi Campbell, Linda Evangelista, and Christy Turlington. Fashion history enters Mizrahi's frames of reference when he visits the costume archives of the Louvre and discovers an eighteenth-century fake fur made of silk, and a corset made of steel and worn with linen that will be incorporated into one of his designs. Last, but not least, clips from home movies and Mizrahi's mother give us insight into the domestic forces that have shaped his creativity and self-expression.

Whereas Mizrahi's initial inspiration is *Nanook of the North*, it is mainstream Hollywood narrative cinema — *The Call of the Wild* — that clinches the fold in his creativity:

> Fifties cheesecake meets (like) Eskimo (kind-of-like-just) crazy fake fur. Very glamorous kind of thing. And I was watching *Call of the Wild* last year and (you know) there's a scene in that movie where (you know) she's kinda abandoned by her husband because she's on the tundra. He goes off looking for food and eventually dies. (And you know) Clark Gable discovers her after (like you know) four days of being frost bitten (you know) and nearly dead. And, of course, when the close-up happens, the make-up is perfect, dewy skin, perfect eyebrows, lip-liner, the hair is (you know) perfection. And I'm thinking if you must freeze on the Tundra, this is the way to do it (you know). So, I made a big note in my book, in my notebook, *Call of the Wild*.

Cutting across the bias of the narrative film, Mizrahi freezes an image and extracts its quintessential performative surrealism. Similarly, the documentary film mimics this moment of cultural reading by showing the viewer the clip in question. Clark Gable and another man find the near frozen body. The other man asks, "Is he dead?" Gable turns the body over to show her perfectly made-up face and responds, "No, he isn't dead, and he isn't a 'he.'" Why does this striking cosmetological epiphany engulfed in fur trigger for Mizrahi, in his own words, a desire for a collection in which the "textures are sort of beastly"? I think that the call of the wild screams for Mizrahi in the beastliness of this ambiguous moment of gender disidentification where "wildness" constitutes a transgressive performativity of gender (the outrageous perfection of a woman's makeup) cagily enclosed by fur, an object of supranatural wildness. The difference between the wild and the domestic, and correlative animal-human relations, is sexual transgression.

The theme of sexual transgression, of gender disidentification, which runs wildly throughout the film is always articulated through agents who embody categories of social reidentification, or domestication, such as "race," "femininity," "orientalism," and "colonial exoticism." Under the caption, *Kitty and Candy*, Mizrahi visits Eartha Kitt, who plays with one of her poodles, named, it would seem, Sheherazade. The scene with Eartha Kitt is cut through with scenes of Mizrahi recounting his meeting with her to someone in his studio, imitating her voice and gestures. During the course of his interview, Kitt launches into a spontaneous performance of a pseudo-oriental dance and song. She belly-dances, wildly vocalizing an orientalist rhythm and sounds that could be identified as an imitation of Arabic phonetics. Her dog growls in the background, adding to the spontaneous wildness of the scene. Several displacements occur through the agency of mimicry: Eartha Kitt imitating orientalist music and dance, Mizrahi imitating Kitt imitating Orson Welles who once bit her on the neck and drew blood because "he got excited." What Mizrahi clearly likes about Kitt is her positive feminine sexuality. He refers to her book *Eartha Kitt: Confessions of a Sex Kitten*, and the viewer is treated to a snippet of a younger Eartha Kitt performing the song "Santa Baby." This pro-sex discourse on feminine sexuality is constituted by an orientalist exoticism in the body of a black female performer. Mizrahi's extraordinary blend of supernatural romanticism and trans/pro-sexuality is dramatized in a skit in which he plays out his encounter with a Ouija Board, which spelled the words "sexy, sexy, dominatrix mixed with Hitchcock, *Marnie*, Mick Jagger, Ouija likes boys at night." "You mean Mick Jagger?" asks Candy Pratts, the fashion director of *Vogue*, who is listening incredulously to this story. "Dominatrix shoes for day, flats for nights." "It works!" claims Mizrahi.[35]

Mizrahi has an acute sense of the political implications of words. When a friend sees the supermodel Naomi Campbell in a fuzzy fake-fur jacket and comments that "it's kind of simian," Mizrahi corrects him, "It's beastly more than simian." It is sexual wildness that Mizrahi is after, not the animalization of women's bodies but a sexual wildness that exists side by side with growling poodles and wild animals. But when the sexually transgressive homoerotic gesture or the pro-sex feminine gesture becomes the only exciting and creatively stimulating moment of a possible cultural, political, and social change in which questions of racism, sexism, and class are subsumed under the libidinal economy of an erotic and exotic wildness, we might well wonder what ideological machinations are afoot that might dissolve the subversive politics of symbolic power into a dominant politics of symbolic appropriation — mostly notably of the "Eskimo" — which, in the final instance, makes money for the fashion industry:

I know what I want to discuss this morning . . . are those embroideries . . . of . . . (um) Eskimos. 'Cause these are simple. These are just going to be put into . . . work . . . and boom, they're done. It's like a [tool? . . .] with a long pony skin skirt. It looks like an Eskimo. I just don't want it to resemble at all those Indian things. And it shouldn't because it doesn't.

The politics of cultural differences do not escape Mizrahi. Other contradictions between his political awareness and the demands of the fashion industry surface. When he has trouble getting hold of some basic corduroy and flannel, he remarks: "It's like I'm asking for some extinct animal skins." When a model informs him about the political implications of the word "Eskimo," he responds, "I didn't know 'Eskimo' was a slur. It means fish-eater, or something." He makes a joke about his own Jewish identity and eating fish.

The cultural politics of fashion as understood by fashion industry critics themselves produce an interesting irony in the film. During a fitting for Mizrahi's show, the supermodel Christy Turlington comments on Jean Paul Gaultier's recent show in which he combined "a punk and Hasidic look." Following this clip, a taped commentary appears with Ingrid Sischy. She says:

> I didn't hear anybody booing, but I certainly heard afterwards, "Oh, my god, Gaultier's gone too far. Now he's done a thing about Hasidic Jews. And people are gonna (you know), Jews are going to be upset. People are going to say (you know) this is a sacred thing." And I completely, completely disagree. I think that what was so fantastic about it, and what's so fantastic about Gaultier, is that he incorporates politics and culture into his fashion.
>
> I think to take something that none of us understands necessarily and mix it up and incorporate it into the culture and show all sorts of different people wearing it, is a way of removing strife. And I think that that was really great. I think that what one sees in Isaac's collections (you know) in a way he sort of does the same thing. He doesn't do it with that subject. But he picks on subjects. He picks on subjects that [for] so many of us are part of life. . . . (You know) his last collection when he did the divorcee and the Hollywood thing. I think to build content into fashion is where fashion is at.

Gaultier is well known for participating in cultural debates where the issue of dress and its political and social symbolic meanings are at issue. For example, in spring 1990 he produced an image of a young woman dressed in the Muslim headscarf, the *hijeb*, following an intense debate in France over whether high school girls should be allowed to wear the *hijeb*.[36] Weeks before Mizrahi's April fashion show an edition of *Women's Wear Daily Beauty*

FIGURE 30. "Gaultier: Eskimo Chic" (1994). Reproduced from *Women's Wear Daily*, 4 March 1994, by permission. "Paris—Nanook of the North had nothing on Jean Paul Gaultier, who's preparing an Eskimo-themed 'trans-Siberian' collection, complete with dramatic real and fake pelts. Here, from the collection he'll show Sunday night, his white inverted sheepskin jacket with a fake-fur lined hood and black and white silk skirt-pants."

Report comes out with a cover preview story on Gaultier's upcoming show. The title reads, "Gaultier: Eskimo Chic," and shows an image of an "Eskimo" woman dressed in "authentic" fur gear (see Figure 30). Mizrahi has been "*Nanooked*"! Has Gaultier stolen Mizrahi's idea? The film does not answer the question.[37]

The unfairness of the competitive capitalist structure of the fashion industry is almost enough to make one forget about all the modes of cultural appropriation, racism, and sexism that pervade, in a contradictory fashion, Mizrahi's "creative process" or bourgeois consciousness. We can all "read the world," but can we read it "critically"? At times yes, and certainly Mizrahi does. In comparison to Gaultier's unabashed appropriation of the image of the "Eskimo woman" and so-called "Eskimo" fashion, Mizrahi's approach to anti-fur activism is to recreate the cultural difference of fur's significance for the Inuit in the cultural and political space of the urban metropolis: he creates fake furs and "a look" that self-consciously mimics an ideology of cultural difference. But his motivation is socially and sexually transgressive, designed to take pleasure in the creative force of disengendering the conventions of sexual difference.

Furs in Disguise

Fine furs are born — not made.

    The Romance of Furs (1936)

*Fetishisms, like the grain of sand in the oyster that produces the pearl,
create social and sexual constructions of things at intractable points
that trouble the social or sexual psyche. If these constructs can be
identified and understood to be symptomatic, their signifiers mark the
delicate points where society and its consciousness lose touch. These are
points where relations between people are liable to become relations
between things.*

    Laura Mulvey, *Fetishism and Curiosity*

*The original inhabitants of the Americas, Australasia and many
other huge areas of the world have suffered an appalling and vicious
colonialism. The surviving aboriginal societies, however, are not
frozen in some archaic condition, but are our contemporaries. Their
existences may be different, but they are modern; they live now,
and — like us, like everyone — have to make accommodations
between their pasts and their present. And if only we could break
out of our political and imaginative constraints, if only we could shed
the monopolistic belief in what might be called United Soviet Man,
then we would see, hear and accept the peoples of the fourth world as
modern societies with their own histories.*

    Hugh Brody, *Maps and Dreams*

In response to increasing pressure from animal rights and welfare organizations to stop fur trapping and the rise of fur farms in newly industrializing countries, such as South Korea, the mainstream fashion industry adjusted its representation of fur in terms of clothing styles, advertising, and fashion spreads in magazines. In September 1992 the *New York Times Magazine* featured a fashion spread titled "Furs in Disguise." [1] Fake furs and "disguised furs" became the vogue as consumers of fashion were given new modes of representation to maintain their access to this luxury good. Furs were disguised, dyed and cut to foreground their "artificiality" as well as to create the illusion that fur resembled fabric — could be woven, textured, and patterned (see Figure 31). The techniques of disguise masked the use of real fur and further abstracted the product from its association with the central anti-fur referent, the fur-bearing animal.

A brief survey of fur fashion spreads in the London *Vogue* magazine from 1984 to 1992 clearly shows a dialogue between anti-fur activism and fur or non-fur fashions. Traditionally, London *Vogue* includes a major fur fashion spread sometime in the months of September, October, or November. These spreads remained quite spectacular well through the early 1980s. In 1989, however, the effects of the anti-fur protest were registered. There was no major spread in the November issue, only minor visual references to accessories, all in fake fur. Fur manufacturers were still advertising in this issue, but there were fewer advertisements than in previous years. In the September issue of 1989, a fashion spread titled "Animal Expressionism" incorporated the pro-animal impulse of the anti-fur activism — "Splashy animal energy unleashed from the studios of London's untamed talents" — thus both drawing on the attack on fur and shifting the pro-animal discourse into the realm of the wild, the savage, the bestial and instinctual. If animal power constituted the new direction, the fashion industry was ready to take up the challenge. [2]

In the December 1990 issue several animal stories appeared. "Now you see them . . . Andrew Powell on the Great Safari Debate" combines the exoticism of African animals with a "politically correct" gesture on the threat of the safari industry to wild animals. A caption reads: "The new animal magic: will the animals or the safari industry disappear first? Here, wild animals in the Masai Mara, Kenya." [3] The resurgence of fake leopard and zebra-skin scarves, furnishings, and clothes in "Animal Expressionism" suggests that such images honor the animals threatened by the safari industry. Another feature article in this issue reproduces a selection of cartoon animals from Andy Warhol's *Colouring Book*. [4] Children of the rich and famous were asked to color in Warhol's outlines of strangely personable animal characters, in a gesture that underlies the infantile association Western

Is it fabric, or is it fur? Patterned in a loose 'crochet weave' or 'printed' in a bold plaid, this fur is cast as cloth.

A mesh of mink overlays a cashmere swing coat (with matching mink scarf wrapped around top hat) from Maximilian Alta Moda, $12,500. At Maximilian fur salon at Bloomingdale's. Ankle boots from Fendi. Hose from Ralph Lauren Hosiery. Top hat by Patricia Underwood.

60

STYLIST: HARRIET MAYS. HAIR: JOE MCDEVITT FOR PIERRE MICHEL SALON. MAKEUP: KERRY WARN. MODEL: LUDMILA.

FIGURE 31. "Furs in Disguise" (1992).
Reproduced from the *New York Times Magazine*, 27 September 1992, by permission of the photographer, Paul Lange. © 1992 by the New York Times Co. Reprinted by permission.

culture makes when fictionalizing the humanlike animal creature. In a further rendition of liberal correctness, another article, titled "The Sublime and the Beautiful: Rare Breeds," features a lament for the demise of small farms and with it the diversity of animal breeds because of corporate standardization:

> Where have all our beautiful animals gone? Why has rationalism conquered aestheticism *again*? Where is the mystery and the sublimity in our farmyards and our lives? We do not want to see only white chickens and pink pigs, we want a variety on which to feast the eye. We have grown tired of the ubiquitous corporate imagery which has spread through our towns and cities, the Tescos, the McDonalds and the BHSs, whose angrily demanding logos invade our private vision and render each high street identical. We have also grown tired of the black and white Friesian cow which has multiplied in hundreds of thousands to populate every field beside the railway and every meadow beside the road. Both the shops with their standardised products and the homogenous hornless cows with their high and watery milk yield have taken an invasive hold of our vision for the same simple reason: to generate the maximum amount of lucre for their owners. This is not a sin. It is just dead boring on the eye of the beholder. Soon we will not be able to bear it. We will have a revolution. We will have to put the small family businesses back in the high streets. . . . Our once instinctive relationship with the country, rusticity, nature and pastoralism has become sanitised, clinical and form-filling.[5]

If the anti-fur rhetoric cuts too close to the bone of fur fashion advertisers and fashion magazines in general, concern for animals can certainly be incorporated into the colonial nostalgia for Africa (a well-worn theme in magazines such as *Vogue* since the 1930s) or into the domestic inscription of the idyllic world of the country gentry and domestic animals and their mutually supportive concern for breeding. The 1990 November issue has no fur spread and only one or two advertisements; one of them, by Philip Hockley, shows a woman in a fur coat and running shoes, taking a furtive glance over her shoulder. Is she meant to be a working woman en route to or from work in her serviceable running shoes and fur coat? Or is it that women who still choose to wear fur must learn to run, especially from spray paint?

The fashion spread "Furs in Disguise" and the selection of animal visuals and stories represent strategic responses to conflicting symbolic and material interests in fur and fur-bearing animals. In 1991 the Fur Council of Canada enlisted D'Arcy Moses, a member of the Gitksan nation of northern British Columbia and commercially successful fur fashion designer based in Montreal, to produce fur coats with aboriginal designs. Commenting on his talents as a fashion designer who "works motifs from his native heritage into his designs," a representative of Industry, Trade, and Technology Canada, explains that Moses is "exploring his own roots and native traditions and finding ways to fit that into fashion."[6] Tailoring their cultural heritage to the needs of the Canadian fur trade, as producers and more recently designers, First Nations are made to figure as a seamless authenticity with which to legitimate the continuing economic policies of the colonial state government. That aboriginal trappers and designers may in fact be fitting these colonial based industries into their own cultural strategies for survival remains unaddressed. It is also possible to see Moses skillfully turning the current field of contestation to his advantage by strategically renegotiating the symbolic dimension of the fur coat by incorporating designs and motifs from the Gitksan while also supporting indigenous fur trappers and traders by using their furs. Nevertheless, the Canadian government and its almost half-a-billion-dollar-a-year fur industry profited from the symbolic value of First Nations designs. Who, in their politically correct mind, would accost a bourgeois women wearing fur with First Nations designs on it?

"Traditional" Fur Fashions (?)

In 1995 and 1996 the Museum of Civilization in Ottawa held an Inuit fashion show in conjunction with "Winterlude," an annual series of events put on by the city and designed to break the tedium of winter, with its mind-numbing cold. The Inuit fashion shows suggest a different kind of response to the politics of cultural difference and contribute another dimension to the cultural politics of fur and fashion. In 1995 the show was part of a larger event devoted to Inuit culture called "Qaggiq," a "celebration of the Inuit culture and tradition." Qaggiq was coordinated by the Inuit Art Foundation, Inuit Broadcasting Corporation, and the Makivik Corporation in collaboration with the Canadian Museum of Civilization (see Figures 32–34).[7]

In 1996 a news release described a fashion show of "traditional and contemporary Inuit clothing, choreographed by Alejandro Ronciera, and sponsored by Pauktuutit, the Inuit Women's Association."[8] This Inuit fashion show was called, in English, "Sanajavut: Our Creations." Seven Inuit women form the core of designers for the show, June Klengenberg from the eastern arctic region of Coppermine, Kitikmeot; Martha Adams and Charlotte St. John, both from the Keewatin area on the west side of Hudson's Bay; Victoria Grey from Kuujjuag, in Nunavik; Lean Wolkie and Annie

Bowkett from the western arctic; and Nellie Winters from Makkovik, the northern tip of Labrador (see Figures 35–37).

The 1996 Inuit fashion show did not conform to the conventions of a mainstream fashion show. The choreographed performance wove cultural activities of hunting, drum dancing, and throat chanting into the display of fashions. Also, groups or pairs of models appeared together, as opposed to the display of an individual model and article of fashion in mainstream fashion shows. These aspects of the performance provided social contexts in which to read the significance of the caribou-skin parkas, cloth parkas trimmed with fur, beaded amautiit (women's parkas), caribou-skin pants and sealskin or caribou-skin boots. The symbolic values attributed to clothing styles are multiple and diverse among the Inuit. They also vary historically in relation to the use of different and changing technologies and high-tech fabrics, as described by Judy Hall, Jill Oakes, and Sally Quimmiu'naaq Webster:

> Inuit now use combinations of traditional and southern-style garments to convey group affiliation, gender, age, role, status, social organization, interaction with neighbouring groups, and changing technology. Regional variations between Copper and Caribou Inuit are less obvious than in the past. Although specific stylistic features, communication

FIGURE 33. Inuit fur fashions, *Qaggiq* (1995).
© Canadian Museum of Civilization, photograph by S. Darby.

FIGURE 34. Inuit fur fashions, *Qaggiq* (1995).
© Canadian Museum of Civilization, photograph by S. Darby.

FIGURE 35. Inuit fur fashions, *Sanajavut* (1996).
© Canadian Museum of Civilization, photograph by S. Darby.

cues, fashion, and materials have changed, clothing still plays an important role at dances, on special occasions, and for jobs. The function of Inuit clothing remains the same: serving as a means of attraction, adornment, communication, and protection (spiritual and physical). Contemporary Inuit clothing provides an intriguing unwritten essay reflecting the social, economic, and technological changes to which Inuit have adapted over the last generation.[9]

Clothing styles as marks of political affiliation, which I noted in the struggle between Puritans and Cavaliers in seventeenth-century England, also play a role in First Nations politics: "At meetings with federal government officials and Dene land-claims organizations, Inuit quietly proclaimed their ethnicity and ties to the land through clothing. Inuit men from the central and eastern Arctic chose undecorated, waterproof sealskin boots. These plain black boots symbolize the negotiator's status as a hunter with expert knowledge of natural resources. Only hunters need waterproof boots today; other members of the community wear rubber boots in wet weather and more elaborately decorated skin boots in cold weather or on special occasions."[10] The symbolic dimension of Inuit fashions must be foregrounded because too often the assumption is that such clothing functions solely in a utilitarian manner and indeed lacks the signifying capacities already associated with "Western dress." Too often contemporary Inuit fashions are

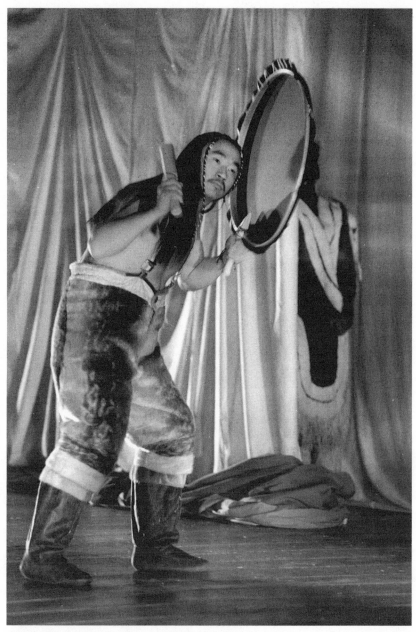

FIGURE 36. Inuit fur fashions, *Sanajavut* (1996).
© Canadian Museum of Civilization, photograph by S. Darby.

FIGURE 37. Inuit fur fashions, *Sanajavut* (1996).
© Canadian Museum of Civilization, photograph by S. Darby.

reduced to "an intriguing unwritten essay reflecting [as opposed to incorporating or producing] the social, economic, and technological changes to
which Inuit have adapted [or contributed] over the last generation." Not
only do Inuit clothing styles require an ability to read their meanings and
values, and therefore constitute a mode of "writing" more broadly understood than the limited notion of roman orthographies, but the Inuit fashion
show, given its location in the Museum of Civilization, initiates a dialogue
with how such institutions have previously confined the values and meanings attributed to Inuit clothing styles.

The museum, writes Douglas Crimp, is an "institution of confinement"
not unlike other modern institutions analyzed by Foucault, such as the asy-
lum, the clinic, and the prison.[11] The corresponding discursive formations
of madness, illness, and criminality are also analogous, according to Crimp,
to the formation and professionalization of the discipline of art history.
The museum can be said to produce a discourse of aesthetics, a grammar
of values and meanings constitutive of the making of art works. But the

apparent coherence of aesthetic judgments, produced upon a metamorphosis of the spatial frontiers of concrete buildings into an abstract reasoning of categories, taxonomies, and classifications, is nothing more than a conjuror's trick, an illusion of confidence in mirrors and trap doors that, when disassembled, reveal the simplicity of empty space filled with virtually meaningless junk. The positive science of artistic categorization — what is and is not art — can be read into and against the semiotics of the museum's or gallery's floor plan, which denotes a devolution to a point of origin, an archaeological or authentic moment in history, usually found under the name of "primitive art" of one sort of another, depending on your classical or paleolithic preferences.

Fashion history texts, when they subscribe to a developmental logic in style, almost always cite a point of origin in the bodily covering of "primitives." Here is James Laver, writing about the origins of clothing:

> The early civilizations of Egypt and Mesopotamia are far from being the whole story. Within recent years a much more primitive documentation has become available, largely owing to the discovery and study of cave paintings. Geologists have made us aware of a succession of Ice Ages when the climate of a large part of Europe was extremely cold. Even in the last of the Palaeolithic cultures (that is, cultures in which tools and weapons were made by chipping hard stones like flints) life was lived, as it were, on the edge of the great glaciers which covered much of the continent. In such circumstances, although details of clothing may have been determined by social and psychological considerations, the main motive in covering the body was to keep out the cold, since nature had proved so niggardly in providing *homo sapiens* with a natural coat of fur.[12]

Utilitarian values are often attributed to aboriginal cultures, and often this attribution conforms to a type of "primitivism" that I imagine is something like what Edward Said refers to as "Orientalism," the discursive construction of a representation by dominant powers to further, through ideological means, the territorial and economic interests of imperialism.[13] Fur's utilitarian value for aboriginal cultures is often said to supersede symbolic value. Conventional historiographies demand that a chronologically delineated line be drawn for fur from the practical to the symbolic, to trace through an "earlier" culture what, if inescapably lost, has never been entirely erased. This Eurocentric bias raises a question about history and the place it allocates for indigenous peoples. In other words, it reveals the persistent need to argue that indigenous peoples are indeed alive and well in the contemporary scene. The point is that no clear, historically developmental line can be traced to mark a shift from the practical to the symbolic values attributed to fur. For indigenous cultures, past and present, fur has symbolic value as well as, for example, value for survival in a cold climate. The utility of fur is often constructed in a way that creates this spurious developmental logic from the "primitive" to the "civilized," from the practical to the symbolic, from use value to exchange value. In the play *Jessica* by Maria Campbell and Linda Griffiths, the lead character expresses her frustration with the ideology of primitivism: "Jessica: I want to show you something. [*she opens her suitcase, pulling things from the mess inside*] We go to ceremonies, I have to change into a skirt. . . . I say, "Why can't women wear pants?" Everyone looks at me like I'm crazy. . . . You see these jeans? They're a part of me. I sit in a room full of sweet grass and animal skins, with rattles and drums, as if I wasn't carrying a walkman and a computer the size of a briefcase. As if it was two hundred years ago. Vitaline, I like spike heels. I read Karl Marx and *People* magazine." [14] More often it is the case that an ideology of fur's utility in twentieth-century fashion discourse is used to hide the symbolic values at work in fur fashions. Of course, at particular historical moments, symbolic or practical values attributed to fur do, indeed, differ for indigenous peoples, as for European cultures. But by and large, the utilitarian function attributed to fur clothing works to situate the paleolithic/primitive as an originary moment, used by the museum to represent a causal and teleological development from the "primitive" to the "civilized" (see Figure 38).

Crimp's use of the following passage from Foucault illustrates that moments of rupture from the presumedly coherent standards that govern aesthetic norms reveal themselves by a self-conscious gesture in which those norms appear, precisely, as "norms":

> Flaubert is to the library what Manet is to the museum. They both produced works in a self-conscious relationship to earlier paintings or texts — or rather to the aspect in painting or writing that remains indefinitely open. They erect their art within the archive. They were not meant to foster the lamentations — the lost youth, the absence of vigor, and the decline of inventiveness — through which we reproach our Alexandrian age, but to unearth an essential aspect of our culture: every painting now belongs within the squared and massive surface of painting and all literary works are confined to the indefinite murmur of writing. [15]

I offer a possible rewriting of Foucault's passage to clarify how the ideological containment of Inuit clothing by the Museum of Civilization comes apart at the seams in the Inuit fashion shows:

> Flaubert is to the library what the Inuit fashion show is to the museum. They both produced works in a self-conscious relationship to earlier artifacts or texts — or rather to the aspect in archaeology or writing that

FIGURE 38. *High Heels in the Arctic*, anonymous, graphite on paper (1959). Reproduced from Jean Blodgett, *Strange Scenes: Early Cape Dorset Drawings* (Kleinburg, Ont.: McMichael Canadian Art Collection, 1993), by permission of the McMichael Canadian Art Collection (CDL.1992.1.239). Copyright permission granted by West Baffin Eskimo Co-operative Limited, Cape Dorset, NWT.

remains indefinitely open. They erect their fashions within the archive. They were not meant to foster lamentations — the lost youth, the absence of vigor, the decline of inventiveness, *the vanishing race* — through which we reproach our postmodern age, but to unearth an essential aspect of our culture; every article of clothing now belongs within the sutured and starched surface of fashion and all textile production is confined to the indefinite murmur of textuality.

Contrary to the description of contemporary Inuit fashions as "an intriguing unwritten essay reflecting the social, economic, and technological changes to which Inuit have adapted over the last generation," I would say that the Inuit fashion show turns up the volume on that indefinite murmur waiting in the shadows to be heard. It loudly and clearly articulates the work of clothing design and adornment that would rival the output of Gaultier and Mizrahi. My exercise in ventriloquism leaves an unsatisfactory feeling that the impulse that generates the disembowelling of aesthetic norms is merely a desire for a change, a new art season waiting to happen, were it not for the existence of that which is indefinitely left open by ideological containment, the realities of different modes of representation that cannot be vanquished but are sustained by the practices of this diverse group of Inuit women. This different mode of representation constitutes a different mode of production in the making of the parkas. The women who make these beautiful clothes do the majority of the design work and sewing themselves. This is not piece work, produced by the labor practice of homeworking that currently dominates the textile industries in North America and Europe. Indeed, the very design of the parkas and the use of fur materials prohibits the division of pieces so central to one of the textile industry's current forms of cheap labor.[16] The Inuit fashion show incorporates a dominant mode of representation, the fashion show, into its so-called traditional clothing styles, making this fashion show something that is far from traditional. Given that one of the essential features of fashion is its theme of change, the notion of traditional fashion which the Inuit fashion show conjures up is as paradoxical as its obverse, the fashionable traditionalism that pervades the postmodern fashions of Gaultier and Mizrahi, whose referents are hardly those of the Inuit, but other images — *Nanook of the North, The Call of the Wild* — and other texts.

The promotional release states that Pauktuutit, the Inuit Women's Association, "is actively involved in assisting Northern women designers who wish to take advantage of business opportunities in the fashion industry." American and French fashion designers' fascination with "Eskimo" clothing styles would certainly suggest that such business opportunities are there for the taking, as would the appearance of the "Siberian-Eskimo" model Irina Pantaeva, who, when asked by another model, if she would sign a petition against fur, is said to have "explained patiently that she would have long ago frozen to death without it"[17] The containment of the Inuit fashion show, however, by the Canadian Museum of Civilization and the Inuit Broadcasting Corporation which aired the shows in Inuktituk to its predominantly Inuit audience raises questions about the use of these "alternative" venues for creating a market for Inuit fashion products that can legitimately compete in the south. It is especially difficult to imagine that Inuit clothing could make a mainstream fashion breakthrough in a place where Isaac Mizrahi worried about getting "stoned off of 7th Avenue like some kind of wanton heretic" if he showed real fur pants.

The pervasive force of an ideology of cultural difference in the fashion industry does very little to overcome the sanctioned ignorance of First Nations involvement in fur trapping and commodity production. Such contradictions reveal the enormous discrepancies that still exist between First Nations material production and that of the dominant fur and anti-fur fashion industries, a discrepancy that is underlined not only by the question of access to particular ideological apparatuses of symbolic production such as the museum or the media, advertising, film, and fashion magazines, but also by the lack of access to organized labor for First Nations in northern Canada.

The Inuit fashion shows and the fur/anti-fur fashions of Mizrahi and Gaultier represent different, if not competing, values and economic interests at stake in the marketing of cultural difference. Ideologies of cultural difference are not only subject to the demands of market forces; they are also productive of meaningful social relations and material conditions, however residual or anticipatory their existence may be.

Storytelling Technologies

For First Nations in northern Canada access to organized labor represents one of the major drawbacks to Inuit and Dene control over the production and distribution of fur fashion products. The exclusion from capital-intensive labor activities in the north such as mining and the extraction of natural resources since the early part of the twentieth century, in conjunction with the revalorization of animal-human and human-land relations, constitutes an aspect of an ideology of cultural difference which emerges in such notable texts as *When the World Was New* and *Life Lived like a Story.*

When the World Was New is George Blondin's collection of stories from the Sahtú Dene, who live in the western Arctic along the Dehcho or what is referred to on official Canadian maps as the Mackenzie River. The text is divided into six parts: "Tales the Elders Told," "Warriors and Medicine Heroes," "The Story of Karkeye," "Paul Blondin," "Edward Blondin," and "George Blondin." The stories are told by and about male heroes, legends, and subjects. "Tales the Elders Told" contains stories of Raven, a trickster figure as difficult to characterize as any complex representation of human life. "He" is a schemer, too smart for his own good, but also a wily strategist, whose intelligence can be put to many uses: to trip up the reader or listener, to put egotism, self-interest, and narcissism in their place.

In the first story, "The Raven's Greed," Raven is hoarding food for himself and refusing to share his abundance with his fellow creatures. The animals "realized that Raven had chased all the caribou off their land into the cave and trapped them there. The animals were angry when they saw this. 'Let's break down his platform and chase all those other ravens away,' they shouted. 'They can work for a living, the same as everyone else!'" (6). An angry mob of creatures breaks the Raven's fortress and sets the caribou, the pent-up animals, free. "Animals on the land are for everyone to share. No one should keep anything just for themselves. You did wrong, Raven" (7). Luckily for Raven, his threat to the survival of the majority is not punished by execution — although it is contemplated — followed by a reign of terror. Instead, Raven is ridiculed and humiliated. The story represents the necessity of reciprocity for survival.

"The Raven's Greed" reads like a marxian allegory of revolutionary practice. The story critiques the idea of a single individual gaining control of natural resources that are necessary for collective survival. The story succeeds because the allegorical figures of Raven and the animals represent the problem of hierarchical differences implicitly through the non-hierarchical difference between human and animal. It is an example of what Julie Cruikshank notes with reference to Tagish and Tlingit storytellers as the use of "symbols from nature to talk about culture."[18] The artifice of the fabula at once creates the conditions in which to recognize the obvious difference between human and animal, and displaces the very artificiality of such a difference for purposes of survival. Supermarkets filled with aisles of prepackaged, plasti-wrapped, processed cuts of meat and mounds of boxed-in vegetables make it difficult to appreciate the inalienable aspects of our relationship to nature. An ecological consciousness that is shaped by a desire to "return to nature" has not yet understood that survival *in nature* demands that we recognize we are *of* and *within* nature and not *at one* with it. As an ideological form, the myth of Raven's greed could be said to resolve a difficult struggle to survive the violence that nature produces over our control of food supplies: "The animals went home," the story concludes, "taking all the meat they could carry" (7).

The second story, "Why Raven Is Black," is about the difference between physical beauty or adornment and narcissism. The animals decide at a political council to have themselves painted beautiful colors, "so we will be nice-looking in this world" (7). Because he is so clever, Raven is asked to paint all the animals' fur and plumage. Raven agrees on condition that the other animals promise to paint him last so he "will be more beautiful than everybody else" (7). The animals agree, but when it comes time to paint Raven, they blindfold him and cover him in coal from the fire until he is completely black. When Raven discovers what has been done to him, he wreaks revenge on the loon and the moose.

The decision to create the variety and diversity of beauty in animals is made at a political council meeting. Contrary to the distinction drawn between political and symbolic modes of power in the modern European tradition, political and symbolic decision-making powers are intertwined in this story through the agency of the animals. Physical differences are celebrated, but an equality in difference is preferred over the use of symbolic display to place one animal above all the rest — like a king who wears his mantle trimmed with ermine to demonstrate his superior power over others and denies others access to beauty through sumptuary legislation, all the while creating conditions to acquire essential commodities to make a spectacle of his absolutism.

One of the theoretical presuppositions informing literary and anthropological study of First Nations stories in print form concerns the politics of cultural difference. In response to the assimilating tendencies on the part of Western critics to frame the cultural practices of indigenous peoples within the familiar paradigms of Western thought ("literature," for example), cultural differences are posited as radically dissimilar across cultural contact and therefore nonassimilable through analogy or comparison.[19] An ideology of cultural difference which insists on reading First Nations stories as belonging to a radically other dimension of self-contained cultural life presupposes that these stories constitute an aesthetic practice removed from political, social, and economic questions. On the contrary, "The Raven's Greed" and "Why Raven Is Black" are as relevant to a critique of environmental exploitation and critical engagement with the history of imperial–First Nations relations as any other produced to critically frame or analyze global/ecological relations of exploitation and narratives of resistance and liberation.[20]

One way to read *Life Lived like a Story* — a book Julie Cruikshank produced in collaboration with the three native elders whose life stories make up the body of the text, Angela Sidney, Kitty Smith, and Annie Ned — is in the context of the politics of cultural difference, as a text that helps us to understand the politics underlying the construction of cultural difference. While this may not be Cruikshank's intention, nevertheless the book's location in Canada's postimperial period, when many First Nations are advocating self-determination and self-government, positions this text at a politico-historical juncture that foregrounds the cultural relationship between First Nations and the remaining citizenry of the country. This text, then, is constitutive of the complexity of the cultural politics of difference, rewriting the dialectic of an increasing specificity in the context of increasing cross-cultural fluidity, the mixedness of all cultural formations, including that which we identify as our "own" or possessed by others. "Perhaps most important," Cruikshank writes, "is the commitment of aboriginal people to record oral accounts from elders which will allow them to document their *own* past in their *own* voice using their *own* oral records."[21]

Another assumption underlying the approach to First Nations cultural productions is an emphasis on the counternarrative of adaptation, a response to a "primitivist" conception of indigenous cultures as static, unchanging, self-enclosed homogeneous entities. Cruikshank's attention to this counternarrative involves focusing on the adaptation of First Nations' cultures to the environment: "Ethnographers have repeatedly documented the ability of Athapaskan Indians to adapt to changing conditions of life, and nowhere is this clearer than in the southern Yukon. Native people living there were aboriginal hunters and fishers whose technology, social customs, and seminomadic lifestyle were admirably adapted to a subarctic environment." Cultural resolutions to the uncontrollable forces of nature can also be found, Cruikshank writes, in the structural determinations of narrative: "Because narratives follow a culturally specific sequence moving through a series of conflicts to some resolution, they are structurally equipped to address dilemmas accompanying change." [22]

Adaptation, however, has its limits in the production of Cruikshank's own text. Even as she privileges her determination to change the academic protocols of ethnographic research and make her endeavor truly collaborative, the multiplicity of narrative adaptations produced by this process is ultimately undermined: "An important part of our collaboration involved jointly reviewing and correcting the transcripts I made from our taped conversations as soon as possible after each session. Older narrators usually responded by listening carefully for a short while, then breaking in to retell the story rather than waiting for me to finish reading it back. Each narrator might tell slightly different versions of a particular story from the others but was so internally consistent that her retelling proved an effective method of checking the transcript." [23]

Collaboration in this context results in a multiplicity of narrative adaptations. Cruikshank, however, redraws the possible differences of renarrativizing into the singularity of an "internal consisten[cy]." The result is an accurate transcript. If the issue is how to undermine outside control by acknowledging the collaboration necessary to the ethnographic enterprise, what new controls are produced by the dissolution of multiplicity and the notion of an accurate text? The relations between herself and these women are, for Cruikshank, principally determined by the exigencies of academic protocols. The academic collaborative adventure is as much an exercise in cross-cultural contact as any involving, for example, missionaries and corporate agents in the north. Academics, missionaries, corporate agents constitute an "outside," a force of change, in many respects a privileged space of subjective-colonial centrality which influences and transforms native cultures, as if such transformation were exceptional or unusual. Contrary to the counternarrative of adaptation (to the environment), transcultural changes brought about by the outside are extraordinary enough that their influence must be self-consciously monitored.

Contrary to Cruikshank's emphasis on adaption, it is incorporation that more closely characterizes cross-cultural relations. And indeed, Cruikshank provides an example of cultural incorporation:

Outwardly, Mrs. Sidney has lived a conservative Tagish life. Yet her account shows how she has accomplished this by reflecting on ideas from other cultures, adapting them (usually by thinking about how they relate to "old stories" she knows), and making them part of her repertoire of ideas. Frequently, when she has faced an unfamiliar situation, she has searched for explanation in a story her mother or an aunt told her. . . . She continues to do this, in her mid-eighties, both when she wants to explain some past decision she has made and when she encounters ideas new to her. Her intellectual drive to formulate consistent links between "old ways" and "new ways" permeates her entire account.[24]

The traffic of ideas between cultures — in a word, "cultural exchange" — would also seem to belie the utilitarian value Cruikshank attributes to the activity of storytelling: "Thus the essential issue addressed in the following pages is how these women *use* traditional narrative to explain their life experiences." Elsewhere she mentions "the importance of looking at how oral tradition is *used* rather than focusing narrowly on its factual contribution." Such utilitarian value ultimately locates itself in the place that constitutes a context of cultural authenticity, where the truth about First Nations storytelling practices can unfold if their usefulness within the proper cultural context is disclosed through rigorous scholarship. Cruikshank is primarily concerned with "how to convey authentically, in words, the experience of one culture to members of another."[25] But what could be more static, more immobile than a "context" that exists in all its propriety "outside" the things that it holds or contains, such as stories? Is there no relation, no exchange, no traffic between text(s) and context(s)?

According to Cruikshank intracultural incorporation may take place between "traditional" and "present-day" aspects of indigenous cultural life: the "special regard for elders as teachers, historians, and sources of authority underlies ethnographic accounts by 'outsiders' as well as contemporary discussion by 'insiders' — *younger Native people concerned about incorporating traditional values into present-day life.*"[26] Cross-cultural incorporation, apparently, does not take place. In this passage, the anthropologist gives herself the name of "outsider." She confirms her externalization, not necessarily from the "other" culture but from her own culture of professional, intellectual, labor. The "other" culture does serve, however, to throw back the alienation of a difference, not without but within — a difference within that is also an (in)difference to the self's other projected "outside" onto an other's self. The politics and poetics of alienation are never so pointedly expressed as in this intimate relationship between an outer self and an other within.

One way to register the effects of storytelling practices on cross-cultural social relations is through the discursive construction of spatial dimensions, which are scripted unto the earth and map our relationship to it. Julie Cruikshank cautions the reader of native stories against the use of these stories as "tangible historical evidence." "Attempts to sift oral accounts for 'facts' may actually minimize the value of spoken testimonies by asserting positivistic standards for assessing 'truth value' or 'distortions.'" Both the notion of history as simply a temporal chronology of events, what Benjamin called "homogeneous, empty time," and the evidential claims that can be asserted based on temporality as the determining modality of historical knowledge, are challenged by storytelling practices that demand, in Cruikshank's term, "contextualization": "An alternative approach treats oral tradition not as evidence but as a window on the ways the past is culturally constituted and discussed in different contexts." Context, a spatially determined concept-metaphor, clearly refers to a notion of place, spatial configurations through which historical knowledge can be perceived. In other words, storytelling helps us to conceive of history as a spatial and graphic configuration rather than a temporal one. Cruikshank observes that by "imbuing place with meaning through story, narrators seemed to be using locations in physical space to talk about events in chronological time." [27]

Cruikshank discusses how each of the three native elders contextualizes her storytelling in terms of place names. In the case of Angela Sidney, "Clan history is narrated as a travelogue. She locates each clan at a specific place and traces a journey to other named places and an eventual fresh beginning in new territory. Although the chronology may be ambiguous, the named locations are not." Cruikshank also records the following telling observation: "Mrs. Sidney has remarked that when she tells some of these stories, she follows the narrative 'like a map,' a comment I have heard from other storytellers." [28]

Cartographies are technologies of space that can be altered or rewritten depending on the demands of the dominant mode of material relations. Cartographies "outside" the system of private property, outside, that is, cartographies of capital, are often conceived of as precartographic when they are in fact written maps that re-present a politics, a history, an economy of writing in the graphic sense of the word. Cartographies can be different. They can bear the imprint of different agencies of land usage. How one stores the land in regulated shapes — and this is the image the map neatly draws — differs from "mapping" that shows movement across space, delineations of mobility that are not quantifiable by measured or striated space. Deleuze and Guattari describe the territorial principal informing nomadic space as variable, incorporating a "polyvocity of directions." [29] When the Sahtú Dene elder George Blondin says, near the conclusion of his stories, that "some Dene say the Earth is our Body. Others say the land is like a big-warehouse" (246), he doubles the image of spatiality, producing one that permits commoditization through the division of space into measurable parts and one that is noncommodifiable, a smooth space, undivided, immeasurable but traversable precisely through its polyvocity of directions.

The spacings of imperialism profoundly altered storytelling practices for the Sahtú-Dene of the western Arctic. The stories collected by George Blondin are introduced in the historical context of the 1940s, after an influenza epidemic in 1928 and the significant shift from living on the land to living in "settlements" had radically changed the conditions of Sahtú Dene life.

The notion of what constitutes an "outside" changes its points of reference in the territoriality of nomadic space. Earlier, I discussed Cruikshank's formation of outside forces, an imperial occupation not simply of land but of knowledges and subjectivities: to be an outsider, to know division between who or what is inside or outside, who or what is outside or inside access to knowledge. In *When the World Was New*, the figure of an "Outside" appears in Paul Blondin's (this is George Blondin's grandfather) late nineteenth-century narrative of a change in condition of wage labor for Sahtú Dene male workers, as a territorial marker. "Outside" is capitalized as if to acknowledge this other space as one would a country or an official place: "The [Hudson's Bay Company] traded the goods from Outside for huge amounts of fur, but the fact was that a year's load didn't go very far among the people in each region. Trade goods were in such short supply that you had to look for the bullet after you shot an animal, because five of the round bullets a muzzle loader fired were supposed to last you a year" (138). The Outside is not given a proper name, like England; yet it is a place name for that which exists beyond Sahtú Dene territory. The HBC does not constitute an Outside because its operations lie within the territorial lands of the Dene. Even though the HBC's relationship to this Outside alters supplies and labor practices in Dene territory, its effects are deemed negligible because of the spatial discontinuity between life in Dene territory and life outside Dene territory. Mass communication becomes the means for dissolving this spatial rupture.[30] As George Blondin writes:

> That fall of 1939, Hitler had invaded Poland, and Great Britain was at war. The manager of the Hudson's Bay Company post gave me some old newspapers that showed soldiers at war. I told my family that a big war was going on, but they didn't believe me. I showed them the pictures, and they still wouldn't believe me. . . . The Second World War didn't affect the Dene much. Most people lived off the land, spending their time in the bush. Few knew how to read, so they didn't know what was happening outside their homeland. Even our supplies were unaf-

fected. Only sugar and shells were rationed. . . . No one in this part of the country spoke English anyway, so no one knew anything about the terrible disasters happening in other parts of the world. The Dene only worried about what they were going to eat each day. It wasn't until years later that everything from Outside began to affect our daily lives. (215)

Two further references in George Blondin's stories confirm the massive changes the space of the Outside brings to Dene life. Solutions to poverty are only on the Outside: "By 1950, we were poor. Fur prices were low, and the Dene had to keep moving all over the country in order to trap enough furs to survive. People were often sick. . . . A priest visited the Dene in hospital and found that their clothes were old. He told the Edmonton welfare office, and people Outside donated big boxes of clothing" (241). Health care, too, can only be found on the Outside: "When I got sick the doctor thought I had kidney trouble, and decided he would have to send me Out to Edmonton. I was sad to leave my wife and four small children, and I grew very worried when the doctor in Edmonton told me I had tuberculosis. I would have to stay there for at least two years, he said" (243).

The Outside, whether England or Edmonton, marked a spatial discontinuity with Dene territory in the late nineteenth and early twentieth century. Eventually, this inside/outside configuration would be permeated by new divisions of space: the Outside would be on the inside. The legal and constitutional battles that many First Nations are fighting with the federal, provincial, and territorial governments over territorial boundaries represent the most recent rewriting of these historically altered cartographies.

The Laws of Culture

In "Yamoría Lives with the Beavers," Yamoría changes himself into a beaver and lives with the beavers in order to learn what he can from them. He learns how they build their houses; social relations among male, female, and infant beavers and with other animals; strategies for survival in winter and avoidance of animals who prey on them, including human hunters. "After his year with the beaver family, Yamoría went back to join the Dene and told them how beavers take care of themselves for the long winter. He pointed out how smart these animals are to plan ahead for a whole year. 'If the beaver family doesn't plan well, starvation sets in before the spring,' he told the people. It was an important lesson for the Dene" (40). There are many references throughout Paul, Edward, and George Blondin's stories that come back to this essential lesson; many lives were saved by planning ahead, making caches of meat and fish in preparation for the scarcity of winter.[31]

Yamoría's acquisition of knowledge for the purposes of establishing a human economy of exchange with the productive forces of nature contrasts sharply with the effects of scientific research in the north, increasing throughout the twentieth century and contributing to the growth of Canada's military and commercial enterprises. During the 1940s, the federal Department of Fisheries brought in three scientists to test fish in Sahtú (Great Bear Lake) to decide whether or not to introduce commercial fishing into the lake. George Blondin and his father Edward worked as guides and hired out their boat to the scientists. Uranium mining began in the early part of this century. During the 1940s, the mine also provided employment and access to a cash economy by hiring Dene to cut cords of wood. George Blondin links the mining operations directly to the atomic bomb: "That year [1945], the mine went at full speed to produce the atomic bomb. Long before the white people came, there were stories about this place. A medicine man in early days prophesied that the mine would develop, and that the atomic bomb would kill many people" (232).[32]

Uranium and pitchblende mining and commercial fishing during the twentieth century brought an expanded economy of wage labor and commodity consumption discontinuous from the previous economy of trapping and trading in furs. The fur trade also marked a "changing time for the North." In the mid-nineteenth century "White people came for the first time to offer the Dene articles in trade for furs. Trading posts sprang up every few hundred kilometres along the Great River, Dehcho (which white men called the Mackenzie). The traders brought merchandise and supplies North by packing them on horses, then travelling by birchbark canoe, and portaging from river to river. Their stores contained things Dene quickly learned to prize, things like matches and muzzle loaders. Some of the native people of that period had never before seen a trading post. As time passed, the traders brought in more and more goods, hoping to get more and more furs" (110). An economy of exchange between human labor and the productive forces of nature, whether in hunting, trapping, commercial fishing, or mining, constitutes the strongest mode of economic practice in the north. Missionaries, the Hudson's Bay Company, the Canadian state, and capital investors, brought new ways of organizing this economy, which in some cases the Dene incorporated but in other cases brought only devastation and destruction of some essential aspects of Dene culture, such as laboring in nature for survival and self-sufficiency rather than for obtaining capital surpluses.

Trapping and fur trading exemplify incorporation. Medicine power adapts to guns and bullets, and stories are told of heroes such as Di (1840–1937) who have medicine powers over bullets used for hunting (109). Kana?i is another hero who has medicine power over bullets. He uses the bullet to test the safety of passage down the Dehcho: "Kanaʔi stood on the shore and shot his rifle down the river. As the bullet raced over the water, Kanaʔi sang and talked. 'I'm watching my whicho (bullet),' he said. 'It's travelling down Dehcho, the Great River. I see someone else watching my whicho also, to be sure it is safe and will not harm anyone. . . . The whicho has arrived at our destination safely. It's travelling back towards us now. Soon I will be able to catch it here, and it will be safe to travel,' he told the people. . . . 'It's red hot! It shouldn't be, but it's hot because someone else is watching it as well. Anyway, since I have it back, it means that it's safe for the journey'" (102). Warriors and hunters are now also glorified for their expertise in trapping and trading, their accumulation of supplies and the generosity with which they share with others in times of need. "Karkeye [b. 1855] was one of the best trappers in the country around Sahtú. The Hudson's Bay Company had great respect for him all his life. It was normal for him to bring in 500 marten pelts to sell at Christmas" (119). "Wherever Karkeye went, there were always many people with him. When they were short of meat and fish, people looked to Karkeye to provide for them. He always had lots of tea, sugar, shells, nets, cloth, and tobacco, because he was one of the best trappers around" (120). Trappers legendary for their reciprocity and generosity and whicho medicine power are two examples of Dene incorporation of significant changes brought about by the economic exigencies of the fur trade and new technologies such as guns and bullets.

There are references that may jar the reader's temporal assumptions throughout the text, such as a remark made in one of the Raven stories about being able to spend a whole day snaring rabbits because it is Sunday; what possible significance Sunday could have in this origin story is not clear, but this reference quite early in the text presumably indicates that missionaries were one of the earliest influences for change. In Karkeye's stories signs of cultural difference begin to appear with greater frequency, framed in a historical context, as a difference between then and now. In Karkeye's time, "people didn't stay in hotels, but with friends or relatives. Instead of paying rent, they helped the people they were staying with to fish, hunt, trap and cut firewood" (115). "In Karkeye's time, the late 1800s, life was hard for Dene who were not good hunters and trappers. You had to travel great distances — usually a hundred kilometres or more — to the trading posts. When you got there, you had to use your furs to buy enough food, supplies and tea to last for at least six months. There was no government to help you in difficult times; there was no welfare and no hospitals. There was just one trader in the country, at the Hudson's Bay Company, and one priest. Even though there were no police, people stayed in line. They didn't shoot one another" (119–20). The effects of overtrapping are also noted: "The country was new, not trapped out as it is today, and there were many good trappers around" (125).

Paul Blondin's stories, which follow Karkeye's, narrate a transition from the incorporation of mercantile modes of economic trade and exchange to more fully developed capitalist demands for itinerant wage labor at the turn of the century. Blondin was hired by the Hudson's Bay Company to paddle the scows upriver. Then, when the HBC converted to steam-powered freighters, "the rivermen could not get jobs any more" (138). At this moment comes the first reference to the notion of an Outside. The effects of the fur trade on economic practices were also felt with the rise of gambling. The "handgame" is traditional among the Dene, but during Paul Blondin's time stories were told of nomadic Dene gamblers who roamed the territory, dispossessing the hardworking trappers of their year's supplies and pelts. Paul Blondin is instrumental in warding off the nomadic gamblers and helping a friend to break a cycle of dependency on this spurious method of commodity acquisition, which appears to mimic capitalism in its exploitative and oppressive effects.

The arrival of the HBC and the fur trade to the north in the mid-nineteenth century marks one of two significant changes in Dene life. The second is the influenza epidemic of 1928, which seemed to open the floodgates on rapid development in Dene territory and throughout the north for the remainder of the twentieth century. Many changes came from the south, including new diseases, but while disease flowed from the south, medical or health care did not.

Edward Blondin's stories are titled "The Dene World Begins to Change." Although the fur trade had already brought many changes, their incorporation into Dene cultural practices seems to have rendered them minor in comparison to those that occurred after the epidemic. Health care, or rather the lack of it, is a persistent theme in Edward Blondin's stories. The mining rush of the 1930s for pitchblende, coal and uranium were also notable events. Government laws concerning wildlife and game hunting were introduced during this time. The story "Change Comes to Dene Life" recounts major changes in diet, health, crime, teenage pregnancies, religion, education, and contact with white people at the turn of the century. The story begins with reference to wildlife laws:

In the old days, the Dene lived simply, off the land. There was little communication with the outside world, and government didn't interfere. People did as they liked. Two Mounties, stationed in Tulít'a by 1921, kept an eye on the Dene, but they didn't enforce government or wildlife laws. The Dene didn't know these laws, anyway. There were very few schools, so most of us didn't speak English. Nevertheless, the people were converting to Christianity. They were religious, and paid attention to the priests. Their own Elders also taught the Dene way of life. (170)

Paul Blondin, Edward's father, anticipates the laws against cutting up beaver houses:

> At that time, there was no law against cutting up beaver houses and people chopped them down to get beavers for food and furs for trading. (Later, the government made a law against doing this, and it was a good law. If the hunter didn't kill the beavers when he chopped down the house, the beavers froze to death.)
>
> People hunted beavers this way for centuries before the white people came. They had learned it from watching the animals. Grizzly bears and wolverines also destroyed beaver houses, but they scratched out the den first. (156–57)

These laws came into effect during Edward's lifetime. Edward notes that one year (around 1936) the new game laws allowed him "to trap only fifteen beaver; trappers had to be at least eighteen years old and have a permit" (195). The laws of culture gave way to government enforced trapping, wildlife, and gaming laws.

George Blondin, Edward Blondin's son, titles his concluding section of stories "Living in Two Worlds." The title can be read ironically as a reference to an already established division between human and animal, dramatized throughout the text by the shifting realities of medicine power. It can also be read with reference to the changing realities of the north during the twentieth century, the development of a mining economy, an expanding government infrastructure, settlements, residential schools run by Roman Catholic or Anglican missionaries, military activity, the pipeline, and so on and so forth. These two worlds, the old world of traveling on the land and the new world of settlement, are constructed in George Blondin's stories through the agency of "cultural difference."[33] Blondin "was born near Horton Lake, at the edge of the Barrens east of K'áhbamítúé, in May 1922" (203). "It was a time when Dene still lived by their own laws and within their own culture" (203). The struggle to hold onto this time began for Blondin during the 1930s, after he had been sent to a residential mission school where he is forbidden to speak his mother tongue and where he forgot "everything [his] grandfather taught [him]" (205). Blondin came back at the request of his mother and father, whose other children had died in the flu epidemic. The stark difference in his experience between the residential school and living on the land is grafted into his narrative:

The Dene lived according to their own laws and culture. They went off in all directions to their hunting areas in winter, and some didn't get to Tulít'a till summer. When they did, the people gathered for a big feast and dance. There were Sahtú Dene, Shihta Got'ine, K'achot'ine, Deh Gah Got'ine at Tulít'a, and they all enjoyed ten days of feasting and fun. Afterward, everybody got supplies and went back to their hunting lands. After they hunted, they would come and trade dry meat and fish for more supplies for the winter. (208)

The positive experience of the past is contrasted to the negative effects of present circumstances, such as alcoholism and the instabilities of wage labor and cash flow: "People were strong then; they never complained about working hard. . . . There were no such things as alcohol and parties. People saw cash only at treaty time. They were wealthy if they stored plentiful supplies — fat, dry meat, berries and fish — for the winter. People worked hard every day. They got up at six in the morning and worked until late at night" (209).

Blondin's narratives repeatedly refer to the devastating effects of wage labor on the Dene way of life. Blondin recounts the difference between the inalienable labor of working the land and the alienated labour of the wage economy: "People expect to be paid for their work nowadays. But at that time, I didn't even know that people in other places worked for money. I was happy, singing to myself as I walked home that night. I had nothing to worry about. It's a big land, and there's plenty of food. You feel free, because nobody tells you what to do" (214). "There was no such thing as government land or people owning land. We hunted and trapped, slept and ate wherever we felt like it. It was a good life" (222).

Working to exchange furs for goods and money did not constitute alienated labor.[34] But the fur trade declined significantly after World War II, and so did its cash flow; wage labor replaced trapping.[35] Blondin records the first time he worked for wages. He was told that the United States army in Łe Góhlini wanted to hire guides. He, along with four other men, were flown in an army plane to Łe Góhlini where they cut line through the thick bush for the summer (224). This work contrasts with organized labor, from which the Dene are excluded: "In May Łe Góhlini was crowded with people from all over the country — private contractors from the United States and Canada, and thousands of soldiers. Mines everywhere were shut down, so people came North to get jobs at Łe Góhlini. But the Dene didn't get jobs in spite of all this activity" (227). George Blondin set up his own business cutting wood and eventually did get a job working for wages: "In the spring of 1956, I got a job at Giant Yellowknife Mines and worked for straight wages — for someone else — for the first time. My best friend had introduced me to the mine superintendent. 'It's our policy not to hire native people in this area,' the superintendent told me. 'But since you've come such a long way, we'll try you out'" (245).

The exclusion of First Nations from organized labor is a major problem, according to George Blondin. He argues that such jobs are necessary if Dene are to survive in the changed north and records the conflict with his father over this point. He decided that he would "live the same way as people did in large centres. [He] would work for wages" (244). When he told his father about his decision, his father "flew into a rage. 'That's all the teaching your grandfather and I gave you? You're going to throw it aside and live the other way.'" Blondin replies that "the Dene would have to change their way of life sooner or later, because the world around them was changing all the time. By then the federal government had set up schools and people were starting to live in settlements. That was the real start of the change. If parents were travelling in the bush, how would their children get properly educated? Besides, getting medical attention was difficult if you lived in the bush. The Dene were now in contact with many new diseases that they had not known before" (244). The introduction of private property, housing, increasing food costs, and the "many things to spend money on: rent, taxis, buses, shows, cafes, alcohol" (245) precipitated an economic crisis. With the decline of the sustainable land-based economy, only access to wage labor could resolve the crisis, and not, as Blondin laments, the compensatory measures of old age pensions, family allowances, and the welfare system. He summarizes the dramatic change in the economy for the Sahtú Dene:

> Once the government put schools in all the settlements, parents had to stay in town so their children wouldn't miss school. Moving to settlements changed our way of life. In the past, the Dene had gone far out on the land, hunting and trapping in areas we had used for centuries. If an area was used too much, we left it for a few years so the animals had a chance to recover. Now the Dene couldn't roam the land the way we used to — but we still hunted every day. Soon there was hardly any game around the settlements. The government made new game laws, set up game warden's offices, and introduced closed seasons for game. This completely disrupted our traditional way of earning a living.
>
> In the past, money hadn't been important to Dene. We knew what cash was, but we hadn't used it much. We had traded our fur for supplies, and it was part of our culture to share what we had. Living in settlements changed all this. Now you needed a steady income. Old age pensions and family allowances helped, but it wasn't enough to live on in town. People tried to get short-term jobs in the summer and trap in the winter.

They did the best they could, but they had problems. The welfare system was created and people became dependent on it.

Dene living on the land carried their homes with them. We lived year-round in tents. But in a settlement, you needed a house. (237)

The spacing of imperialism, the spacing of the flows of capital and private ownership of the land, create the need for access to organized labor. That access is still denied to many First Nations in the north. Blondin concludes his stories by underlining that "few Dene hunt and trap full time, so their relationship to the land is also changing. They live in communities, so they need jobs to make money. But there aren't many jobs" (246).

The discourse of cultural difference also changes at the conclusion to Blondin's narratives. Whereas cultural difference signified the spatial transition in labor and human, land, and animal relations, by the end of Blondin's stories it has become abstracted into a discourse on ethics and values which might provide a residue of hope in an otherwise difficult set of circumstances. "Some things do not change," writes Blondin, "Many younger Dene no longer live the traditional life, but they know it and understand its values. They try to use this heritage in their work, and to maintain control over the changes that affect our land and people. They are creating Dene lives in new ways" (246).

Texts such as *When the World Was New* inscribe different modes of representation and thus produce ideologies of cultural difference. Relations among humans, nature, and labor find their symbolic re-presentation in the Raven stories. Furthermore, the economies of the storytelling technique narrate a cultural politics of difference that illustrates how those relations shape material practices of reciprocity with the earth's resources and are in turn shaped by the dominant material practices of capital extraction of natural resources in the north.

Woman the Hunter, Woman the Gatherer

The stories collected in *When the World Was New* attend to male hunters and legendary figures. The consequences of eclipsing aboriginal women as subjects in and for themselves, both for First Nations decolonization and the feminist movement, are enormous, particularly as feminism's relationship to the struggle of aboriginal women in Canada is a subject of some ethical and political concern.[36] I find myself brought full circle to the question of the uneven relationship that exists between an examination of the libidinal investments in the psychic fantasy of the European bourgeois woman (in the Lynx campaign, for example) and the lack of attention to the specificity of Inuit and Dene women's labor in Hugh Brody's competing

FIGURE 39. Woman the Hunter: Ida Aivek wearing a fabric Mother Hubbard (1988).
Reproduced by permission of the Northwest Territories Archives, photograph by Tessa MacIntosh: 2089/NWT Archives.

ecologial discourse, *Living Arctic* discussed in Chapter 1. It is this question, of the representation of "woman" and women's social and material existence that, I think, will make or break the impasse that currently exists between northern hunters and gatherers and animal rights organizations such as Lynx. Answering it would involve rethinking the relations among social categories such as gender, culture, and labor. I want to begin to do some of this rethinking by turning to images and texts by aboriginal women. Angela Sidney, the Tagish/Tlingit elder whose words were recorded and transcribed by Julie Cruikshank, recounts a somewhat different story about woman the gatherer/man the hunter: "Sometimes I would hunt

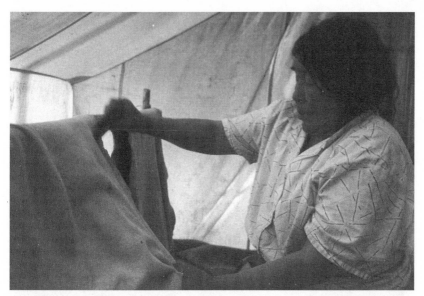

FIGURE 40. Elizabeth Chocolate scraping a hide at a camp south of Edzo (1990). Reproduced by permission of the photographer, Dorothy Chocolate.

just for fun, I guess. Trap gophers with a snare. . . . All women worked on skins, those days: women trapped around while men hunted. Then they made fur — when a woman fixes skin, then it belongs to her and she can trade it. Most women don't hunt big animals — my mother did, though. One year when she was still well she got fourteen caribou!" [37] This figure of woman the hunter or, more specifically, mother the hunter, introduces another competing dimension into the current configuration of debates between animal rights and welfare advocates and northern indigenous struggles for self-determination where the "hunter" is generally perceived to be male (see Figure 39). What are we to make of Angela Sidney's "mother the hunter"? How, as a feminist trained in the universalizing narratives of women's oppression, am I to understand this example, which both delimits a gender division of labor between Tagish/Tlingit women and men and yet transgresses the symmetrical relationship of that division? The contradictions raised by these questions are graphically contained by Dorothy Chocolate's photograph of her mother working an animal hide. The picture is taken by a Dene woman, a professional photographer, using photographic technology to "capture" an image of her mother working here and now and not in some nostalgic regime of the past on an animal skin. As her mother does the work of a gatherer in her treatment of the caribou hide, Dorothy Chocolate gathers images of her people, the Dene (see Figures 40 and 41).

FIGURE 41. Hide drying in the open air (1990).
Reproduced by permission of the photographer, Dorothy Chocolate.

First Nations women's access to print and photographic media intervenes in the cultural contest over fur. Through the use of accessible media to shape political subjects and subjectivities, these storytelling technologies inscribe a veritable cartography of difference, narrative spacings with which to navigate the ebbs and flows of postmodern politics. Access to technologies of representation are an important consideration for any struggle interested in assembling the political affinities that are becoming and coming into being in and across the disparate worlds of postmodernism.[38] In relation to the politics of images, I imagine positioning Dorothy Chocolate's photographs against Lynx's representations; against the cold and cruel depiction of the fantastical bourgeois "woman," I would place these images of the labor of an indigenous woman — the images themselves signs of labor, the activity of women in their daily lives. This dialectical image shores up the contradictions of its modern technological form and its paleolithic technologies of tanning hides. I read these images beside Walter Benjamin's demand of art, that it "*undo* the alienation of the corporeal sensorium, to *restore the instinctual power of the human bodily senses for the sake of humanity's self-preservation,* and to do this, not by avoiding the new technologies, but by *passing through* them."[39] Dorothy Chocolate's image of her mother restores those human bodily senses to indigenous women's labor in preparing animal skins; as a photograph this image simulates an experience, for the photographer, her subject, and this spectator, which transgresses and yet affirms the potential for egalitarian gendered relations in women's work in these paleolithic late modern times.

Afterword

There is interest, often unperceived by us, in not allowing transnational complicities to be perceived.

Gayatri Chakravorty Spivak,
Outside in the Teaching Machine

Canada was founded on the desire for warmth, the search for Cathay. When the Orient didn't materialize explorers pursued the warmest object of all: they followed the lush climate that animals carry on their backs.

Elizabeth Hay, *Crossing the Snow Line*

In 1993 the Montreal-based fashion designer Mariouche Gagné incorporated an environmentalist concern for biodegradable products into her fashion designs. According to a Fur Council of Canada press release on their 1993 fur design competition, she recycled fur into fashion accessories and ski wear. Fur is a "natural fiber" and will, therefore, live out a shorter life span than those Doc Martens boots and shoes, made with "the finest non-leather material available," which Lynx determined would make an excellent contribution to the "green" marketplace. Which is more ecologically correct? "Natural" fur or anti-fur synthetic products that protect animal life but use up other natural resources such as oil and wood? In either case the struggle over what constitutes a proper object for environmental defense cannot be isolated from the symbolic history of meanings and material or discursive values ascribed to that object. In part, the dominance assigned to fur as an ecologically correct object is not unrelated to the current battle over other natural resources, such as oil, a sign of international contest whose importance to the global economy seems far more urgent, cause of a major war, not the microideological war waged over the significance of fur.

The current conflict over fur indicates, however, just how complex the field of power relations has become in our contemporary moment. Here is a social movement — environmentalism — with a common interest in combating an intolerable form of symbolic and material exploitation and, yet, set in an antagonistic and contradictory relationship to the antiimperial struggle of aboriginal people. Perhaps one should not be so surprised. The increasingly integrated global dimensions of economic, political, and social forces, supported by advanced communication technologies, will, no doubt, reveal problems hitherto unforeseen or, at any rate, unacknowledged. The point is, these problems can no longer be ignored. The contradictions and conflicts between social movements and decolonization constitute productive sites of tension — productive in that they enable dialogue, new forms of political praxis, theoretical insights, agency, and action. Productive tensions expand the limits of the political field, on which, more often than not, players are sharply polarized, divided by simple or reductive exclusivities based in seemingly identifiable class, gender, sex, race, or "World" (First/ Third, New/Old, East/West) differences. To delimit this politically circumscribed space involves drawing out both the limits of the field *and* the limitations of operating within that field. Cultural politics must continually assert the conditions of possibility for articulation among radical democratic movements by cutting across their respective regimes of difference so as to disclose how specific differences are constituted in relation to one another.

In his essay "Socialism and Ecology" (1982) Raymond Williams maintains that the conflict between labor support for new industrial development and environmentalist calls for the preservation of nonindustrial lands could be resolved only through "equitable negotiation" and, furthermore, that socialists could make the necessary articulation. Any negotiation must also include equitable representation of indigenous communities and feminist organizations. But adding more chairs to the table may not be a sufficient solution; the very agenda may have to undergo transformation. The challenge is enormous but not impossible, its seeming impossibility a charged reminder of the necessity for making it possible.

For Williams, writing ten years before the Gulf War, one of the more compelling arguments to make in attempting to convince the (middle-class First World/Third World) consumer of the necessity for equitable ecological solutions is that increasingly "we" will have to choose between more violence and more peace. In the global contest over resources, it would appear that someone else's war and violence temporarily ensures someone else's peace and prosperity. This is one way in which to allow transnational complicities to be perceived.

The historical and cultural specificity of the meanings and values attributed to fur fashions has always been negotiated in the context of social modes of differentiation. Indeed, what gives symbolic value its *value* is precisely the mode of social differentiation most actively deployed to retain the necessary charge of ideological violence. The question of ideology and its influence in the realm of cultural materialisms can be rethought in the context of the tension between symbolic and political powers over which one will dominate access to and control over commodity and property wealth. Ideologies in material culture are most animate when this tension is at work and yet, ironically, appear frozen, solid, intemporal, and immutable — in short, fetishistic. By turning to the question of symbolic as well political agency, we mobilize the fetishism attributed to sexual and cultural differences. The history of symbolic powers contained in juridical discursive practices, such as sumptuary legislation, and supplementary texts on fashion, femininity, the clergy, and women points to a mode of power heavily circumscribed by ideas about material accumulation and expenditure. The multiple effects of power — political, symbolic, religious, libidinal — demand that we disentangle the many strands comprised in the text of power. It is also important to track the many discursive and nondiscursive avenues of trade in which objects of material culture and the meanings and values ascribed to them circulate. Finally, we might stop to consider the figure of the human agent, actively involved in shaping the traffic of significations between herself, the "world," other social, human and animal relations, and objects of desire. How is the agency of the bourgeois women, the principle agent of symbolic display, written into the history of gender, feminine and masculine notions of power, access to economic capital and the accumulation of symbolic and cultural capitals? How are cultural codes of libidinal accumulation and expenditure written into women's bodies and social practices? It is one of the paradoxical consequences of symbolic agency that in the hardness of truth can be found the fluidity of its dissolution. In the most unlikely places — the phantasm of the fur-clad bourgeois woman, for example — we can locate an agent of change, a potential metamorphosis from the symbolic/political complicity of legitimate/illegitimate agency to a notion of agency that is free of an identifiable "truth" or fetishistic value, if not the problem of fetishism itself.

Feminist cultural studies must acknowledge the complex relations in the very constitution of identifiable social differences. It is not enough, however, to know the ensemble of social modes of differentiation as they exist at any given time in a given institution of knowledge and power. They must be known genealogically, in the movement and dynamism of their discursive and pictorial conditions of emergence. For each material signifier, such as the fur-clad woman, is the accumulation not only of existing social differences but of the history of its contradictory and contestatory relations. Fur, fur fashions, fur producers and consumers are constitutive of all the past in their present and future metamorphoses.

Notes

INTRODUCTION

1. Colin Smith, "A City Slowly Bludgeoned to Death," *Observer*, 14 June 1992: 17.

2. Mark Harris usefully distinguishes between animal *welfare* and animal *rights* positions: "Traditional welfare organizations such as the Humane Society work to improve the conditions of animals used for human ends, allowing for their use in research and as food as long as they are treated humanely in the process. Advocates for animal rights oppose animal exploitation of any kind. In popular rhetoric, animal welfarists work to clean cages, while animal rightists work to empty them." Mark Harris, "The Threat from Within: Will Infighting Weaken the Animal-Rights Movement?" *Vegetarian Times*, February 1995: 64.

3. For a summary of the decline of fur sales in Europe due to the anti-fur movement, see Kathryn M. Olson and G. Thomas Goodnight, "Entanglements of Consumption, Cruelty, Privacy, and Fashion: The Social Controversy over Fur," *Quarterly Journal of Speech* 80.3 (1994): 249–76, especially 256.

4. See Raymond Williams, "Socialism and Ecology," in *Resources of Hope: Culture, Democracy, Socialism*, ed. Robin Gayle (London: Verso, 1989), 221.

5. Hugh Brody, *Living Arctic: Hunters of the Canadian North* (London: Faber and Faber, 1987), 85.

6. Ibid.

7. How an object, such as fur, is constituted by these conflicting, if not competing, conceptions depends, as Chantal Mouffe and Ernesto Laclau argue, on its discursive conditions of emergence: "The fact that every object is constituted as an object of discourse has *nothing to do* with whether there is a world external to thought, or with the realism/idealism opposition. . . . What is denied is not that such objects exist externally to thought, but the rather different assertion that they could constitute themselves as objects outside any discursive condition of emergence." Ernesto Laclau and Chantal Mouffe, *Hegemony and Socialist Strategy* (London: Verso, 1985), 108.

8. Harold A. Innis, *The Fur Trade in Canada: An Introduction to Canadian Economic History*, rev. ed. (Toronto: University of Toronto Press, 1970), 3.

9. Writing on European activities in the fur trade from 1540 to 1600, Bruce Trigger considers the material importance of beaver hat fashions among the nobility and middle classes of Western Europe. He notes, for example, citing J. F. Crean, that "more research is needed to determine whether the felting industry expanded more because of the new fashions, which increased demand for beaver pelts, or because of the growing availability of the pelts." Bruce G. Trigger, *Natives and Newcomers: Canada's "Heroic Age" Reconsidered* (Kingston: McGill-Queen's University Press, 1985), 135–36. See also Murray G. Lawson, *Fur: A Study in English Mercantilism, 1700–1775*, foreword by Harold A. Innis, History of Economics Series 9 (Toronto: University of Toronto Press, 1943).

10. For an important analysis of symbolic production in the field of cultural artifacts, see Pierre Bourdieu, "The Field of Cultural Production, or: The Economic World Reversed," in his *Field of Cultural Production: Essays on Art and Literature*, ed. Randal Johnson (New York: Columbia University Press, 1993).

11. See *The Marx-Engels Reader*, ed. Robert C. Tucker, 2d ed. (New York: Norton, 1978), 170, quoted by Donna Landry and Gerald MacLean, *Materialist Feminisms* (Oxford: Blackwell, 1993), 67.

12. Gayatri Chakravorty Spivak, "Scattered Speculations on the Question of Value," in *In Other Worlds: Essays in Cultural Politics* (New York: Methuen, 1987), 158.

13. The following passage is, arguably, the most influential and critical formulation of women as objects of exchange in the writings of Lévi-Strauss: "Now, these results can be achieved only by treating marriage regulations and kinship systems as a kind of language, a set of processes permitting the establishment, between individuals and groups, of a certain type of communication. That the mediating factor, in this case, should be the *women of the group*, who are *circulated* between clans, lineages, or families, in place of the *words of the group*, which are *circulated* between individuals, does not at all change the fact that the essential aspect of the phenomenon is identical in both cases. . . . It is generally recognized that words are signs; but poets are practically the only ones who know that words were also once values. As against this, women are held by the social group to be values of the most essential kind, though we have difficulty in understanding how these values become integrated in systems endowed with a significant function. This ambiguity is clearly manifested in the reactions of persons who, on the basis of the analysis of social structures referred to, have laid against it the charge of 'anti-feminism,' because women are referred to as objects. Of course, it may be disturbing to some to have women conceived as mere parts of a meaningful system. However, one should keep in mind that the processes by which phonemes and words have lost — even though in an illusory manner — their character of value, to become reduced to pure signs, will never lead to the same results in matters concerning women. For words do not speak, while women do; as producers of signs, women can never be reduced to the status of symbols or tokens." Claude Lévi-Strauss, "Language and the Analysis of Social Laws," in *Structural Anthropology*, trans. Claire Jacobson and Brooke Grundfest Schoepf (New York: Basic Books, 1963), 61.

14. In her essay "Marginality in the Teaching Machine" Spivak writes that "gender determinacy is the coding of the value-differential allowing for the possibility of the exchange of affective value, negotiating 'sexuality' rather than sexual identity. . . . The operation of the value-form makes every commitment negotiable, however urgent it might seem or be. For the long haul emancipatory social intervention is not primarily a question of redressing victimage by the assertion of (class- or gender- or ethnocultural) identity. It is a question of developing a vigilance for systemic appropriations of the unacknowledged social production of a *differential* that is one basis of exchange into the networks of the cultural politics of class- and gender-*identification*." Spivak, "Marginality in the Teaching Machine," in *Outside in the Teaching Machine* (New York: Routledge, 1993), 63.

15. Hanif Kureishi, *"Sammy and Rosie Get Laid": The Screenplay and the Screenwriter's Diary* (Markham, Ontario: Penguin, 1988), 79.

16. Audre Lorde, "Eye to Eye: Black Women, Hatred, and Anger," in *Sister Outsider* (Freedom, Calif.: Crossing Press Feminist Series, 1984), 147–48.

17. To add to the urgency of the project, recently a French anti-racist group contemplated taking action against Brigitte Bardot, who "denounced Muslim sheep-slaughtering rituals during what she called the 'atrocious' Aid-el-Kebir feast of the sacrifice." She is reported to have said: "And now my country, France, my home-

land, my land, is with the blessing of successive governments again invaded by a foreign, especially Muslim, over-population to which we pay allegiance . . . We have to submit against our will to this Muslim overflow. From year to year, we see mosques flourish across France, while our churchbells fall silent because of a lack of priests." See "Former Sex Queen Slammed for Bashing Muslims," *Prince George Citizen,* 27 April 1996: 2. Raymond Williams understood all too well the degree to which ecological pressures would increase "the possibility of recruiting wide areas of public opinion to cast as enemies the poor countries which have been assigned the role of supplying the raw materials, the oil, the whole range of basic commodities, at prices which are convenient to the functioning, in received terms, of the older industrial economies." Williams, "Socialism and Ecology," 223. In the case of Bardot's racism, we have an instance of recasting that enemy "within."

18. See Gustave Flaubert, *"Bouvard and Pécuchet" with the "Dictionary of Received Ideas,"* trans. A. J. Krailsheimer (Markham, Ontario: Penguin, 1976), 306.

19. Herbert S. Parmet, *Richard Nixon and His America* (Toronto: Little, Brown, 1990), 247.

20. See *Gentlemen Prefer Blondes,* dir. Howard Hawks, perf. Jane Russell, Marilyn Monroe, Charles Coburn, Twentieth Century Fox, 1953; and Madonna, "Material Girl," in *Madonna: The Immaculate Collection,* Warner Reprise Video, 1990.

21. Edward W. Said, *Culture and Imperialism* (New York: Knopf, 1993), 7.

22. Whether the models used for these paintings were from this class or not is not the issue here. Rather, it is the "re-presentation" of female bodies belonging to specific class categories that is in question.

23. For an excellent account of women workers in the global textile industry, see Cynthia Enloe, *Bananas, Beaches, and Bases: Making Feminist Sense of International Politics* (Berkeley: University of California Press, 1990). See especially "Blue Jeans and Bankers," 151–76.

24. Karl Marx, *Capital: A Critique of Political Economy,* trans. Ben Fowkes, vol. 1 (New York: Vintage, 1977), 163.

25. Walter Benjamin, "Theses on the Philosophy of History," in *Illuminations,* ed. Hannah Arendt, trans. Harry Zohn (New York: Schocken, 1969), 261.

26. George Blondin, *When the World Was New: Stories of the Sahtú Dene* (Yellow-knife, Northwest Territories: Outcrop, 1990); Julie Cruikshank, in collaboration with Angela Sidney, Kitty Smith, and Annie Ned, *Life Lived like a Story: Life Stories of Three Yukon Native Elders* (Vancouver: University of British Columbia, 1990).

27. On misrecognition, see Pierre Bourdieu, *Outline of a Theory of Practice,* trans. Richard Nice (Cambridge: Cambridge University Press, 1977), 5–6.

28. As Olson and Goodnight observe: "Status symbols reflecting a relatively high class position are valued both for their scarcity and their distinction as an 'expressive' vehicle." "Entanglements of Consumption," 254.

29. Leslie C. Smith, "Ecologically Correct: For Today's Fashions, We'd Rather Dance with Wolves Than Skin Them," *Globe and Mail* [Toronto], 10 October 1991: D4.

CHAPTER 1. SIMULATED POLITICS

1. See, for example, James M. Jasper and Dorothy Nelkin, *The Animal Rights Crusade: The Growth of a Moral Protest* (New York: Free Press, 1992).

2. To draw the anti-fur/pro-fur distinction, as I do, between animal liberationist and decolonial movements differs from Olson and Goodnight's characterization of the political outlines of this debate in the United States. In "Entanglements of Consumption," Olson and Goodnight discuss the fur debate during the late 1980s and early 1990s as an example of the media construction of controversy in the public domain. They divide the political field between an animal liberationist struggle and a beleaguered fur industry that must support its capitalist interests. Dividing the political field along different axes of "entanglement" would appear to depend on differing historical and geopolitical contexts. Olson and Goodnight's approach emphasizes an ideological concern for "constitutional rights," especially those of the consumer who purchases fur. In addressing this issue, Olson and Goodnight fail to highlight its obvious importance to the case of animal rights. Donna Landry and Gerald MacLean note that "in the US context especially, it should come as no surprise that the debate [over animal rights] is often couched in terms of a discourse of legal rights, explicitly invoking the example of the Civil Rights and other social movements. An 'Animal Bill of Rights,' such as that proposed by the Animal Legal Defense Fund (ALDF), would assure 'that animals, like all sentient beings,' be 'entitled to basic legal rights in our society. Deprived of legal protection, animals are defenseless against exploitation and abuse by humans.'" Landry and MacLean, *Materialist Feminisms*, 215. By failing to note how the discourse of rights plays itself out on both sides of the debate, Olson and Goodnight miss the opportunity to constitute the shared ground on which this polarized field ultimately rests. It is perhaps because of this shared interest in the question of political "rights" that other potentially more conflicted interests such as those of American transnational capital interests in fur factories in developing nations and indigenous trappers in northern Canada, Greenland, and Siberia, remain seemingly "marginal" to, if not outside, the bounds of their own argument. Nevertheless I have found their article to be enormously informative about the U.S. anti-fur lobby, and I would agree with their conclusion that "such oppositional argument seems to promise thus far only a limited discussion: one focused on a single issue or identity to the exclusion of others, one that asks for civility for the oppressed while not extending such respect across a community of interlocutors, and one that functions in a narrow time span driven by the tempo of argumentative performances and the changing seasons." Olson and Goodnight, "Entanglements of Consumption," 267–68, 272.

3. Paleonomy captures the complex weaving of meanings and values that make up a text. Spivak elaborates its meaning as "the charge which words carry on their shoulders." In other words, textuality carries a history of a different mode of discursive production, a charged reminder that even though a capitalist economy of meanings and values dominates, residual economies such as those that characterize a nomadic way of life still survive. See Gayatri Chakravorty Spivak, interview with Geoffrey Hawthorn, Ron Aronson, and John Dunn, "The Post-modern Condition: The End of Politics?" in *The Post-colonial Critic: Interviews, Strategies, Dialogues*, ed. Sarah Harasym (New York: Routledge, 1990), 17–34, especially 25.

4. As announced in "Campaign against furs," *Times* [London], 8 August 1984: G2.

5. Lynx ceased to exist in early 1993. Another organization "Respect for Animals" has been set up to resume the anti-fur campaigns. As they write in their newsletter: "On November 5th, following a five week trial, Lynx, along with Mark Glover and Stefan Ormrod lost the libel action brought against it, ostensibly by

Swalesmoor Mink Farm Ltd., and were ordered to pay £40,000 damages and the plaintiffs' legal fees. Unable and unwilling to pay over such money to the fur trade, Lynx became insolvent and thus ceased to operate." See "Crushed but Unbowed," *Fur Campaign Review* 1 (January–March 1993): 1.

6. Richard Maracle, "The European Union's Import Restrictions on Wild Fur, EU Regulation 3254/91: Impacts on the Indigenous Peoples of Canada," sponsored by Old Massett Village Council of Haida Gwaii, Internet, December 1995.

7. Benetton, "Fall/Winter 1992 Advertising Campaign," bulletin mailed to author, December 1992.

8. In *The Fashion System*, Roland Barthes insists that "without discourse there is no total Fashion, no essential Fashion." Indeed, for Barthes, no "system of objects . . . can dispense with articulated language," for it is the linguistic signifying order that constitutes fashion's meanings. See Roland Barthes, *The Fashion System*, trans. Matthew Ward and Richard Howard (New York: Hill and Wang, 1983), xi.

9. See Williams, "Socialism and Ecology," 221: "Even at the simplest material level the notion of an indefinite expansion of certain kinds of production, but even more of certain kinds of consumption, is going to have to be abandoned."

10. Susan Stewart, *On Longing: Narratives of the Miniature, the Gigantic, the Souvenir, the Collection* (Durham: Duke University Press, 1993), 32.

11. The emergence of anti-racist, anti-imperialist, feminist, and lesbian/gay movements in Britain during the 1970s in conjunction with the acceleration of "the decline in the role of bourgeois political parties and the ideological basis on which these parties were founded" would indicate that Lynx, as a simulated political movement with strong interests in commoditization and composed largely of a white, middle-class, liberal-minded, and well-educated constituency, is part of the broader political forces and contradictions that emerged in response to the profound changes in the equilibrium of post-WWII British hegemony. See John Solomos et al., "The Organic Crisis of British Capitalism and Race: The Experience of the Seventies," in *The Empire Strikes Back: Race and Racism in 70s Britain*, ed. Centre for Contemporary Cultural Studies (London: Hutchinson with the Centre for Contemporary Cultural Studies, University of Birmingham, 1982), especially 20.

12. René Descartes, *Discourse on Method*, in *The Philosophical Writings of Descartes*, trans. John Cottingham, Robert Stoothoff, and Dugald Murdoch (Cambridge: Cambridge University Press, 1985), 1: 139–40.

13. Ibid., 140.

14. Like Walt Disney after him, Descartes privileges the talking parrot as an example of the mechanistic properties inherent in animal speech. The mechanical singing parrots of Disney invention constitute a spectacular simulacrum of Descartes's notion that animals figure as natural automata; that is, they make natural subjects for imitation precisely because they are essentially imitative and, therefore, mechanistic. Descartes insists that "we must not confuse speech with the natural movements which express passions and which can be imitated by machines as well as by animals" (140–41). And lest we succumb to the protoscientific underachievement of a Dr. Dolittle, Descartes also insists, "Nor should we think, like some of the ancients, that the beasts speak, although we do not understand their language" (141).

15. Cathy Griggers, "A Certain Tension in the Visual/Cultural Field: Helmut

Newton, Deborah Turbeville, and the *Vogue* Fashion Layout," *Differences: A Journal of Feminist Cultural Studies* 2.2 (1990): 96.

16. Griggers notes that "consumption functions now, and has since the early decades of this century, as a form of social discourse, a means of communication and of differentiating consumer communities, and also as a means of perpetually constructing and reconstructing that first and most important product of advanced consumer culture — the ideal (if no longer unified) social self" (ibid., 98) — in which case, if certain material goods such as a mink coat once consolidated the unified bourgeois female self, the moral values of not wearing the fur coat, coupled with the purchase of alternative "green" consumer goods, gives rise to the politically ideal social self.

17. See this image and other grafitti-bedecked signs of the early to mid-eighties in Britain in Jill Posener, *Louder Than Words* (London: Pandora Press, 1986). Annie Razor notes that this image in particular "'ignores the role of men who control the profits and the killing of the fur trade. Greenpeace shouldn't have produced slick sexism in its opposition to a bloody trade.'" Posener adds: "Neither should the Body Shop, whose range of natural beauty products sell primarily to women, have sponsored some of the advertising sites" (13).

18. See Christine Fellingham, "Are Fur Coats Becoming Extinct?" *Glamour*, December 1992: 183–84.

19. Gail Faurschou theorizes a "'specular logic' of abstraction" at work in the fashion system "in which the concrete dimensions of social life and the symbolic world are increasingly reduced, recoded, and smoothly reprocessed into the one-dimensional, glossy (or increasingly fluorescent) signifying surfaces of their photographic (or televisual) equivalent." "Obsolescence and Desire: Fashion and the Commodity Form," in *Postmodernism: Philosophy and the Arts*, ed. Hugh J. Silverman, Continental Philosophy 3 (New York: Routledge, 1990), 257.

20. For an excellent account of the recent history of these movements and their impact on feminist theories and methods, see Landry and MacLean, *Materialist Feminisms*.

21. Middle- to upper-class women do, of course, have a choice whether or not to wear fur coats; nevertheless, their "complicity" is, to some extent, overdetermined by the libidinal investments of capitalism.

22. For another video representation of the anti-fur position, see *Pelts: Politics of the Fur Trade*, dir. Nigel Markham, National Film Board of Canada, 1989.

23. The distinction between wild and domesticated is implicated in another culturally encoded symbolic system of differentiation, the edible and the nonedible. In his discussion of the cultural inscription of objects Marshall Sahlins demonstrates the significance American culture encodes in the (non)edibility of dogs. Dogs and horses, Sahlins notes, "participate in American society in the capacity of subjects." Such is the anthropocentric configuration of dogs as "one of the family" that to eat this animal would constitute a form of cannibalism, and as Sahlins goes on to elaborate, "evokes some of the revulsion of the incest tabu." The distinction between the edible and the inedible may also encode ethnic or racial differences, rendering the status of persons and cultures in terms of their general ordering within a schema of "civilization." See Marshall Sahlins, "La Pensée Bourgeoise: Western Society as Culture," in *Culture and Practical Reason* (Chicago: University of Chicago Press, 1976), 174, 175, and 176.

24. The image of the Holocaust persists as a key trope in animal rights discourse.

In 1996, British Labour MP Tony Banks, in an attempt to bolster British support for a European Union ban on Canadian fur (which was to come into effect in January 1997), was quoted: "'And if anyone says to me "It means jobs," well so did killing Jews in gas ovens in concentration camps mean jobs, probably for the gas oven lighters,' Banks said. 'It's barbarous. It's got to be stopped. And that's what we're going to try and do.'" Helen Branswell, "U.K. Activists Push Trap Ban," *Vancouver Sun*, 18 October 1996: A11.

25. Solomos et al., "Organic Crisis," 11.

26. See also Gayatri Chakravorty Spivak's discussion of unexamined imperialism in bourgeois feminist interpretations of gender relations between South Korean men and women in the context of the multinational electronics corporation Data Control. The complexities of the multinational theater demand that we run discontinuous channels of investigation simultaneously. See Gayatri Chakravorty Spivak, "Feminism and Critical Theory," in *In Other Worlds*, especially 90–92. For an ecofeminist discussion of Spivak's critique, see Lee Quinby, "Ecofeminism and the Politics of Resistance," in *Reweaving the World: The Emergence of Ecofeminism*, ed. Irene Diamond and Gloria Feman Orenstein (San Francisco: Sierra Club Books, 1990), 122–27.

27. Donna J. Haraway, "A Cyborg Manifesto: Science, Technology, and Socialist-Feminism in the Late Twentieth Century," in *Simians, Cyborgs, and Women: The Reinvention of Nature* (New York: Routledge, 1991), 161 and on the distinction between modernist and postmodernist tropes, 161–62.

28. Brody, *Living Arctic*, 83, 85.

29. John Best, "Canada Fur Trade under Fire," *Times* [London], 22 December 1986: D7. See also Canada, House of Commons, Standing Committee on Aboriginal Affairs and Northern Development, *Minutes of Proceedings and Evidence of the Standing Committee on Aboriginal Affairs and Northern Development, the Fur Issue: Cultural Continuity and Economic Opportunity*, December 1986, issue 1 (Ottawa: Queen's Printer, 1986); Canada, Department of Indian and Northern Affairs, *Evaluation Report of the Fur Industry Defence Program* (Ottawa, November 1991). A more recent newspaper article values the Canadian fur industry at $120 million. See Branswell, "U.K. Activists Push Trap Ban."

30. The labor of women in the domestic sphere and the labor of indigenous peoples are represented by the established order through a similar technique of exclusion. On women's domestic labor, see Christine Delphy, "For a Materialist Feminism," *Feminist Issues* 1.2 (1981): 69–76.

31. Brody, *Living Arctic*, 221.

32. For a description of the exhibition, see "On the Move in the Arctic," *Bulletin* of the British Museum Society, Autumn 1987: 3–5.

33. See Peter Kulchyski, "The Postmodern and the Paleolithic: Notes on Technology and Native Community in the Far North," *Canadian Journal of Political and Social Theory* 13.3 (1989): 49–62.

34. Although, as Raymond Williams points out, the industrial revolution may have dramatized better than any other period in history the effects of ecological disaster, it is an all too common error to assume that substantial tampering with the natural environment began only with this major historical change. During the industrial revolution itself, Williams notes, "environmentalist" debates took place in which "people idealized the pre-industrial order and supposed, for example, that there had been no significant and destructive intervention in the natural environ-

ment before industrialism. In fact of course — and this probably goes back to neo-lithic times — certain methods of farming, over-grazing, destruction of forests, had produced natural physical disasters on an enormous scale." Williams, "Socialism and Ecology," 212.

35. See, for example, Diamond and Orenstein, eds., *Reweaving the World;* and Judith Plant, ed., *Healing the Wounds: The Promise of Ecofeminism* (Toronto: Between the Lines, 1989).

36. Haraway, "A Cyborg Manifesto," 181, 151.

37. Kulchyski, "The Postmodern and the Paleolithic," 50, 58, 59.

38. Mona Etienne and Eleanor Leacock, eds., *Women and Colonization: Anthro-pological Perspectives* (New York: Praeger, 1980), 9–10.

39. Haraway, "Teddy Bear Patriarchy," in *Primate Visions: Gender, Race, and Na-ture in the World of Modern Science* (New York: Routledge, 1989), 48, 33, 45. For a reading of "men in fur" and the libidinal constructions of masculinity in the writ-ings of Jack London, see Mark Seltzer, "The Love-Master," in *Engendering Men: The Question of Male Feminist Criticism,* ed. Joseph A. Boone and Michael Cadden (New York: Routledge, 1992), 140–58.

40. Susan Sontag, *On Photography* (New York: Delta, 1977), quoted in Haraway, "Teddy Bear Patriarchy," 42.

41. Leacock and Etienne's thesis made significant gains in feminist theory by foregrounding the difference between gendered and sexed notions of the division of powers in aboriginal cultures, but feminist theorists, thanks to Judith Butler's seminal work *Gender Trouble,* have now come to understand that sex, and by exten-sion the notion of a sexual division of labor, cannot be taken as an unmediated ground on which to contruct gender differences, for "sex" too is a constructed so-cial and gender formation. See Judith Butler, *Gender Trouble: Feminism and the Sub-version of Identity* (New York: Routledge, 1990). For a working through of this prob-lematic from the question of political agency and the egalitarian thesis in aboriginal women's writings, discussed with reference to a colonial archive from the 1940s, see my article "The Power in Written Bodies: Gender, Decolonization, and the Ar-chive," in *Bodies of Writing, Bodies in Performance,* ed. Thomas Foster, Carol Siegel, and Ellen E. Berry, *Genders* 23 (Winter 1996): 184–211.

CHAPTER 2. THE SUMPTUOUS DETAILS OF HISTORY

1. Frances Elizabeth Baldwin, *Sumptuary Legislation and Personal Regulation in England,* Johns Hopkins University Studies in Historical and Political Science 44 (Baltimore: Johns Hopkins University Press, 1926).

2. Ibid., 10.

3. Chandra Mukerji, *From Graven Images: Patterns of Modern Materialism* (New York: Columbia University Press, 1983), 2, 4.

4. Claire Sponsler, "Narrating the Social Order: Medieval Clothing Laws," *Clio* 21.3 (1992): 267, 275, 279.

5. Ibid., 266–67.

6. *The Statutes of the Realm,* 11 vols. in 12 (1810–28; London: Dawsons, 1963), 1:381.

7. J. Anderson Black, *A History of Fashion* (London: Orbis, 1975), 70.

8. François Boucher, *20,000 Years of Fashion: The History of Costume and Personal*

Adornment, 2d ed. (New York: Abrams, 1987), 214. The primary source for the history of British fur fashions is Joseph Strutt, *A Complete View of the Dress and Habits of the People of England, from the establishment of the Saxons in Britain to the present time, illustrated by engravings taken from the most authentic remains of antiquity; to which is prefixed an Introduction containing a general description of the ancient habits in use among mankind from the earliest period of time to the conclusion of the seventeenth century*, 2 vols. (London, 1796–99), see especially 2 : 138–39.

9. Elspeth M. Veale, *The English Fur Trade in the Later Middle Ages* (Oxford: Clarendon Press, 1966), 138, 140.

10. Laura Hodges, "A Reconsideration of the Monk's Costume," *Chaucer Review* 26.2 (1991): 137. Hodges also cites an interesting ecclesiastical origin story to explain the inside/outside configuration of fur's placement: "The possibility exists that the purfled sleeves are part of the fur-lined sub-tunica commonly worn by the clergy which signified the skins of animals worn by Adam after the Fall over which the surplice signifying purity was worn" (137).

11. Boucher, *20,000 Years*, 214.

12. Sponsler, "Narrating the Social Order," 268.

13. *Statutes of the Realm*, 1: 380.

14. Ibid., 3 :430.

15. Pierre Bourdieu, *Distinction: A Social Critique of the Judgement of Taste*, trans. Richard Nice (Cambridge: Harvard University Press, 1984), 24.

16. Hodges, "Reconsideration," 141.

17. *Fellini's Roma*, dir. Federico Fellini, screenplay Federico Fellini and Bernardino Apponi, 1972. MGM/UA Video, 1991.

18. Baldwin, *Sumptuary Legislation*, 34–35, quoting John Stowe, *Annales: or, A General Chronicle of England* (ed. of 1631), 94.

19. Ibid., 41, 44, 61, 122, and see 257.

20. Ibid., 116, 166, and see 68.

21. Diane Owen Hughes, "Regulating Women's Fashion," in *A History of Women in the West*, vol. 2: *Silences of the Middle Ages*, ed. Christiane Klapisch-Zuber (Cambridge: Belknap Press of Harvard University Press, 1992), 140.

22. Phillip Stubbes, *Phillip Stubbes's Anatomy of the Abuses in England in Shakspere's Youth*, ed. Frederick J. Furnivall (London: New Shakspere Society, 1876–79); John Evelyn, *Tyrannus, or The Mode; In a Discourse of Sumptuary Lawes* (London, 1661). The full title of Stubbes's original work is *The Anatomie of Abuses: Contayning A Discoverie, or briefe Summarie, of such Notable Vices and Imperfections, as now raigne in many Christian Countreyes of the Worlde: but (especiallie) in a verie famous Ilande called Ailgna* [England]*: Together, with most fearefull Examples of Gods Iudgementes, executed vpon the wicked for the same, aswell in Ailgna of late, as in other places elsewhere. Verie Godly, to be read of all true Christians, euerie where; but most needeful, to be regarded in Englande. Made dialogue-wise by* Phillip Stubbes. *The Anatomie of Abuses* (part 1) was originally published 1 May 1583. Further editions were published in 1583, 1585, and 1595. The New Shakspere Society republished part 1 in 1876 and in 1879 republished parts 1 and 2 with extracts from other works by Stubbes, a scholarly commentary on the work and its reception in the late sixteenth century as well as some woodcuts of Elizabethan fashions. F. J. Furnivall edited these works for the society.

23. Thomas Dekker, *Seven Deadly Sinnes of London* (1606; Arber, 1879), 36–37; as quoted in Stubbes, *Anatomy of the Abuses*, 77*.

24. Stubbes, *Anatomy*, 44.

25. Ibid., 32–33, 70, 82.

26. Ibid., 33–34.

27. Ibid., 35.

28. Ibid., 64.

29. Ibid., 54–55, 73.

30. Ibid., 65, 69.

31. Baldwin, *Sumptuary Legislation*, 91–92.

32. Stubbes, *Anatomy of the Abuses*, 75.

33. Ibid.

34. Baldwin, *Sumptuary Legislation*, 264.

35. W. W. Cunningham argues that British sumptuary legislation of the late fourteenth century, particularly in regard to fur, was enlisted in support of domestic monopolies, providing protectionist measures against imports. Wool manufacturers, as the principal source of warm clothing, had the most to gain from such measures. See W. W. Cunningham, *The Growth of English Industry and Commerce during the Early and Middle Ages*, vol. 1 (New York: Augustus M. Kelley, 1968), 308.

36. Evelyn, *Tyrannus*, 2, 29.

37. Ibid., 4–5.

38. Ibid., 15, 18, 20.

39. Ibid., 24. The 1818 edition reads: "There may be much said (I confess) concerning customs and opinion which render all things supportable; but we in this nation can plead neither of these for our fantastical and often changes; if tis true they have prevailed amongst us, let us remember whose act it is; *Meddle not with those who are given to change*. We have suffer'd enough by these Lunatics, and been brought to nothing but our inconstancies, which however allowable in the weaker, becomes not the viriler Sex." See William Bray, ed., *Memoirs, Illustrative of the Life and Writings of John Evelyn* (London, 1818), 2: 329–30.

40. Ibid., 24–25.

41. Ibid., 21–22.

42. See Samuel Johnson, *English Dictionary*, vol. 2, additions by Rev. H. J. Todd, 2d ed. (London, 1827).

43. Evelyn, *Tyrannus*, 19–20, 28, 9. "I have heard say, that when a *Turk* would execrate one that displeases him, he wishes him as unstable as a *Christian Hat*" (27).

44. See Burris Meyer, *This Is Fashion* (New York: Harper and Brothers, 1943), 131.

45. See Eric R. Wolf, *Europe and the People without History* (Berkeley: University of California Press, 1982), 159–60.

46. Stubbes, *Anatomy of the Abuses*, 50.

47. J. Anderson Black and Madge Garland, *A History of Fashion*, ed. Frances Kennett (London: Orbis, 1980), 180, 196.

48. In the late nineteenth century the Paris arcades represented the best example of commodity display for the consumer-spectator. In her discussion of Walter Benjamin's critical reading of the arcades, in his *Passagen-Werk*, Anne Friedberg writes that the "relation between the reading room and the library stack, which offers the reader a clear view of the articles in stock, became a spatial model for the department store, where the consumer also had a clear view of the commodities on display. The shopper, like the library reader, was on a mission for knowledge, computing the relations between the social hieroglyphs of goods on display." Anne Friedberg,

Window Shopping: Cinema and the Postmodern (Berkeley: University of California Press, 1993), 79. In the late twentieth century the window display has all but erased its historical debt to the reading room; commodities and images now preoccupy our "reading" habits.

49. *Canada's Fur Bearers; containing Notes on the Principal Fur Bearing Animals of Canada, Trapping, and the Preparation of Furs for the Market* (Winnipeg: Fur Trade Department, Hudson's Bay House, 1933), 15.

50. Ibid., 3.

CHAPTER 3. THE MASOCHIST'S GIFT

1. Leopold von Sacher-Masoch, *Venus in Furs*, in *Masochism*, trans. Jean McNeil (New York: Zone, 1989), 179–80, hereafter cited in the text.

2. Richard von Krafft-Ebing, *Psychopathia Sexualis: A Medico-Forensic Study*, intro. Ernest van den Haag, trans. Harry E. Wedeck (New York: Putnam's, 1965), 127–28.

3. Masoch, "A Childhood Memory and Reflections on the Novel," in *Masochism*, 274.

4. Ibid., 275.

5. Krafft-Ebing, *Psychopathia Sexualis*, 197, 149.

6. Ibid., 234, 238 n. 1.

7. Sigmund Freud, "Fetishism" (1927), *The Standard Edition of the Complete Psychological Works of Sigmund Freud*, trans. James Strachey et al. (London: Hogarth Press, 1935–74), 21: 152, 155.

8. Kaja Silverman, *The Acoustic Mirror: The Female Voice in Psychoanalysis and Cinema* (Bloomington: Indiana University Press, 1988), 21.

9. Freud, "The Economic Problem of Masochism," *Standard Edition*, 19: 161, 162.

10. Masoch, "A Childhood Memory and Reflections on the Novel," in *Masochism*, 273.

11. Silverman, *Acoustic Mirror*, 28, 16, 20.

12. Krafft-Ebing, *Psychopathia Sexualis*, 142.

13. Elizabeth Grosz, "Lesbian Fetishism?" *Differences: A Journal of Feminist Cultural Studies* 3.2 (1991): 44, 42–43. Reprinted in *Fetishism as Cultural Discourse*, ed. Emily Apter and William Pietz (Ithaca: Cornell University Press, 1993).

14. Ibid., 45.

15. Gilles Deleuze defines masochism as a syndrome and not a symptom, "the meeting-place or crossing-point of manifestations issuing from very different origins and arising within variable contexts." See Deleuze, "Coldness and Cruelty," in *Masochism*, trans. Jean McNeil (New York: Zone, 1989), 14.

16. Another late nineteenth-century incarnation of the female sadist is the ubiquitous femme fatale. Like the feminine despot, the femme fatale "has power *despite herself*," precisely because, as Mary Ann Doane elaborates, she "is attributed with a body which is itself given agency independently of consciousness." *Femmes Fatales: Feminism, Film Theory, Psychoanalysis* (New York: Routledge, 1991), 2. The sort of false agency attributed to the sexually powerful and aggressive feminine despot in Masoch's novel is, not surprisingly, similar to the "power accorded to the femme fatale," which as Doane further observes is "a function of fears linked to the notions

of uncontrollable drives, the fading of subjectivity, and the loss of conscious agency — all themes of the emergent theories of psychoanalysis" (2). Doane echoes my own concern that the sexual power invested in these late nineteenth-century figures makes them especially important to feminist inquiries into the history of women and their access to economic, political, and symbolic modes of power: "Because she seems to confound power, subjectivity, and agency with the very lack of these attributes, her relevance to feminist discourses is critical. Since feminisms are forced to search out symbols from a lexicon that does not yet exist, their acceptance of the femme fatale as a sign of strength in an unwritten history must also and simultaneously involve an understanding and assessment of all the epistemological baggage she carries along with her" (3). Doane confirms that the feminine despot or female sadist, like the femme fatale, "is not the subject of feminism but a symptom of male fears about feminism" (2–3).

17. Krafft-Ebing, *Psychopathia Sexualis*, 127.

18. Angela Carter, *The Sadeian Woman: A Exercise in Cultural History* (London: Virago Press, 1979), 20.

19. Biddy Martin, *Woman and Modernity: The (Life)Styles of Lou Andreas-Salomé* (Ithaca: Cornell University Press, 1991), 2–3. Martin notes that the sharp polarization of the sexes characteristic of Wilhelminian Germany was sustained through an intensified intolerance of gender ambiguity. She quotes George L. Mosse's illustrative point that "by mid-nineteenth century the androgyne as an aggressive and almost masculine *femme fatale* had become a familiar figure in popular literature. . . . By the *fin de siècle* the androgyne was perceived as a monster of sexual and moral ambiguity, often identified with other 'outsiders' such as masochists, sadists, homosexuals, and lesbians" (3–4).

20. Arjun Appadurai, "Introduction: Commodities and the Politics of Value," in *The Social Life of Things: Commodities in Cultural Perspective*, ed. Appadurai (Cambridge: Cambridge University Press, 1986), 5.

21. Anne McClintock, *Imperial Leather: Race, Gender and Sexuality in the Colonial Contest* (New York: Routledge, 1995), 202, 203.

22. Michel Foucault, *The History of Sexuality*, vol. 1: *An Introduction*, trans. Robert Hurley (New York: Pantheon, 1978), 90.

23. Indeed, in the words of Wanda von Sacher-Masoch, Leopold's onetime wife, the bonds administered by state and church in the religious marriage ceremony represented a far greater restriction and degree of cruelty than those enforced by law: "If Sacher-Masoch and I had not married in a church but had gone to a notary and had a contract drawn up specifying (in the event of divorce) terms which would do the least possible harm to us and our children, and what should be my situation and that of the children — if we had done this, not only the ridiculous farce of the religious marriage ceremony but the cruel, repugnant procedure of divorce would have been spared me. . . . A notarized contract would have assured my future and that of my children better than was done by the State and the Church." Wanda von Sacher-Masoch, *The Confessions of Wanda von Sacher-Masoch*, ed. V. Vale and Andrea Juno, trans. Marian Phillips, Caroline Hébert, and V. Vale (San Francisco: Re/search, 1990), 119, hereafter cited in the text.

24. Masoch is playing with the historical investment in Greece as a utopian site of libidinal excess and its social forms of slavery which are the conditions of such sexual mastery and freedom. What is different, if not ironic, about Masoch's re-pre-

sentation of this ideological investment is that the figure of mastery is not a European man, as might be expected, but a European bourgeois woman. Naomi Schor comments that "fetishism necessarily speaks in tropes, but if it does, irony and not metaphor is the trope of fetishism." See "Fetishism and Its Ironies," in *Fetishism as Cultural Discourse*, ed. Apter and Pietz, 97.

25. Said, *Culture and Imperialism*, 132.

26. Alain Grosrichard, *Structure du serail* (Paris: Seuil, 1979), 156, as quoted by Barbara Harlow, in her Introduction to Malek Alloula, *The Colonial Harem*, Theory of History of Literature 21, trans. Myrna Godzich and Wlad Godzich (Minneapolis: University of Minnesota Press, 1986), xxi.

27. Alloula, *Colonial Harem*, 122.

28. Winifred Woodhull, "Unveiling Algeria," *Genders* 10 (1991): 124, 126. This essay appears in a revised form in Winifred Woodhull, *Transfigurations of the Maghreb: Feminism, Decolonization, and Literatures* (Minneapolis: University of Minnesota Press, 1993), see especially chap. 1.

29. For an extended discussion of the feminization of the Orient, see Julia V. Emberley, *Thresholds of Difference: Feminist Critique, Native Women's Writings, Postcolonial Theory* (Toronto: University of Toronto Press, 1993), especially 35–39.

30. There is also the correspondence between Severin and a mysterious person, whose "sex" is never confirmed. The appendix to *Masochism* contains an excerpt from *The Confessions of Wanda von Sacher-Masoch* which insists on Masoch's heterosexual orientation: "Whereas the exaltation of his correspondent seemed quite genuine, my husband knew that his own was not, and that although he did not admit it to himself, he was entirely fabricating it. Besides, 'The Love of Plato' was not his style at all, and the man who wrote under the name of Anatole must have known very little about Sacher-Masoch to have imagined otherwise. Leopold believed and sincerely hoped that it was a woman, but because he was afraid of creating a conflict between us, he pretended to believe and to desire quite the opposite. . . . our correspondent seemed to know nothing of Sacher-Masoch's personal life. How could he be ignorant, for example, of the fact that he was *married?* Plato married! Anatole had certainly never dreamt of that." "The Adventure with Ludwig II" (told by Wanda), in *Masochism*, 283.

31. Interestingly, slave figures represented in other novels such as *Uncle Tom's Cabin* and *Robinson Crusoe* also appear in the narratives of Krafft-Ebing's masochistic subjects, particularly in relation to female masochists who must imagine themselves as black slaves and not just (white) women in order to conjure the necessary feelings of humiliation: "Often I have dreamed that I was his slave — but, mind you, not his female slave! For instance, I have imagined that he was Robinson and I the savage that served him. I often look at the pictures in which Robinson puts his foot on the neck of the savage. I now find an explanation of these strange fancies: I look upon woman in general as low, far below man; but I am otherwise extremely proud and quite indomitable, whence it arises that I think as a man (who is by nature proud and superior). This renders my humiliation before the man I love the more intense. I have also fancied myself to be his female slave; but this does not suffice, for after all every woman can be the slave of her husband." Krafft-Ebing, *Psychopathia Sexualis*, 179 and see 137.

32. Deleuze, "Coldness and Cruelty," 31.

33. William Pietz, "The Problem of the Fetish," part 1, *Res* 9 (Spring 1985): 6.

34. Elizabeth Alexander, *The Venus Hottentot*, Callaloo Poetry Series 9 (Charlottesville: University Press of Virginia, 1990), 4. Reprinted with permission of University Press of Virginia.

35. McClintock argues that fetishes "may not always be disruptive or transgressive and can be mobilized for a variety of political ends — some progressive, some subversive, some deeply reactionary." *Imperial Leather*, 202. For my purposes, it is important to note how fetishes are generally always mobilized to inscribe a radical difference.

36. Ibid., 155.

37. Franz Kafka, *The Metamorphosis/Die Verwandlung*, trans. Willa Muir and Edwin Muir (New York: Schocken, 1946), 7.

38. See Gilles Deleuze and Félix Guattari, *Kafka: Toward a Minor Literature*, trans. Dana Polan (Minneapolis: University of Minnesota Press, 1986), chap. 2.

39. Ibid., 13, 14–15.

40. Angela Carter, *The Sadeian Woman*, 20–21.

41. In "Coldness and Cruelty," Deleuze's reading of the significance of the mother is heavily indebted, I think, to Wanda von Sacher-Masoch's *Confessions* and her own idealization of the figure of the mother, but what Deleuze interprets as the mother's preoedipal positioning conforms to a general infantilization of women that persistently refuses to acknowledge the powerful logic of such a teleology in covering over woman's exclusion from the symbolic (i.e., her entry into language and the law) as an effect of relations of power and domination. For an interesting reading of Deleuze's essay on masochism see Gaylyn Studlar, "Masochism, Masquerade, and the Erotic Metamorphoses of Marlene Dietrich," in *Fabrications: Costume and the Female Body*, ed. Jane Gaines and Charlotte Herzog (New York: Routledge, 1990), especially 233–34.

42. Jeffrey Mehlman, *Walter Benjamin for Children: An Essay on His Radio Years* (Chicago: University of Chicago Press, 1993), 83–84.

43. The real-life Wanda's feminism, or at least the agent of female empowerment she creates in the mother figure, stands in direct contrast to the figure of female empowerment represented by the imaginary Wanda, Leopold von Sacher-Masoch's feminine despot. On feminism, the real-life Wanda writes: "Why does the *feminist movement* not intervene here? Why does it not advance to the root of the evil, so as to sweep away all this old rotten institution of marriage — so contrary to our modern thoughts and feelings? Or if it cannot sweep it away, then ignore it? As long as women have not the courage to manage, without the intervention of State or Church, that which concerns them alone — their relations with men — they will not be free. Whatever this movement may have produced or *will* produce will not endure, because it tends to bring the woman out of the sphere which is hers, and which nature has destined to her; and nothing which is contrary to nature can endure or bring happiness" (119). The feminine despot and the maternal woman stand in opposition to each other and yet constitute similarly circumscribed notions of female agency in late nineteenth-century Europe: the mother is linked to education and the intellect, the feminine despot to a body without consciousness.

CHAPTER 4. THE FECUNDITY OF FUR

1. John Berger, *Ways of Seeing* (London: British Broadcasting Corp. and Penguin, 1972), especially 60–61.

2. Ibid., 61.

3. Anne Hollander, *Seeing through Clothes* (Berkeley: University of California Press, 1975), xiii.

4. Berger, *Ways of Seeing*, 61.

5. Hollander, *Seeing through Clothes*, xii.

6. The embroidered bodice is described as follows: "linen embroidered with silver and silver-gilt thread and silks in detached button-hole, stem, chain, plaited braid, knotted and speckling stitch, trimmed with silver and silver-gilt bobbin lace and spangles. *English, about 1620.* The bodice was worn by Margaret Laton when she sat for the portrait painted by Marcus Gheeraerts." Natalie Rothstein, ed., *Four Hundred Years of Fashion*, text by Madeleine Ginsburg, Avril Hart, Valerie D. Mendes, and other members of the Department of Textiles and Dress, photography by Philip Barnard (London: Victoria and Albert Museum, 1984), 17. The bodice also appears in Millia Davenport, *The Book of Costume* (New York: Crown, 1948), 2: 565.

7. Hollander, *Seeing through Clothes*, xii.

8. Ibid., xiii.

9. Bourdieu, *Distinction*, 3 (emphasis added), 5.

10. Two excellent books that combine images of actual clothing with photographic images are Rothstein, *Four Hundred Years*, and the catalog for the Metropolitan Museum of Art exhibition to commemorate the fiftieth anniversary of the founding of the Costume Institute at the Museum of Costume Art, Jean L. Druesedow, ed., *In Style: Celebrating Fifty Years of the Costume Institute* (New York: Metropolitan Museum of Art, 1987).

11. Druesedow, *In Style*, 3. See Cesare Vecellio, *Vecellio's Renaissance Costume Book: All 500 Woodcut Illustrations from the Famous Sixteenth-Century Compendium of World Costume* (New York: Dover, 1977).

12. In this seminal essay, "The Work of Art in the Age of Mechanical Reproduction," first published in German in 1936, Walter Benjamin traces the "developmental tendencies of art" under the effects of early twentieth century European conditions of economic capitalism and the rising political power of fascism. His analysis is dialectical, in that Benjamin's interest in reading the historical change in modes of perception and conception from "the work of art" to "mechanical reproduction" lies in tracing an emancipatory potential within ideologies of art under capitalism which is indicative of the very conditions capital creates, however inadvertently, "to abolish capitalism itself." In other words, Benjamin sees within this historical shift an impending crisis for a nineteenth-century ideology of aesthetics. Although that crisis may be managed, eventually, within the terms of mechanical reproduction, there nevertheless exists an interstitial space of difference where the seeds of an emancipatory potential begin to grow. Benjamin also traces residual aspects of an ideology of the aesthetic as they survive in a different form within the media of film and photography. Furthermore, he accounts for the present conditions of dominance which exploit the media of mechanical reproduction. Residual, dominant, and emergent modes of perception/conception are dialectically interwoven in Benjamin's text on the developmental interrelatedness of class and politics

in mechanical reproduction. See Walter Benjamin, "The Work of Art in the Age of Mechanical Reproduction," in *Illuminations*, 217.

13. Ivins insists on print culture as a form of visual communication: "This means that, far from being merely minor works of art, prints are among the most important and powerful tools of modern life and thought. Certainly we cannot hope to realize their actual role unless we get away from the snobbery of modern print collecting notions and definitions and begin to think of them as exactly repeatable pictorial statements or communications, without regard to the accident of rarity or what for the moment we may regard as aesthetic merit. We must look at them from the point of view of general ideas and particular functions, and, especially, we must think about the limitations which their techniques have imposed on them as conveyors of information and on us as receivers of that information." William M. Ivins Jr., *Prints and Visual Communication* (Cambridge: MIT Press, 1969), 3.

14. Katherine S. Van Eerde, *Wenceslaus Hollar: Delineator of His Time*, published for the Folger Shakespeare Library (Charlottesville: University Press of Virginia, 1970), 23. See also George Vertue, *A Description of the Works of the Ingenious Delineator and Engraver Wenceslaus Hollar disposed into Classes of Different Sorts with Some Account of His Life* (London, 1745); and Arthur M. Hind, *Wenceslaus Hollar and His Views of London and Windsor in the Seventeenth Century* (London: Bodley Head, 1922). Catalogs of Hollar's works include Gustav Parthey, *Kurzes Verzeichniss der Hollar'schen Kupferstiche* (Berlin, 1853); and Richard Pennington, *A Descriptive Catalogue of the Etched Work of Wenceslaus Hollar, 1607–1677* (Cambridge: Cambridge University Press, 1982).

15. Van Eerde, *Wenceslaus Hollar*, 6, 23, 21, 17, 22, 5.

16. Jacqueline Burgers, *Wenceslaus Hollar: Seventeenth-Century Prints from the Museum Boymans–Van Beuningen, Rotterdam* (Alexandria, Va.: Arts Service International, 1994), 57, 71.

17. Ibid., 81.

18. Benjamin, "The Work of Art," in *Illuminations*, 220.

19. Ibid., 221.

20. Ibid., 223.

21. R. Turner Wilcox, *The Mode in Furs* (New York: Scribner's, 1951), 91. Wilcox links the fashion in furs to the rise of the fur trade in the seventeenth century, the founding of the Hudson's Bay Company (1665), and its two-hundred-year monopoly on the trade of beaver fur especially.

22. Black and Garland, *History of Fashion*, 191, 188.

23. Davenport, *Book of Costume*, 579, 579a, 580. The French fashion historian François Boucher also reproduces the full-length female figures of *The Four Seasons*. With reference to *Winter* he notes that the "mask is typical of the period, as was the sable muff, an indispensable accessory in winter, and the fur cravat, which does not seem to have been worn in France at this time." Boucher, *20,000 Years*, 272.

24. Ibid., 587a–88, 616a.

25. Benjamin, "The Work of Art," in *Illuminations*, 218.

26. Dion Calthrop, *English Costume* (London: Adam and Charles Black, 1906), vol. 3, n.p.

27. Roland Barthes, "The Photographic Message" in *Image/Music/Text*, trans. Stephen Heath (New York: Hill and Wang, 1977), 25–26.

28. Color films, developed in the 1930s, were certainly available when Benjamin wrote his essay, but color was not to become the extraordinary device for replacing

an earlier perception of "realism" until the 1960s, when television converted to color. Graeme Turner notes that color's function was originally "not to create the illusion of the real, but to signify artifice, decoration, the cinema as story-teller. In *The Wizard of Oz*, colour is used in the fantasy world of Oz, while the 'real' world of Dorothy's Kansas home is shot in black and white. As colour became part of current affairs programmes and news reporting on television it lost its association with fantasy and spectacle." Graeme Turner, *Film as Social Practice* (London: Routledge, 1988), 17–18.

29. Boucher, *20,000 Years*, 7a.

30. To note that reproduced images serve such functions is by no means to reduce those images exclusively to functionality. What is important is that such images, in particular contexts, are deployed for various purposes.

31. Benjamin, "The Work of Art," in *Illuminations*, 226.

32. Boucher, *20,000 Years*, 191.

33. H. W. Janson with Dora Jane Janson, *History of Art: A Survey of the Major Visual Arts from the Dawn of History to the Present Day* (New York: Abrams, 1969), 292.

34. Boucher, *20,000 Years*, 198a.

35. James Laver, *Costume and Fashion: A Concise History*, 2d ed. (London: Thames and Hudson, 1982), 64.

36. Boucher, *20,000 Years*, 191.

37. Laver, *Costume and Fashion*, 84, 86, 85.

38. Helen Langdon, with notes by James Malpas, *Holbein*, 2d ed. (London: Phaidon Press, 1993), 19.

39. Malpas, ibid., 64, 66.

40. Benjamin, "The Work of Art," in *Illuminations*, 225.

41. Ibid., 232.

42. Ibid., 234, 237 (emphasis added), 232, 239, 241.

43. Suzanna Danuta Walters, *Material Girls: Making Sense of Feminist Cultural Theory* (Berkeley: University of California Press, 1995), 89.

44. Valerie Steele, *Fetish: Fashion, Sex, and Power* (New York: Oxford University Press, 1996), 42.

45. See Judy Olausen, *Mother*, intro. Karin Winegar (Toronto: Penguin, 1996), for the complete collection of images.

CHAPTER 5. HOW TO MISREAD FASHION

1. Hudson's Bay Company, *General Court of the Governor and Company of Adventurers of England trading into Hudson's Bay was held at the City Terminus Hotel, Cannon Street, London, EC4, on Tuesday, the 29th Day of June, 1926, Mr. Charles V. Sale (the Governor), presiding* (London: Hudson's Bay Company, 1926), 9.

2. Great Britain, House of Commons, *Parliamentary Debates*, 10 February 1926: 1169.

3. Hudson's Bay Company, *General Court*, 9–10.

4. Virginia Woolf, *Three Guineas*, in *A Room of One's Own/Three Guineas*, ed. Michèle Barrett (Toronto: Penguin, 1993), 134.

5. Michèle Barrett, Introduction, ibid., xxx–xxxi, quoting *Three Guineas*, 138.

Barrett's wonderful edition provides the reader with the opportunity to see fragments from Woolf's scrapbook of newspaper clippings and images that represent her critical catalog of the male-invested symbolic capital in ritual clothing.

6. Woolf, *Three Guineas*, 137. Also worth commenting on here is Woolf's attention in this paragraph to "primitive fetishism" and the double standard that exists for the imperial male elite: "And still the tradition, or belief, lingers among us that to express worth of any kind, whether intellectual or moral, by wearing pieces of metal, or ribbon, coloured hoods or gowns, is a barbarity which deserves the ridicule which we bestow upon the rites of savages. A woman who advertised her motherhood by a tuft of horsehair on the left shoulder would scarcely, you will agree, be a venerable object" (137). Meanwhile, men of high social, professional, or intellectual standing advertise their status through signs and symbols on their bodies, very similar, Woolf points out, to forms of symbolic display which such men attribute to and ridicule in the indigenous cultures of the colonies — as well as bourgeois women.

7. James Laver notes that in Paris in the 1890s fur fashions were worn principally by women, contrary to previous practice: "The Russian fleet visited Toulon in 1893, and three years later the Tsar himself came to Paris amid scenes of the greatest enthusiasm. This inaugurated a vogue for furs, which were adopted by women as well as by men: in former ages fur had been almost entirely a male prerogative. The position was now somewhat reversed, in that women wore furs in the form not only of trimmings, but of whole fur coats, whereas men's fur coats had the fur on the inside, the fur being visible only in the collar and the cuffs." Laver, *Costume and Fashion*, 210–11. Marybelle Bigelow writes that the "first fur coats [for women] appeared in 1808 and are believed to have been introduced by Russians visiting Paris. Two names were used for this garment, each described the use made of the fur. If the exterior were fur and the lining silk, it was called the *witzchoura* and was of Russian origin. However, when spelled *witchoura*, it was of Polish design and was a heavy woolen coat with a fur lining. In both instances, this warm outer garment was styled like a redingote." See Marybelle S. Bigelow, *Fashion in History: Western Dress, Prehistoric to Present* (Minneapolis: Burgess, 1979), 218.

8. For an excellent collection of essays that foreground women as astute readers of cultural and social fashion practices, see Gaines and Herzog, *Fabrications*. See also Elizabeth Wilson, *Adorned in Dreams: Fashion and Modernity* (London: Virago Press, 1985).

9. See Barthes, *Fashion System*, and Lévi-Strauss, "The Structural Study of Myth" in his *Structural Anthropology*.

10. Barthes, *Fashion System*, 247, see also 236–37.

11. Ibid., 231–32.

12. Simone de Beauvoir, *The Second Sex*, trans. H. M. Parshley (New York: Vintage, 1952), 702, 706.

13. Maximizing these tensions is ultimately productive to the extent that elaborating the terrain contested by symbolic, economic, and political agencies brings into focus class as well as cultural differences among women, hence demystifying feminist theories of the universal oppression of women, which make it virtually impossible to comprehend, for example, the politics of contestation between many indigenous or aboriginal women's movements and their colonial counterparts.

14. On the melodramatic conventions of the film, see Patrice Petro, *Joyless*

Streets: Women and Melodramatic Representation in Weimar Germany (Princeton: Princeton University Press, 1989), especially 199–219.

15. Mary Ann Doane, "The Erotic Barter: *Pandora's Box*," in her *Femmes Fatales*, 142, 143, 144.

16. Petro, *Joyless Streets*, 204.

17. It is as if the contempt Pabst displays in the film for the callous brutality of rich men has metamorphosed into self-loathing for his work as a fiction film director and not a political film documentarist. Perhaps that is why the film ends with the restoration of middle-class values, the middle ground between destitution and enormous wealth, an interstitial space of enormous distance that protects the wealthy from any visible confrontation with the poor, while it provides the poor with a moral frontier to strive to conquer in place of material comfort.

18. The similarities between *The Joyless Street* and *Pandora's Box* are striking on this point. Mary Anne Doane observes that "Alwa's two addictions in the film are Lulu and gambling, linking a peculiarly modern conceptualization of free sexuality with the idea of unrestrained speculation at the economic level; in both cases the returns can be either pleasurable or unpleasurable." "The Erotic Barter," in *Pandora's Box*, 156.

19. Stephen Heath, "Lessons from Brecht," *Screen* 15. (1970): 107, as quoted in Silverman, *Acoustic Mirror*, 6.

20. Why do women who wear fur not have hands? It is curious that fashion images of women in fur, at least during the twentieth century, rarely show their hands. They are always buried in the sensuous depth of the fur or some undisclosed deep pocket. I have already noted Kafka's exaggerated reference to Freud's ideas on sexual fetishism and his traditional oedipal interpretation of women's hands disappearing into the folds of fur, like the longed-for penis that has already disappeared into the vaginal muff. For Pabst, hands represent a destructive greed, a grabbing at things and women, a murderous desire. Hands also represent a site of the body's labor. The disappearing hands re-present, on the one hand, the disappearance of labor, on the other hand, their reactivation as instruments of greed and accumulation. The disappearance of the male laboring body and its subsequent metonymic displacement onto the female body finds a historical link to the emergence of the femme fatale in the late nineteenth century. Mary Ann Doane, citing Christine Buci-Glucksmann, notes that "this is the moment when the male seems to lose access to the body, which the woman then comes to *overrepresent*. The 'working body' is 'confiscated by the alienation of machines' and 'submitted to industrialization and urbanization.' At the same time, in a compensatory gesture, the woman is made to inhere even more closely to the body." Doane, *Femmes Fatales*, 2, citing Buci-Glucksmann, *La raison baroque: de Baudelaire à Benjamin* (Paris: Éditions Galilée, 1984). To put another spin on the disappearance of labor in the contemporary context of fur fashion production: the disappearance of the laboring hands represents the disappearance of the laboring class of workers in the fur industry as that laboring class has been systematically moved to the fur factories of the "new industrializing countries."

21. Doane, "The Erotic Barter," in *Femmes Fatales*, 144.

22. Petro, *Joyless Streets*, 207.

23. Pabst was very interested in the use of the flashback technique to convey the psychic and mental processes of a character. It was especially notable in his next

film, *Secrets of the Soul* (1926), which deals explicitly with the application of Freudian theories and practices. Maureen Turim points out that in this film "dream sequences and flashbacks serve important narrative functions, churning and distorting narrative events already seen. Later, these events are isolated and rearranged as connections and meanings are provided for them. Flashbacks are used to display the verbalizations by the patient during the psychoanalytic sessions, an innovation of historical and theoretical importance." Maureen Turim, *Flashbacks in Film: Memory and History* (New York: Routledge, 1989), 85. In *The Joyless Street* the susceptibility of Maria to fantasy, romanticism, and delusion is also revealed by the "confessional" context in which the flashback occurs.

24. Petro, *Joyless Streets*, 209.

25. See Marjorie Garber, *Vested Interests: Cross-Dressing and Cultural Anxiety* (New York: Routledge, 1992). For a discussion of positions and position takings, see Pierre Bourdieu, "The Field of Cultural Production; or, The Economic World Reversed," in *Field of Cultural Production*, especially 30.

26. See Bourdieu, "The Field of Cultural Production," 32.

27. The House of LaBeija, House of Xtravaganza, House of Chanel, House of Pendavis, and the House of Saint Laurent — all these "houses" mimic the fashion houses of Paris, but they also function to house homeless boys whose families have rejected them because they are gay. The houses shift the discourse from the traditional family of filiative bonds to an affiliative bonding, a "sisterhood." Dorian Corey says, "It's not a question of a man, a woman, and children which we grew up knowing as a family. It's a question of a group of human beings in a mutual bond. . . . You know what a house is? I'll tell you what a house is. A house is a gay street gang. Now, a street gang gets their reward from street fighting. A gay house street fights at a ball, and you street fight at a ball by walking in the categories. The house is started because you want a name. The people that the houses are named after were ball walkers who became known for winning. After the first few houses were started and named after people who had won trophies, they would create houses like a new group of kids would create a house and work at building its name up."

28. Ironically and tragically, Venus Xtravaganza's mimicry comes off as the most reactionary use of language in the film. She rarely gets beyond woman-as-whore: "If you are married, a woman in the suburbs . . . if she wants a washer or dryer, she has to go to bed with him to get what she wants."

29. The film contains one time break, from 1987 to 1989. In 1989 we are told that Venus Xtravaganza has been murdered. She was found four days after she died, under a bed in a seedy New York hotel. No midnight cowboy came to her rescue.

30. "We assassinate," says Willy, like the Ninja from whom he takes his name.

31. Madonna brought vogue-ing into the arena of popular culture with her music video "Vogue." See *Madonna: The Immaculate Collection*. This video collection also contains a live version of "Vogue" from the 1990 MTV Awards Show in which Madonna and dancers reinvent a sumptuous display of a seventeenth-century French court, dressed in period costumes.

32. James Van Der Zee's photograph titled *A Couple Wearing Raccoon Coats with a Cadillac, Taken on West 127th Street* (1932), from his collection of images of Harlem during the 1920s and 1930s, depicts a black middle-class couple in fur. This photographic image placed beside the popular image of the black pimp in fur dramatizes the racist visual imagery of the latter, designed to criticize an aspiring

so-called underclass for "wrongly" appropriating symbolic power. See Deborah Willis-Braithwaite, ed., *Van Der Zee: Photographer, 1886–1983* (New York: Abrams, 1993), 12.

33. Marshall Berman illuminates this point in his dialectical critique of Marx on the issue of free trade: "This society is driven by its unprincipled principle of free exchange to open itself to movements for radical change. The enemies of capitalism may enjoy a great deal of freedom to do their work — to read, write, speak, meet, organize, demonstrate, strike, elect. But their freedom to move transforms their movement into an enterprise, and they find themselves cast in the paradoxical role of merchants and promoters of revolution, which necessarily becomes a commodity like everything else. Marx does not seem to be disturbed by the ambiguities of his social role — maybe because he is sure that it will become obsolete before it can ossify, that the revolutionary enterprise will be put out of business by its rapid success. A century later, we can see how the business of promoting revolution is open to the same abuses and temptations, manipulative frauds and wishful self-deceptions, as any other promotional line." See Marshall Berman, *All That Is Solid Melts into Air: The Experience of Modernity* (London: Verso, 1983), 114.

34. On the aristocratic values of Reagan's era, see Debora Silverman, *Selling Culture: Bloomingdale's, Diana Vreeland, and the New Aristocracy of Taste in Reagan's America* (New York: Pantheon, 1986).

35. The next block of scenes shows Mizrahi in Paris under the caption "A voyage and a vision." In the background Eartha Kitt is singing "Je Cherche un Homme." Mizrahi sits with the boys in a Paris café including André Léon Talley, creative director of *Vogue*, someone reads his Tarot cards, and the scene ends with a shot of Mizrahi holding a romantic glance in somebody's direction. We can only guess toward whom the loving and sexually inspired glance is directed. At the beginning of this charged scene of homoeroticism, Mizrahi bemoans the necessity of pursuing his fashion business in a foreign place. He prefers the domestic comforts of home. In another narrative segment titled "Back to front," Mizrahi says that living in New York is all he needs and wants. He doesn't have to go to Australia or India to do his collections. He can watch a *Flintstones* episode that was set in Australia if he wants some ideas. The enclosed, domestic production of popular and high culture serves equally well as source of inspiration. Why leave New York or America when the fantasy of cultural difference is itself so uniquely American? Nevertheless, Mizrahi manages to find some pleasure in crossing the border of the domestic into the foreign.

36. The image appears in *Vogue* [Paris], March 1990: 170. Winifred Woodhull explains that "in the fall of 1989 high-school girls defending their right to wear the Muslim headscarf, the *hijeb*, in school met with intense opposition from many groups — groups that are often at odds with each other — despite support from civil rights advocates and antiracist liberals (including many Maghrebians) who refused to single out the *hijeb* (as opposed to the cross or the yarmulke) as an intolerable intrusion of religion into public education. Among their opponents were school administrators defending what they claimed was France's commitment to the separation of church and state." Woodhull, *Transfigurations of the Maghreb*, 48.

37. Since Gaultier's and Mizrahi's spring fashion shows, the fascination with the Eskimo and *Nanook of the North* has reached a high level of exoticism and market value in the fashion industry which extends to new trends in "magazine actresses" (compared as they are to silent film actresses such as Louise Brooks). Irina Pantaeva

is one such model, self-described in an article in *New Yorker* as a "Siberian Eskimo." In the article, "Irina Rising," Pantaeva's movielike existence is considered in light of "the high-concept 'Nanook' premise." Jay McInerney, "Irina Rising," *New Yorker* 21 and 28 August 1995: 70. See also a brief interview with Pantaeva and a preface on the concept of the "magazine actress" in Richard Pandiscio, "What a World," *Interview*, February 1996: 82–83.

CHAPTER 6. FURS IN DISGUISE

1. "Furs in Disguise," *New York Times Magazine*, 27 September 1992: 56–61.
2. See "Animal Expressionism," *Vogue* [London], September 1989: 350–57.
3. "Now You See Them . . . Andrew Powell on the Great Safari Debate," *Vogue* [London], December 1990: 119, 124.
4. "Andy Warhol's *Colouring Book*," *Vogue* [London], December 1990: 160–78.
5. Candida Lycett Green, "The Sublime and the Beautiful: Rare Breeds," photographed by Snowdon, *Vogue* [London], December 1990: 198–200.
6. "Getting a Jump on Spring," *Toronto Star*, 3 October 1991: D4.
7. "Official Program," *Qaggiq '95*, 18–19 February 1995, Canadian Museum of Civilization.
8. Promotional release from the Canadian Museum of Civilization, 30 November 1995, for Winterlude, 17 and 18 February 1996.
9. Judy Hall, Jill Oakes, and Sally Qimmiu'naaq Webster, eds., *Sanatujut, Pride in Women's Work: Copper and Caribou Inuit Clothing Traditions* (Hull, Quebec: Canadian Museum of Civilization, 1994), 122.
10. Ibid., 122.
11. Douglas Crimp, "On the Museum's Ruins," *The Anti-Aesthetic: Essays on Postmodern Culture*, ed. Hal Foster (Port Townsend, Wash.: Bay Press, 1983), 45.
12. Laver, *Costume and Fashion*, 8.
13. See Edward W. Said, *Orientalism* (New York: Vintage, 1978).
14. Maria Campbell and Linda Griffiths, *The Book of "Jessica": A Theatrical Transformation* (Toronto: Coach House Press, 1989), 121.
15. Michel Foucault, "Fantasia of the Library," in *Language, Counter-Memory, Practice*, trans. Donald F. Bouchard and Sherry Simon (Ithaca: Cornell University Press, 1977), 92–93, as quoted in Crimp, "On the Museum's Ruins," 47.
16. For an excellent account of homeworking in Britain, see Annie Phizacklea, *Unpacking the Fashion Industry: Gender, Racism, and Class in Production* (London: Routledge, 1990).
17. See McInerney, "Irina Rising," 70.
18. Cruikshank, *Life Lived like a Story*, 354.
19. In "Decolonizing the Mind — September 1994" Edward Said addresses the question of how writers, intellectuals, and citizens "confront the question of how as people living and working in one culture they relate to other cultures." See *Peace and Its Discontents* (London: Vintage, 1995), 91. Said argues that the problem of monolithic configuration of a large community or nation-state is especially acute in the context of a postimperial contest. Homogenizing tendencies exist on both sides of the imperial/antiimperial divide. The irony is that this divided consciousness must map itself onto a complex cultural formation, already fluid, hybrid, and mixed. On the one hand, discourses of difference, with their attendant codes of particu-

larity, specificity, and diversity, successfully alleviate the homogenizing tendencies produced by the imperial/antiimperial "mind." Increasing specificity, if not a uniqueness attributed through "cultural difference," confounds the reductive effects of universal categorization. On the other hand, diversity permeates the borders of a contradictorily divided consciousness. A cultural politics of difference, as Said conceives it, must re-*mind* its audience that cultural vitality has always depended on diversity and that such diversity is a creative site of interconnection and not, as is often assumed, a privileged site of radical otherness where no connection is desirable or feasible. As Julie Cruikshank observes: "The intensive fur trade during the late nineteenth century, fueled by the demands of international fur markets, led to considerable blurring of linguistic and cultural boundaries." *Life Lived like a Story*, 5.

20. Recalling my discussion in Chapter 1 of the problem of positioning aboriginal cultures as signs of a redemptive faculty there to cure the West of its ills, I want here to insist that aboriginal storytelling practices are nevertheless important to environmental issues, and their relevance should not be foreclosed by an ideology of cultural difference which persists in bracketing off this critical importance.

21. Cruikshank, *Life Lived like a Story*, 346, emphasis added.

22. Ibid., 8, 344.

23. Ibid., 15. Cruikshank elaborates the ethics of academic research: "Documenting life histories has always been an approved fieldwork *method* in anthropology, particularly in North America. Until recently, though, such accounts were treated as supplementary material, possibly a corrective to ethnographic description or a way to breathe life into academic writing. Renewed anthropological interest in life histories coincides with increasing attention to analysis of symbolism, meaning, and text. The expectation seems less that such accounts will clarify social structure and more that they may show how individuals use what Sapir called the "scaffolding of culture" to talk about their lives. The present volume is based on the premise that life-history investigation provides a model for research. Instead of working from the conventional formula in which an outside investigation initiates and controls the research, this model depends on ongoing collaboration between interviewer and interviewee. Such a model begins by taking seriously what people say about their lives rather than treating their words simply as an illustration of some other process. By looking at ways people use the traditional dimension of culture as a resource to talk about the past, we may be able to see life history as contributing to explanations of cultural process rather than as simply illustrating or supplementing ethnographic description" (1–2). I would still question whether the attention to the ethics of academic protocols is sufficient to transform a long history of colonial relations.

24. Ibid., 355.

25. Ibid., 2, 4, 1.

26. Ibid., 10, emphasis added.

27. Ibid., 346, 347.

28. Ibid., 347, 350.

29. Gilles Deleuze and Félix Guattari, *Nomadology: The War Machine*, trans. Brian Massumi (New York: Semiotext(e), 1986), 54.

30. The issue of mass communication is important here. In his essay, "The Storyteller," Walter Benjamin traces the transition from feudalism to capitalism through the figure of the storyteller. Specifically, Benjamin narrates the decline of

the storytelling craft in feudalism and the emergence of the novel form in capitalism. By the mid-nineteenth century, the storytelling that was nurtured by feudal
relations and mercantile wealth exists only as a residual element in the novel form.
For the most part, storytelling's use value had been vacated for the exchange value
of information retrieval in the beginning stages of mass-mediated communication
systems.

There are two kinds of storytellers for Benjamin — one local, full of homebound
experience, and a bearer of traditional knowledge, history, and folklore, the other
from far away, carrying the stories of journeys to and from exotic places. "If one
wants to picture these two groups through their archaic representatives, one is embodied in the resident tiller of the soil, and the other in the trading seaman. Indeed,
each sphere of life has, as it were, produced its own tribe of storytellers. Each of
these tribes preserves some of its characteristics centuries later. . . . The actual
extension of the realm of storytelling in its full historical breadth is inconceivable
without the most intimate interpenetration of these two archaic types. Such an interpenetration was achieved particularly by the Middle Ages in their trade structure. . . . If peasants and seamen were past masters of storytelling, the artisan class
was its university. In it was combined the lore of faraway places, such as a much-
travelled man brings home, with the lore of the past, as it best reveals itself to natives
of a place." "The Storyteller," in *Illuminations*, 84–85. Both modes of storytelling
are characterized by a spatial orientation toward social relations, whether local or
distant. Fernand Braudel notes that it was not until "1857 with the laying of the
first intercontinental maritime cable" that mass communication achieved a world-
scale effect. This achievement marks for Braudel, quoting Ernst Wagemann, "the
defeat of space." Braudel, *Capitalism and Material Life, 1400–1800*, trans. Miriam
Kochan (New York: Harper and Row, 1973), 310. With the novel, then, time begins
to dominate as the organizing principle of narrative structure. The rise of capitalism
and the novel form leads Benjamin to lament: "It is as if something that seemed
inalienable to us, the securest among our possessions, were taken from us: the
ability to exchange experiences." "The Storyteller," 83.

The emergence of communication systems increases information exchange,
which is not only incompatible with the "spirit of storytelling," says Benjamin, but
also brings about the crisis the novel must ideologically resolve. As storytelling
technologies, the novel form and mass media information systems clearly dominate
exchange value, helping to make storytelling practices obsolete, not to mention
the social relations such storytelling practices make possible. Those relations are,
for the most part, nostalgically feudal. Storytelling is one of "the oldest forms of
craftsmanship," and yet, perhaps, not so much feudal as palaeolithic: "Thus traces
of the storyteller cling to the story the way the handprints of the potter cling to the
clay vessel" (92). There is another, residual mode of storytelling production that
weaves its way into Benjamin's account of the seemingly feudal, mercantile storyteller. What is missing from Benjamin's account are the people with whom those
seaman and merchants of the sea came into contact. Were not these people the
subject of stories? Did their existence not constitute for the traffic in stories a veritable treasure house of images, meanings, values, symbols, and so on, for the European traveler-cum-storyteller? One thinks here of the novels of Joseph Conrad
such as *Heart of Darkness* and *Lord Jim*. And would not the tiller of the soil, the
decisive figure of the neolithic revolution, have soaked up these exotic stories as
confirmation of overcoming their "archaic," if not savage, way of life? Or perhaps

these stories from far away began to compete with the local traditions and histories; what to Benjamin looked like a necessary combination achieved through "interpenetration" may indeed have been a hybrid mode of storytelling practice in which could be read the contradictions that the traffic in mercantile wealth might have produced for the peasant's existence.

31. See "The Dogs Bark Mysteriously in the Night" and "Edward Rides a Caribou," in Blondin, *When the World Was New*, 151–58.

32. See also "An Oldtimer's Prophesy," in Blondin, *When the World Was New*, 78–79.

33. Changing attitudes toward cultural differences between Dene and Inuit are also noted briefly: "'Oh, you're Edward Blondin's son,' the man exclaimed. My dad travelled all over the country, and everyone knew him. 'At first, I thought you were Inuit, and I got scared. You know, we used to fight wars a long time ago and we're enemies. That's why I wouldn't talk to you at first.' The Dene sometimes used to have strange ideas about other people. A long time ago, there were lots of different groups speaking different languages; they lived hundreds of kilometres apart, and never saw one another. The people passed down stories about using medicine power against other groups or of wars fought a long time ago." Blondin, *When the World Was New*, 233.

34. Cash exchange for furs increased throughout the twentieth century. George Blondin mentions one incident: "When it got warm, we packed our traps and fur, and moved to Sahtú. When we got there, a trader wanted to buy our fur, but Dad said we should get at least $1,300, while the trader offered only $1,000. The next day, a plane came in from Sòmbak'è carrying Sam Barr, who offered us $1,500. We sold the furs to him." Blondin, *When the World Was New*, 222.

35. "Fur prices dropped during the War. The Hudson's Bay Company was paying $5 for mink, $7 for marten, $5 for red fox, $12 for beaver and 50 cents for muskrat. In the meantime, the price of food was going up. It was hard to make a good living." Blondin, *When the World Was New*, 228.

36. The problem of female representation in aboriginal communities is addressed in a discussion paper released by the Nunavut Implementation Commission, titled *Two-Member Constituencies and Gender Equality: A "Made in Nunavut" Solution for an Effective and Representative Legislature*, Iqaluit, December 1994.

37. Cruikshank, *Life Lived like a Story*, 84–85.

38. On the significance of technologies of representation in the late twentieth century, see Terry Eagleton, *Literary Theory: An Introduction* (Minneapolis: University of Minnesota Press, 1983), 216.

39. As paraphrased by Susan Buck-Morss, "Aesthetics and Anaesthetics: Walter Benjamin's Artwork Essay Reconsidered," *October* 62 (1992): 5.

Bibliography

Alexander, Elizabeth. *The Venus Hottentot.* Callaloo Poetry Series 9.
Charlottesville: University Press of Virginia, 1990.
Alloula, Malek. *The Colonial Harem.* Theory of History of Literature. 21. Trans.
Myrna Godzich and Wlad Godzich. Minneapolis: University of Minnesota
Press, 1986.
"Andy Warhol's *Colouring Book.*" *Vogue* [London], December 1990: 160–78.
"Animal Expressionism." *Vogue* [London], September 1989: 350–57.
Appadurai, Arjun, ed. *The Social Life of Things: Commodities in Cultural Perspective.*
Cambridge: Cambridge University Press, 1986.
Apter, Emily, and William Pietz, eds. *Fetishism as Cultural Discourse.* Ithaca:
Cornell University Press, 1993.
Baldwin, Frances Elizabeth. *Sumptuary Legislation and Personal Regulation in
England.* Johns Hopkins University Studies in Historical and Political Science
44. Baltimore: Johns Hopkins University Press, 1926.
Barthes, Roland. *The Fashion System.* Trans. Matthew Ward and Richard Howard.
New York: Hill and Wang, 1983.
——. *Image/Music/Text.* Trans. Stephen Heath. New York: Hill and Wang, 1977.
Beauvoir, Simone de. *The Second Sex.* Trans. H. M. Parshley. New York: Vintage,
1952.
Benetton, "Fall/Winter 1992 Advertising Campaign," bulletin mailed to author,
December 1992.
Benjamin, Walter. *Illuminations.* Ed. Hannah Arendt. Trans. Harry Zohn. New
York: Schocken, 1969.
Berger, John. *Ways of Seeing.* London: British Broadcasting Corp. and Penguin,
1972.
Berman, Marshall. *All That Is Solid Melts into Air: The Experience of Modernity.*
London: Verso, 1983.
Best, John. "Canada Fur Trade under Fire," *Times* [London], 22 December
1986: D7
Bigelow, Marybelle S. *Fashion in History: Western Dress, Prehistoric to Present.*
Minneapolis: Burgess, 1979.
Black, J. Anderson. *A History of Fashion.* London: Orbis, 1975.
Black, J. Anderson, and Madge Garland. *A History of Fashion.* Rev. ed. by Frances
Kennett. London: Orbis, 1980.
Blondin, George. *When the World Was New: Stories of the Sahtú Dene.* Yellowknife,
Northwest Territories: Outcrop, 1990.
Boucher, François. *20,000 Years of Fashion: The History of Costume and Personal
Adornment.* Rev. 2d ed. New York: Abrams, 1987.
Bourdieu, Pierre. *Distinction: A Social Critique of the Judgement of Taste.* Trans.
Richard Nice. Cambridge: Harvard University Press, 1984.
——. "The Field of Cultural Production, or: The Economic World Reversed."
Trans. Richard Nice. In *The Field of Cultural Production: Essays on Art and
Literature,* ed. Randal Johnson, 29–73. New York: Columbia University
Press, 1993.
——. *Outline of a Theory of Practice.* Trans. Richard Nice. Cambridge: University
of Cambridge Press, 1977.

Branswell, Helen. "U.K. Activists Push Trap Ban." *Vancouver Sun,* 18 October 1996: A11.

Braudel, Fernand. *Capitalism and Material Life, 1400–1800.* Trans. Miriam Kochan. New York: Harper and Row, 1973.

Bray, William, ed. *Memoirs, Illustrative of the Life and Writings of John Evelyn.* 2 vols. London, 1818.

Brody, Hugh. *Living Arctic: Hunters of the Canadian North.* London: Faber and Faber, 1987.

——. *Maps and Dreams: Indians and the British Columbia Frontier.* Toronto: Douglas and McIntyre, 1981, 1988.

Brooks, Peter. *The Melodramatic Imagination: Balzac, Henry James, Melodrama, and the Mode of Excess.* New Haven: Yale University Press, 1976.

Buci-Glucksmann, Christine. *La raison baroque: de Baudelaire à Benjamin.* Paris: Éditions Galilée, 1984.

Buck-Morss, Susan. "Aesthetics and Anaesthetics: Walter Benjamin's Artwork Essay Reconsidered." *October* 62 (1992): 3–41.

Burgers, Jacqueline. *Wenceslaus Hollar: Seventeenth-Century Prints from the Museum Boymans–Van Beuningen, Rotterdam.* Alexandria, Va.: Arts Service International, 1994.

Butler, Judith. *Gender Trouble: Feminism and the Subversion of Identity.* New York: Routledge, 1990.

Calthrop, Dion. *English Costume.* 4 vols. London: Adam and Charles Black, 1906.

"Campaign against furs." *Times* [London], 8 August 1984: G2.

Campbell, Maria, and Linda Griffiths. *The Book of "Jessica": A Theatrical Transformation.* Toronto: Coach House Press, 1989.

Canada, Department of Indian and Northern Affairs. *Evaluation Report of the Fur Industry Defence Program.* Ottawa, November 1991.

Canada, House of Commons, Standing Committee on Aboriginal Affairs and Northern Development. *Minutes of Proceedings and Evidence of the Standing Committee on Aboriginal Affairs and Northern Development, the Fur Issue: Cultural Continuity and Economic Opportunity.* December 1986. Issue 1. Ottawa: Queen's Printer, 1986.

Canada's Fur Bearers; containing Notes on the Principal Fur Bearing Animals of Canada, Trapping, and the Preparation of Furs for the Market. Winnipeg: Fur Trade Department, Hudson's Bay House, 1933.

Carter, Angela. *The Sadeian Woman: A Exercise in Cultural History.* London: Virago Press, 1979.

Clinch, George. *English Costume from Prehistoric Times to the End of the Eighteenth Century.* London: Methuen, 1909.

Crimp, Douglas. "On the Museum's Ruins." In *The Anti-Aesthetic: Essays on Postmodern Culture,* ed. Hal Foster, 43–56. Port Townsend, Wash.: Bay Press, 1983.

Cruikshank, Julie, in collaboration with Angela Sidney, Kitty Smith, and Annie Ned. *Life Lived like a Story: Life Stories of Three Yukon Native Elders.* Vancouver: University of British Columbia, 1990.

"Crushed but Unbowed." *Fur Campaign Review* 1 (January–March 1993): 1.

Cunningham, W. W. *The Growth of English Industry and Commerce during the Early and Middle Ages.* Vol. 1. New York: Augustus M. Kelley, 1968.

Davenport, Millia. *The Book of Costume.* Vol. 2. New York: Crown, 1948.

Davey, Richard. *Furs and Fur Garments*. London: International Fur Store and the Roxburghe Press, 1895.

Deleuze, Gilles. "Coldness and Cruelty." In *Masochism*. Trans. Jean McNeil. New York: Zone, 1989.

Deleuze, Gilles, and Félix Guattari. *Kafka: Toward a Minor Literature*. Trans. Dana Polan. Minneapolis: University of Minnesota Press, 1986.

——. *Nomadology: The War Machine*. Trans. Brian Massumi. New York: Semiotext(e), 1986.

Delphy, Christine. "For a Materialist Feminism." *Feminist Issues* 1.2 (1981): 69–76.

Descartes, René. *Discourse on Method*. In *The Philosophical Writings of Descartes*. Trans. John Cottingham, Robert Stoothoff, and Dugald Murdoch. 3 vols. Cambridge: Cambridge University Press, 1985.

Diamond, Irene, and Gloria Feman Orenstein, eds. *Reweaving the World: The Emergence of Ecofeminism*. San Francisco: Sierra Club Books, 1990.

Doane, Mary Ann. *Femmes Fatales: Feminism, Film Theory, Psychoanalysis*. New York: Routledge, 1991.

Druesedow, Jean L., ed. *In Style: Celebrating Fifty Years of the Costume Institute*. New York: Metropolitan Museum of Art, 1987.

Eagleton, Terry. *Literary Theory: An Introduction*. Minneapolis: University of Minnesota Press, 1983.

Emberley, Julia V. "The Power in Written Bodies: Gender, Decolonization, and the Archive." In *Bodies of Writing, Bodies in Performance*. Ed. Thomas Foster, Carol Siegel, and Ellen E. Berry. *Genders* 23 (Winter 1996): 184–211.

——. *Thresholds of Difference: Feminist Critique, Native Women's Writings, Postcolonial Theory*. Toronto: University of Toronto Press, 1993.

Enloe, Cynthia. *Bananas, Beaches, and Bases: Making Feminist Sense of International Politics*. Berkeley: University of California Press, 1990.

Etienne, Mona, and Eleanor Leacock, eds. *Women and Colonization: Anthropological Perspectives*. New York: Praeger, 1980.

Evelyn, John. *Tyrannus, or The Mode; In a Discourse of Sumptuary Lawes*. London, 1661.

Faurschou, Gail. "Obsolescence and Desire: Fashion and the Commodity Form." In *Postmodernism: Philosophy and the Arts*, ed. Hugh J. Silverman, 234–59. Continental Philosophy 3. New York: Routledge, 1990.

Fellingham, Christine. "Are Fur Coats Becoming Extinct?" *Glamour*, December 1992: 183–84.

Fellini's Roma. Dir. Federico Fellini. Screenplay Federico Fellini and Bernardino Apponi. 1972. MGM/UA Video, 1991.

Flaubert, Gustave. *"Bouvard and Pécuchet" with the "Dictionary of Received Ideas."* Trans. A. J. Krailsheimer. Markham, Ontario: Penguin, 1976.

"Former Sex Queen Slammed for Bashing Muslims." *Prince George Citizen*, 27 April 1996: 2.

Foucault, Michel. *The History of Sexuality*. Vol. 1: *An Introduction*. Trans. Robert Hurley. New York: Pantheon, 1978.

——. *Language, Counter-Memory, Practice*. Trans. Donald F. Bouchard and Sherry Simon. Ithaca: Cornell University Press, 1977.

——. *The Order of Things*. New York: Random House, 1970.

Freud, Sigmund. "The Economic Problem of Masochism." 1924. *The Standard Edition of the Complete Psychological Works of Sigmund Freud*, 19: 155–70. Trans. James Strachey et al. London: Hogarth Press, 1935–74.
——. "Fetishism." 1927. *The Standard Edition*, 21: 147–57.
Friedberg, Anne. *Window Shopping: Cinema and the Postmodern*. Berkeley: University of California Press, 1993.
Fur Council of Canada. *1993 Canada Fur Design Competition, Mariouche Gagné: A Retreat to Quality*. Press Release, Montreal, 5 May 1993.
Fur Factories. Lynx. Videocassette. Campaign Video, 1990.
"Furs in Disguise." *New York Times Magazine*, 27 September 1992: 56–61.
Gaines, Jane, and Charlotte Herzog, eds. *Fabrications: Costume and the Female Body*. New York: Routledge, 1990.
Garber, Marjorie. *Vested Interests: Cross-Dressing and Cultural Anxiety*. New York: Routledge, 1992.
Gentlemen Prefer Blondes. Dir. Howard Hawks. Perf. Jane Russell, Marilyn Monroe, Charles Coburn, 1953. Videocassette. Fox Video and Twentieth Century Fox, 1992.
"Getting a Jump on Spring." *Toronto Star*, 3 October 1991: D4.
Great Britain, House of Commons, *Parliamentary Debates*.
Green, Candida Lycett. "The Sublime and the Beautiful: Rare Breeds." Photo. Snowdon. *Vogue* [London], December 1990: 197–201.
Griggers, Cathy. "A Certain Tension in the Visual/Cultural Field: Helmut Newton, Deborah Turbeville, and the *Vogue* Fashion Layout." *Differences: A Journal of Feminist Cultural Studies* 2.2 (1990): 76–104.
Grosrichard, Alan. *Structure du serail*. Paris: Seuil, 1979.
Grosz, Elizabeth. "Lesbian Fetishism?" *Differences: A Journal of Feminist Cultural Studies* 3.2 (1991): 39–54.
Hall, Helen Forrist, ed. *The Romance of Furs*. Chicago: Cramer-Tobias, 1936.
Hall, Judy, Jill Oakes, and Sally Qimmiu'naaq Webster, eds. *Sanatujut, Pride in Women's Work: Copper and Caribou Inuit Clothing Traditions*. Hull, Quebec: Canadian Museum of Civilization, 1994.
Haraway, Donna J. "A Cyborg Manifesto: Science, Technology, and Socialist-Feminism in the Late Twentieth Century." In *Simians, Cyborgs, and Women: The Reinvention of Nature*, 149–81. New York: Routledge, 1991. Previously published as "Manifesto for Cyborgs: Science, Technology, and Socialist Feminism in the 1980s." *Socialist Review* 80 (1985): 65–108.
——. *Primate Visions: Gender, Race, and Nature in the World of Modern Science*. New York: Routledge, 1989.
Harris, Mark. "The Threat from Within: Will Infighting Weaken the Animal-Rights Movement?" *Vegetarian Times*, February 1995: 62–72.
Hay, Elizabeth. *Crossing the Snow Line*. Windsor, Ontario: Black Moss Press, 1989.
Heath, Stephen. "Lessons from Brecht." *Screen* 15.4 (1970): 107.
Hind, Arthur M. *Wenceslaus Hollar and His Views of London and Windsor in the Seventeenth Century*. London: Bodley Head, 1922.
Hodges, Laura. "A Reconsideration of the Monk's Costume." *Chaucer Review* 26.2 (1991): 133–46.
Hollander, Anne. *Seeing through Clothes*. Berkeley: University of California Press, 1975.
Hollar, Wenceslaus. *Aula veneris; sive, Varietas foeminini sexus*. London, 1644.

———. *Ornatus Muliebris Anglicanus; or, The Several Habits of English Women from the Nobility to the Countrywoman as They Are in These Times.* London, 1640.

———. *Theatrum muliebrum.* London, 1643.

Hudson's Bay Company, *General Court of the Governor and Company of Adventurers of England trading into Hudson's Bay was held at the City Terminus Hotel, Cannon Street, London, EC4, on Tuesday, the 29th Day of June, 1926, Mr. Charles V. Sale (the Governor), presiding.* London: Hudson's Bay Company, 1926.

Hughes, Diane Owen. "Regulating Women's Fashion." In *A History of Women in the West.* Vol. 2: *Silences of the Middle Ages,* 136–58. Ed. Christiane Klapisch-Zuber. Cambridge: Belknap Press of Harvard University Press, 1992.

Innis, Harold A. *The Fur Trade in Canada: An Introduction to Canadian Economic History.* Rev. ed. Toronto: University of Toronto Press, 1970.

Ivins, William M., Jr. *Prints and Visual Communication.* Cambridge: MIT Press, 1969.

Janson, H. W., and Dora Jane Janson. *History of Art: A Survey of the Major Visual Arts from the Dawn of History to the Present Day.* New York: Abrams, 1969.

Jasper, James M., and Dorothy Nelkin. *The Animal Rights Crusade: The Growth of a Moral Protest.* New York: Free Press, 1992.

Johnson, Samuel. *English Dictionary.* Vol. 2. Additions by Rev. H. J. Todd. 2d ed. London, 1827.

The Joyless Street. (Die freudlose Gasse. 1925). Dir. G. W. Pabst. Perf. Greta Garbo, Asta Nielsen, Werner Krauss. Restoration Catherine Gaborit, Connaissance du Cinéma, 1981. Videocassette. Kino International Corp. 1990.

Kafka, Franz. *The Metamorphosis/Die Verwandlung.* Trans. Willa Muir and Edwin Muir. New York: Schocken, 1946.

Krafft-Ebing, Richard von. *Psychopathia Sexualis: A Medico-Forensic Study.* Intro. Ernest van den Haag. Trans. Harry E. Wedeck. New York: Putnam's, 1965.

Kulchyski, Peter. "The Postmodern and the Paleolithic: Notes on Technology and Native Community in the Far North." *Canadian Journal of Political and Social Theory* 13.3 (1989): 49–62.

Kureishi, Hanif. *"Sammy and Rosie Get Laid": The Screenplay and the Screenwriter's Diary.* Markham, Ontario: Penguin, 1988.

Laclau, Ernesto, and Chantal Mouffe. *Hegemony and Socialist Strategy: Towards a Radical Democratic Politics.* London: Verso, 1985.

Landry, Donna, and Gerald MacLean. *Materialist Feminisms.* Oxford: Blackwell, 1993.

Langdon, Helen, with notes by James Malpas. *Holbein.* 2d ed. London: Phaidon Press, 1993.

Laver, James. *Costume and Fashion: A Concise History.* 2d ed. London: Thames and Hudson, 1982.

Lawson, Murray G. *Fur: A Study in English Mercantilism, 1700–1775.* Foreword by Harold A. Innis. History of Economics 9. Toronto: University of Toronto Press, 1943.

Lévi-Strauss, Claude. *Structural Anthropology.* Trans. Claire Jacobson and Brooke Grundfest Schoepf. New York: Basic Books, 1963.

Lorde, Audre. *Sister Outsider.* Freedom, Calif.: Crossing Press Feminist Series, 1984.

Madonna. *Madonna: The Immaculate Collection.* Videocassette. Warner Reprise Video, 1990.

Maracle, Richard. "The European Union's Import Restrictions on Wild Fur, EU Regulation 3254/91: Impacts on the Indigenous Peoples of Canada." Sponsored by Old Massett Village Council of Haida Gwaii. Internet. December 1995.

Martin, Biddy. *Woman and Modernity: The (Life)Styles of Lou Andreas-Salomé*. Ithaca: Cornell University Press, 1991.

Marx, Karl. *Capital: A Critique of Political Economy*. Vol. 1. Trans. Ben Fowkes. New York: Vintage, 1977.

McClintock, Anne. *Imperial Leather: Race, Gender and Sexuality in the Colonial Contest*. New York: Routledge, 1995.

McInerney, Jay. "Irina Rising," *New Yorker*, 21 and 28 August 1995: 67–71.

Mehlman, Jeffrey. *Walter Benjamin for Children: An Essay on His Radio Years*. Chicago: University of Chicago Press, 1993.

Meyer, Burris. *This Is Fashion*. New York: Harper and Brothers, 1943.

Mosse, George L. *Nationalism and Sexuality: Middle-Class Morality and Sexual Norms in Modern Europe*. Madison: University of Wisconsin Press, 1985.

Mukerji, Chandra. *From Graven Images: Patterns of Modern Materialism*. New York: Columbia University Press, 1983.

Mulvey, Laura. *Fetishism and Curiosity*. Bloomington: Indiana University Press and the British Film Institute, 1996.

———. *Visual and Other Pleasures*. Bloomington: Indiana University Press, 1989.

"Now You See Them . . . Andrew Powell on the Great Safari Debate." *Vogue* [London], December 1990: 119–24.

Nunavut, Nunavut Implementation Commission. *Two-Member Constituencies and Gender Equality: A "Made in Nunavut" Solution for an Effective and Representative Legislature*. Iqaluit, December 1994.

Olausen, Judy. *Mother*. Intro. Karin Winegar. Toronto: Penguin, 1996.

Olson, Kathryn M., and G. Thomas Goodnight. "Entanglements of Consumption, Cruelty, Privacy, and Fashion: The Social Controversy over Fur." *Quarterly Journal of Speech* 80.3 (1994): 249–76.

"On the Move in the Arctic." *Bulletin* of the British Museum Society, Autumn 1987: 3–5.

Pandiscio, Richard. "What a World." *Interview*, February 1996: 82–83.

Paris Is Burning. Dir. Jennie Livingston. Off White Productions, 1991.

Parmet, Herbert S. *Richard Nixon and His America*. Toronto: Little, Brown, 1990.

Parthey, Gustav. *Kurzes Verzeichniss der Hollar'schen Kupferstiche*. Berlin, 1853.

Pelts: Politics of the Fur Trade. Dir. Nigel Markham. Videocassette. National Film Board of Canada, 1989.

Pennington, Richard. *A Descriptive Catalogue of the Etched Work of Wenceslaus Hollar, 1607–1677*. Cambridge, 1982.

Petro, Patrice. *Joyless Streets: Women and Melodramatic Representation in Weimar Germany*. Princeton: Princeton University Press, 1989.

Phizacklea, Annie. *Unpacking the Fashion Industry: Gender, Racism, and Class in Production*. London: Routledge, 1990.

Pietz, William. "The Problem of the Fetish," part 1. *Res* 9 (Spring 1985): 5–17.

Plant, Judith, ed., *Healing the Wounds: The Promise of Ecofeminism*. Toronto: Between the Lines, 1989.

Posener, Jill. *Louder Than Words*. London: Pandora Press, 1986.

Quinby, Lee. "Ecofeminism and the Politics of Resistance." In *Reweaving the*

World: The Emergence of Ecofeminism, Ed. Irene Diamond and Gloria Feman
  Orenstein, 122–27. San Francisco: Sierra Club Books, 1990.
The Roar of Disapproval. Lynx. Videocassette. 1989.
Rothstein, Natalie, ed. *Four Hundred Years of Fashion*. Text by Madeleine Ginsburg,
  Avril Hart, Valerie D. Mendes, and other members of the Department of
  Textiles and Dress. Photography by Philip Barnard. London: Victoria and
  Albert Museum, 1984.
Sacher-Masoch, Leopold von. *Venus in Furs*. In *Masochism*. Trans. Jean McNeil.
  New York: Zone, 1989.
Sacher-Masoch, Wanda von. *The Confessions of Wanda von Sacher-Masoch*. Ed. V.
  Vale and Andrea Juno. Trans. Marian Phillips, Caroline Hébert, and V. Vale.
  San Francisco: Re/search, 1990.
Sahlins, Marshall. *Culture and Practical Reason*. Chicago: University of Chicago
  Press, 1976.
Said, Edward W. *Culture and Imperialism*. New York: Knopf, 1993.
——. *Orientalism*. New York: Vintage, 1978.
——. *Peace and Its Discontents*. London: Vintage, 1995.
Sammy and Rosie Get Laid. Dir. Stephen Frears. Screenplay Hanif Kureishi. Perf.
  Shashi Kapoor, Claire Bloom, Ayub Khan Din, and Frances Barber, 1988.
Schor, Naomi. "Fetishism and Its Ironies." In *Fetishism as Cultural Discourse*,
  ed. Emily Apter and William Pietz, 92–100. Ithaca: Cornell University
  Press, 1993.
Seltzer, Mark. "The Love-Master." In *Engendering Men: The Question of Male
  Feminist Criticism*, Ed. Joseph A. Boone and Michael Cadden, 140–58. New
  York: Routledge, 1992.
Silverman, Debora. *Selling Culture: Bloomingdale's, Diana Vreeland, and the New
  Aristocracy of Taste in Reagan's America*. New York: Pantheon, 1986.
Silverman, Kaja. *The Acoustic Mirror: The Female Voice in Psychoanalysis and Cinema*.
  Bloomington: Indiana University Press, 1988.
Smith, Colin. "A City Slowly Bludgeoned to Death." *Observer*, 14 June 1992: 17.
Smith, Leslie C. "Ecologically Correct: For Today's Fashions, We'd Rather
  Dance with Wolves Than Skin Them." *Globe and Mail* [Toronto], 10 October
  1991: D4.
Solomos, John, Bob Findlay, Simon Jones, and Paul Gilroy. "The Organic Crisis
  of British Capitalism and Race: The Experience of the Seventies." In *The
  Empire Strikes Back: Race and Racism in 70s Britain*, ed. Centre for
  Contemporary Cultural Studies, 9–46. London: Hutchinson with the
  Centre for Contemporary Cultural Studies, University of Birmingham, 1982.
Sontag, Susan. *On Photography*. New York: Delta, 1977.
Spivak, Gayatri Chakravorty. *In Other Worlds: Essays in Cultural Politics*. New York:
  Methuen, 1987.
——. *Outside in the Teaching Machine*. New York: Routledge, 1993.
——. *The Post-colonial Critic: Interviews, Strategies, Dialogues*. Ed. Sarah Harasym.
  New York: Routledge, 1990.
Sponsler, Claire. "Narrating the Social Order: Medieval Clothing Laws." *Clio*
  21.3 (1992): 265–83.
The Statutes of the Realm. 11 vols. in 12. 1810–28; rpt. London: Dawsons, 1963.
Steele, Valerie. *Fetish: Fashion, Sex, and Power*. New York: Oxford University
  Press, 1996.

Stewart, Susan. *On Longing: Narratives of the Miniature, the Gigantic, the Souvenir, the Collection*. Durham: Duke University Press, 1993.

Strutt, Joseph. *A Complete View of the Dress and Habits of the People of England, from the establishment of the Saxons in Britain to the present time, illustrated by engravings taken from the most authentic remains of antiquity; to which is prefixed an Introduction containing a general description of the ancient habits in use among mankind from the earliest period of time to the conclusion of the seventeenth century*. 2 vols. London, 1796–99.

Stubbes, Phillip. *Phillip Stubbes's Anatomy of the Abuses in England in Shakspere's Youth* (1583). Ed. Frederick J. Furnivall. London: New Shakspere Society, 1876–79.

Studlar, Gaylyn. "Masochism, Masquerade, and the Erotic Metamorphoses of Marlene Dietrich." In *Fabrications: Costume and the Female Body*, ed. Jane Gaines and Charlotte Herzog, 229–49. New York: Routledge, 1990.

Trigger, Bruce G. *Natives and Newcomers: Canada's "Heroic Age" Reconsidered*. Kingston: McGill-Queen's University Press, 1985.

Tucker, Robert C., ed. *The Marx-Engels Reader*. 2d ed. New York: Norton, 1978.

Turim, Maureen. *Flashbacks in Film: Memory and History*. New York: Routledge, 1989.

Turner, Graeme. *Film as Social Practice*. New York: Routledge, 1988.

Unzipped. Dir. Douglas Keeve. Miramax Films, 1995.

Van Eerde, Katherine S. *Wenceslaus Hollar: Delineator of His Time*. Folger Shakespeare Library. Charlottesville: University Press of Virginia, 1970.

Veale, Elspeth M. *The English Fur Trade in the Later Middle Ages*. Oxford: Clarendon Press, 1966.

Vecellio, Cesare. *Vecellio's Renaissance Costume Book: All 500 Woodcut Illustrations from the Famous Sixteenth-Century Compendium of World Costume*. New York: Dover, 1977.

Vertue, George. *A Description of the Works of the Ingenious Delineator and Engraver Wenceslaus Hollar disposed into Classes of Different Sorts with Some Account of His Life*. London, 1745.

Walters, Suzanna Danuta. *Material Girls: Making Sense of Feminist Cultural Theory*. Berkeley: University of California Press, 1995.

Wilcox, R. Turner. *The Mode in Furs*. New York: Scribner's, 1951.

Williams, Raymond. "Socialism and Ecology." In *Resources of Hope: Culture, Democracy, Socialism*, ed. Robin Gayle, 210–26. London: Verso, 1989.

Willis-Braithwaite, Deborah, ed. *Van Der Zee: Photographer, 1886–1983*. New York: Abrams, 1993.

Wilson, Elizabeth. *Adorned in Dreams: Fashion and Modernity*. London: Virago Press, 1985.

Wolf, Eric R. *Europe and the People without History*. Berkeley: University of California Press, 1982.

Woodhull, Winifred. *Transfigurations of the Maghreb: Feminism, Decolonization, and Literatures*. Minneapolis: University of Minnesota Press, 1993.

——. "Unveiling Algeria," *Genders* 10 (1991): 112–31.

Woolf, Virginia. *Three Guineas*. In *A Room of One's Own / Three Guineas*. Notes and Intro. Michèle Barrett. Toronto: Penguin, 1993.

Index

master-slave dialectic, 220–21n24; sexualized, 11, 75, 76, 78–79, 81, 83–85, 93, 100
material signifier: fur as, 4–5; fur-clad woman as, 208
McCartney, Linda, 30–31, 33
McClintock, Anne, 82, 91, 222n35
Mehlman, Jeffrey, 98–99
Metamorphosis, The, 93, 94
methodological fetishism, 82
mink coats, 9, 158, 214n16
mink fur, 33, 35, 233n35
Mizrahi, Isaac, 16, 18, 154, 160, 161–69, 183, 184, 185, 229n35, 229n37
Mode in Furs, The, 121, 224n21
Morris, Desmond, 33–34
Moses, D'Arcy, 173–74
Mukerji, Chandra, 44–45
Museum of Civilization (Ottawa), exhibition at, 18, 174, 180, 182, 184
muskrat fur, 47, 233n35

Nanook of the North (film, 1922), 161, 164, 165, 169, 184, 229–30n37
New York Times Magazine, The, 1992 fashion spread, 171

Olausen, Judy, 133
Orient: European trade with, 59, 64; Western image of, 84–86, 90, 181
Oriental despotism: European fantasy of, 11, 83, 85, 87; related to feminine despotism, 11, 87
Orientalism, 166, 181
Ornatus Muliebris Anglicanus (1640), 111, 123
otter fur, 47

Pabst, G. W., 16, 142–52, 227n17, 227n20, 227–28n23
Pandora's Box (*Die Büchse der Pandora*, film, 1929), 144–45, 149–52, 227n18
Paris is Burning (film, 1991), 16, 153–60
People for the Ethical Treatment of Animals (PETA), 12
Philosophy of the Bedroom, The (painting), 155–56
Pietz, William, 89–90, 90–91
political agency. *See* political power

political power, 12, 27, 53, 88, 223n12; of aboriginal peoples, 216n41; and fur, 7, 81; and masculinity, 65, 70; v. symbolic power, 7, 50, 64, 139, 207; of women, 135
Presence through Absence (installation, 1994), 156
primitivism, 181, 182, 187
pro-fur/anti-fur debate, 3, 6–7, 22, 212n2
Psychopathia Sexualis, 75
Puritanism: and adornment, 57–64, 67, 178; and sumptuary legislation, 63

rabbit fur, 47
race, 7–8, 141, 214n23; in anti-fur campaign, 23, 26, 33; in art, 112; and ethnographic fetishism, 80, 91; and fur, 15; in literature, 89; and sumptuary legislation, 61, 66. *See also* social differentiation
Rembrandt, 12
Roar of Disapproval, The (video, 1989), 33, 34
Rubens, 12, 103–4, 108

sable fur, 7, 47, 93, 224n23; fake, 164
Sacher-Masoch, Leopold von, 11, 72, 73–76, 80, 81, 100, 101, 104, 220n23, 220–21n24, 222n43
Sacher-Masoch, Wanda von, 95–98, 101, 220n23, 222nn41,43
sadism, 11, 75, 80–81, 99
sadomasochism (s/m), 81, 91. *See also* masochism; master/slave dialectic; sadism
safari industry, 171
Said, Edward, 11, 181, 230–31n19
Sadeian Woman, The, 94–95
Sammy and Rosie Get Laid (film, 1987), 7, 30
sexual difference, 5, 8, 72, 79, 81, 83; and origins of fashion, 127; related to fur clothing, 5–6, 9, 152, 169; among women, and fur production, 42. *See also* social differentiation
sexual fetishism, 75, 77, 142, 152, 227n20; and fur, 4, 5, 18, 73, 114, 120, 150; and fur-clad bourgeois woman, 11–12, 104; and fur coats, 19